CIUTI-Forum
New Needs, Translators & Programs

Martin Forstner & Hannelore Lee-Jahnke
(eds)

CIUTI-Forum
New Needs, Translators & Programs

On the Translational Tasks
of the United Nations

PETER LANG
Bern · Berlin · Bruxelles · Frankfurt am Main · New York · Oxford · Wien

Bibliographic information published by Die Deutsche Bibliothek
Die Deutsche Bibliothek lists this publication in the Deutsche Nationalbibliografie; detailed bibliographic data is available on the Internet at ‹http://dnb.ddb.de›.

British Library and Library of Congress Cataloguing-in-Publication Data: A catalogue record for this book is available from The British Library, Great Britain.

Library of Congress Cataloging-in-Publication Data

CIUTI-Forum (2011)
CIUTI-Forum new needs, translators & programs : on the translational tasks of the United Nations / Martin Forstner & Hannelore Lee-Jahnke (eds).
p. cm.
Papers in English, German, French and Spanish.
ISBN 978-3-03911-623-2
1. Translating and interpreting–Congresses. I. Forstner, Martin.
II. Lee-Jahnke, Hanna.
P306.C56 2011
418'.02–dc22

2011003739

Nous remercions nos généreux sponsors: Université de Genève; Formation Continue de l'Université de Genève; ONU, CIUTI, CLS Communication, Zürich; Dr. François Massion, D.O.G. Leonberg (D).

Cover design: Thomas Jaberg, Peter Lang, Berne

ISBN 978-3-03911-623-2

Hochfeldstrasse 32, CH-3012 Bern, Switzerland
info@peterlang.com, www.peterlang.com, www.peterlang.net

Printed in Switzerland

Content

Préface

Il n'est certes pas trop tôt et il semble plus qu'évident de consacrer un Forum de la CIUTI aux différentes tâches que les Nations Unies, partenaires dès le début des Fora CIUTI, ont prioritairement à accomplir dans le cadre de leurs services linguistiques et de conférences.

Les questions préliminaires posées par ce Forum sont, entre autres, l'efficacité de communication de la part des traducteurs et interprètes des Nations Unies et, dans ce contexte, plus spécifiquement ce qui suit:

1. En quoi consiste la communication des services linguistiques des Nations Unies?
2. Quelles répercussions ces besoins peuvent avoir sur les Universités qui forment des traducteurs et interprètes?
3. Quel rôle la CIUTI peut-elle jouer?

1) La communication des services linguistiques

En ce qui concerne la première question au sujet de la communication, il faut tenir compte du fait que la société du futur basée sur le savoir, dépendra forcément de la communication et, dans ce contexte l'organisation des Nations Unies représente un sous-système basé sur le savoir. Un sous-système qui produit, utilise et diffuse un savoir spécifique en utilisant des techniques d'information et de communication particulières. Dans la présentation d'Erich Prunč il est clairement indiqué que chaque société d'information possède sa propre culture communicative avec, également, des formes de communications spécifiques. L'Organisation des Nations Unies, quant à elle, possède ces formes de communications culturelles spéciales en six langues et dans des domaines les plus divers: la politique, le droit, l'économie et l'éducation pour n'en citer que quelques-uns. Tâche hautement intéressante, mais exigeante.

De plus, deux types de communication sont à prendre en compte: une communication interne et une externe. La communication interne étant une communication entre experts ce qui engendre une tâche complexe qui consiste à créer des textes en six langues. Quant à la communication externe, elle s'adresse à un large public. La grande difficulté des traducteurs est donc la création de textes qui s'adressent aux experts et à un large public avec un excellent niveau de compétence traductologique.

2) Quelles sont donc les répercussions de ces besoins sur les universités qui forment les traducteurs et interprètes?

Dans un premier temps, il me semble évident qu'efficacité et efficience doivent être définies d'un point de vue académique et professionnel. Le monde académique conçoit l'efficacité de la communication dans le sens de la compétence de traduire et l'efficience semble jouer un moindre rôle.

Le monde professionnel, par contre, exige que la communication se fasse de manière efficiente. C'est pour cela que le monde du travail, donc les Nations Unies, exigent de le part des traducteurs diplômés une combinaison entre efficacité et efficience sous forme de compétence du traducteur.

Afin que les universités puissent au mieux répondre au monde du travail, il faut une plateforme pour un échange d'idées, des besoins et de la faisabilité pour permettre aux formateurs de corriger, rectifier ou anticiper les contenus des cours, répondant ainsi au mieux aux besoins et à la demande des futurs employeurs.

L'objectif principal du Forum est de rendre attentives les universités qui forment des traducteurs et interprètes sur les besoins ressentis et auxquels les Nations Unies n'ont peut-être pas encore trouvé une réponse chez les jeunes diplômés.

Il serait certes utile que les Nations Unies définissent un profil idéal de leurs médiateurs linguistiques qui seront nécessaires dans les vingt années à venir pour répondre aux exigences et aux besoins de la quantité et qualité du travail requis.

3) Quel est le rôle que CIUTI pourrait jouer?

D'emblée il s'agit de cerner quelques problèmes d'ordre général: nous savons tous qu'il est très facile de prêcher la coopération mais, bien plus difficile de l'exécuter. Formellement, les services linguistiques des Nations Unies sont hautement centralisés tandis que les systèmes éducatifs des universités sont décentralisés au plus haut degré. Il serait utile et certes souhaitable que, similairement aux différents Masters introduits par la Commission Européenne, les Nations Unies pourraient – en coopération avec la CIUTI – établir un réseau en créant une formation: Traduire pour les Nations Unies. Un tel réseau serait en ligne avec le *higher education management*, et correspondrait au nouveau paradigme d'une recherche collaborative dans une société basée sur le savoir. CIUTI dans ce contexte pourrait servir d'interface entre les services linguistiques des Nations Unies et les Universités qui forment des traducteurs et interprètes pour introduire un *Master en traduction/interprétation internationale*.

Le présent volume est divisé en quatre parties: à la suite de la séance d'ouverture par Vladimir Gratchev et Mariana Fiorito, la section 1) *Communication as a necessity* comporte les contributions de Nicolas Tate qui souligne la formation linguistique à l'école, Marie-Josée de Saint Robert qui aborde plus spécifiquement la problématique de la traduction à l'ONU et Martin Forstner qui insiste sur les tâches de communications particulières des traducteurs à l'ONU. Cette partie se termine par l'article d'Erich Prunč sur le lien étroit entre langue et pouvoir.

La section suivante 2) *Practical experiences* regroupe trois états des lieux en Chine: Lidi Wang et Jianhua Yuan ainsi que Min Lu et une expérience russe: celle de Natalia Sigareva et Tatiana Yudina.

Avec la section 3) *New Visions* nous abordons le *European Master in Translation* par Reinhard Hoheisel, une esquisse d'un Master pour les Nations Unies par Mohammed Didaoui et une recherche nouvelle par Annie Sturm qui dessine une approche novatrice de la recherche interdisciplinaire avec des aphasiques.

La section 4) *Answers & solutions* comporte des articles par Marcel Thelen, Information technology, Diane Howard sur la sélection de textes, Suzanne Ballansat et Gunhilt Perrin sur la comparaison de textes de loi et Jiang Lu sur la problématique des traductions d'enseignes en Chinois.

Nous espérons avoir donné au lecteur de cet ouvrage une vue d'ensemble aussi complète que possible et lui souhaitons de prendre plaisir à sa lecture.

Fait à Genève le 24 octobre 2010

Martin FORSTNER
Hannelore LEE-JAHNKE

Opening Speeches

Vladimir GRATCHEV

Mrs President
Mr. Vice-President of the Swiss Confederation State Council,
Mr. Rector of the University of Geneva,
Ladies and Gentlemen,
Dear Colleagues,

I am honored to address, on behalf of the Conference Services Division, this gathering of scholars and practitioners.

The Palais des Nations is hosting this forum for the third time. Since the Employment Market, held on 23 May 2003, remarkable inroads in the language profession have been made.

Driven by new possibilities offered by computer technology, the United Nations is exploring new vistas: relocation of services or off-shoring, contracting out to external providers or outsourcing, and allowing translators to work off-site at a distance or tele-working. Indeed, the translational scene at the United Nations is changing thus requiring a new approach to the training of translators and interpreters.

Meanwhile, on one hand, a demographic change is taking place which requires careful planning of vacancy management taking into account retirements and new recruitment. The pool of skilled linguists with a potential to work as international translators and interpreters is ominously shrinking as witnessed by the decline in the number of qualified applicants for the UN competitive examinations.

The vacancy rate requires a proactive approach in order to cope efficiently with this state of affairs and pave the way to bring to life new policies and new visions, through active training. The success will be determined by the qualification of candidates to UN language posts.

Staff at the entry level have been traditionally recruited to work for the United Nations exclusively through competitive examinations. It should be mentioned, however, that administering those examinations has proven to be cumbersome and costly and a downward trend has been noticed in their yield. This may be attributed to the small number of language experts trained by educational institutions and having the requisite competencies. Jointly and commonly held examinations for translators, interpreters, editors and verbatim reporters were organized for the sake of economies of scale and to enable multi-talented candidates to take examinations in all these fields.

The only formal group training sponsored by the United Nations was the Training Programme for African Translators, established in the 1970s to remedy the Economic Commission for Africa's chronic and severe vacancy problem and meet its needs for Arabic, English and French translators. It was discontinued in 1996 due to financial constraints. Also, many international organizations offered graduate internships and traineeships, some in this profession.

The language training and experience gained in Russia and China is worth-mentioning whose representatives will elaborate on these training courses, which have been very instrumental in supplying the United Nations with competent translators.

However, a permanent solution is needed for training better-suited to the specific demands of the United Nations and other organizations. Relatively minor adjustments to the curricula of training entities would be sufficient to increase the numbers of would-be UN translators and interpreters.

The post-recruitment training is very important and should be addressed permanently. Until now, it has been carried out through revision as a quality control tool or by training sessions with a training officer, as it is usually the case at the UN Headquarters.

In this regard, a new concept is being contemplated. It would consist of the establishment, within the Economic and Social Commission for Western Asia, in Beirut, of an Arabic Language Centre, which will have among its goals to organize training workshops "for the continuous learning of in-house translators and eligible free lance translators". Perhaps, this option should be generalized to cover all the UN official languages and language professions.

Finally, the Executive Session of the International Annual Meeting on Language Arrangements, Documentation and Publications, held in Vienna last June, issued a statement in which it "advocated closer cooperation between the international organizations and universities and other reputable academic institutions to promote the training of conference and language service professionals".

It is in this spirit that we are gathered here and we are looking forward to fruitful and mutually beneficial exchanges.

Universities and the Sworn Translators' Association of the City of Buenos Aires: A Common Goal

Mariana FIORITO

First of all, let me thank Ms Hannelore Lee-Jahnke for her kind invitation to make this presentation. It's an honour for me to be able to address all of you here today to let you know what we do in Argentina concerning the link between the university and the professional association, and through that link, between graduate translators and the increasingly demanding world of work.

To begin with, let me introduce the Sworn Translator's Association of the City of Buenos Aires, or *"Colegio de Traductores Públicos de la Ciudad de Buenos Aires"*. After that, I'll describe the activities of the University Affairs Committee of the *"Colegio"*. Finally (last but most definitely not least), I'll tell you how we connect training and market; that is, the student and his or her dreamed professional achievements on the one hand, and society and the satisfaction of its needs on the other.

Considering that there are differences among countries concerning the denomination and functions of "sworn" or "public" or "certified" translators, let me first of all explain what a sworn translator is in Argentina. A sworn translator is one we call *"traductor público"*, who must be trained at university, and then become a member of the *Colegio*, and whose signature must be registered there, for it to be certified every time a client has had a translation made by such sworn translator, provided that translation is to be submitted to official agencies at home or abroad. Certified translation is governed by a law, unlike literary and technical or scientific translation.

The translator's profession has been a companion on the road of technological and social evolution. The new demands of contemporary society place us face to face with the need to optimise results and improve efficiency. Too often, services are sought from people who, despite their fluency in a foreign tongue, cannot guarantee effective results. Argentina is privileged in the sense that the profession of sworn translators currently functions within a regulatory-legal framework that protects the translator as well as the user public requiring the translator's services. It is this particular difference that places the sworn translator in a privileged position with respect to other settings in the vast realm of translation, either at the national or at the international level.

The first degree of Sworn Translator was granted in our country by the University of Buenos Aires in 1868. The National Association of Sworn Translators, a non-commercial body that evolved into a professional certifying board was organised in 1946. Finally, in 1973, Act 20,305 established the status of the profession and of its members' association: "*Colegio de Traductores Públicos de la Ciudad de Buenos Aires*" (the Sworn Translators' Association I am representing today), which means we are 34 years old. Its roster consists now of nearly 5,000 registered members representing 34 languages. Its registered members vote for the members of the Executive Board every 4 years.

The Association has so far had 12 working committees: Legal Experts for Lawsuits, Terminology, Defense of the Profession, Interpreters, International Relations, CAT Tools, Culture, Newly Graduates, and University Affairs, are some of them. This year we're planning to start new committees according to areas of specialisation: legal, financial and medical translation, to start with. The Newly Graduates Committee has recently launched a "Mentoring Programme", where experienced, established translators guide and help those who are treading the initial steps towards becoming accomplished translators. Since last November, one member of the Newly Graduates Committee was elected to integrate the seven-member Executive Board of our Association.

The *Colegio de Traductores Públicos* has a scholarship programme aiming at aiding experienced translators as well as young graduates to pursue master degrees in Argentina, of which there are still a few, but from the Association we are encouraging the creation of new postgraduate studies, and are also starting to do some research abroad, to be able to offer that information to our members.

We also hold International Congresses every two years. In July last year we organised the First International Subject-Specific Translation Conference, which gathered 1,200 people, including visitors and lecturers from other Latin American countries as well as from Germany, France, Romania, the United States, and Spain among others. On that occasion, the University Matters Committee organized a Round Table which discussed "The University and Its Role in Providing Specialization for Professional Translators".

At the same time, the Association regularly organises one- or two-day conferences on certain aspects of the profession, where also would-be translators doing the last subjects of their careers at university were invited to show their research projects on a couple of occasions.

Argentina is a huge country and distances are a problem. When we (from Buenos Aires) go to the seaside, we travel 400 km; when we go to the high mountains, 1,500 km; when we go to the southernmost part, 3,000 km; when a translator from dramatically beautiful Patagonia wants to specialize or take courses to improve his or her professional performance... the vastness of our country becomes a handicap due to time consumption and very high travelling costs. This is why we started studying "e-learning" and the "*Colegio*" implemented a virtual classroom to shorten the distance between wanting to receive further training and being able to actually do it regardless of geography and time availability. We plan, in this way, to expand the reach of our work countrywide and worldwide. Even though last year our Association offered 171 courses, only 2 of them were virtual, because of course, instructors must be trained and the general public must get used to the new way of learning. So we are getting ready for a very "course-active" 2007.

But I came here more specifically to tell you about the activities of the Committee I chair: the University Affairs Committee. The purpose of this Committee is to establish (and maintain) fruitful relationships with the 16 universities where translation is currently taught in our country. And my presence here may well initiate our contact with European universities as well.

We aim at gathering information about curricula being used, faculty, students, research and alumni; and we also aim at very actively participating in the process of improving and updating existing curricula. We have on various occasions – and at the request of the authorities of some university translation departments-studied and given our opinion and advise concerning new curricula both for ordinary university courses and postgraduate projects.

We usually hold regular meetings with translation departments' authorities in order to strengthen our relationship with them, and also to interchange information, comment on university problems and training, common concerns, etc.

Apart from that, we visit universities with a view to meeting students before they graduate and showing them the end of their university studies is definitely not the end of their training. In that way a strong connection is then established between the university and the association that watches the profession and counsels its registered members. But not only do we go to universities; we also have students come and visit us at the *Colegio*. In this way they get acquainted with the functioning of the institution, the legislation governing their future profession (still not every university trains would-be translators in this area), they get to know the *Colegio's* library where they can attend in order to work on their papers and projects, etc.

We also organize special conferences to contribute to the training not of the translator herself or himself, but of the one in charge of training the future translator. But what I've said is incomplete, for professors and lecturers know a lot. Therefore, another aim of next March's conference is to provide them with some time to tell each other what their experience has taught them, so that everyone will be able to profit from everyone else's expertise.

Finally, concerning the activities of the University Affairs Committee, let me mention a project we have been involved in, which we expect will be officially implemented in the future. It is true that every university has its characteristics, and it is also true that in a free country there should be freedom to engineer curricula without restrictions. But the search after individuality and originality combined with inexorable budget restrictions has led to a varied offer of translation diplomas where certain key aspects of translator training have been neglected, given that time and resources had to be allotted to courses inherent to the character of the universities containing them.

Thus it is very hard for students who start their courses at one university and want (or need) to continue them in another. This, coupled with the growth of *Mercosur,* (whose component parts have the same problems of diversity I am describing to you now, and which is still a commercial association of Latin American countries, but which aims in the long run at legislative, educational and political union) has led us to believe that the establishment of minimum contents that should be common to every career of translation – regardless of the character of every university – is a must.

So we drew up the list of what we consider are "minimum contents" that the *Colegio* recommends should be considered when updating or creating curricula. The list contains a series of contents concerning five areas: language, translation, juridical area (don't forget we are training sworn translators), professional practice, CAT tools, and introduction to new specializations.

Such minimum contents have been discussed by the University Affairs Committee, by other committees of the *Colegio*, and by other registered members who attended an "open day" debate. We are currently waiting for translation departments' authorities to approve of them before we submit them to the Ministry of

Education. Our aim is to guarantee end users of translation services that every translator in our country has received a basic common training to which every university has been free to add what their faculty and authorities have considered proper.

The last aspect of this presentation has to do with the connection between training and market, and the obvious role that the *Colegio* has taken up in order to be a vehicle, to facilitate this passage from student to actual performer, sort of from worm to butterfly.

Universities produce graduates every year, but they need these graduates to return to them in the form of professors and researchers. On the other hand, the market demands experienced as well as newly trained graduates to satisfy its hungry needs. We feel it is our duty to do our bit to be of assistance to both of them.

It is through a wide assortment of postgraduate specialization courses, through the Scholarship Programme I have already described to you, thorough the disinterested work of the members of the Committees, that the *Colegio* encourages valuable graduates to return to their alma maters to help train future colleagues.

It is through the Mentoring Programme, through the Defense of the Profession Committee and its talks with official agencies and private institutions for these bodies to resort to professional translators (and also of course to the work of all the other committees), through the constant monitoring of market needs, through our untiring encouragement to our registered members to develop an area of specialization, through the Communications Committee, which is always striving to let people and institutions know that professional translators know better than untrained "people who translate", that the *Colegio* contributes with universities by helping graduates in their hard transition after university into their professional lives.

When I was a student at university I had no idea what the Association was for. Then, twenty years ago, I became a lecturer, and as such I didn't want my students to be unaware that there is an institution which can actually help them after the protective wing of the university has turned to other new students. Being a bridge between training and market, that is between personal projects and professional realization, is perhaps one of the most rewarding and compromising roles our Association – the *Colegio* – can take upon itself in terms of training.

1. *Communication as a Necessity*

Language Issues in School Education*

Nicolas TATE

It is with great pleasure that I address this conference, as the head of a local educational institution here in Geneva and as a former education policy-maker.

As director-general of a school with nearly 4000 students who come from 133 nationalities and speak 98 mother tongues, language education issues are rarely far from my mind. Indeed we started the present school term with a one-day conference last week on languages and education, with a particular focus on bilingual education, which was held just up the road from here at the International Labour Office. It was a bilingual conference, in English and French, with excellent interpretation throughout. We were also fortunate enough to attract a number of extremely distinguished speakers who included two from the University of Geneva's school of translation and interpretation, Professor Lee-Jahnke and Professor François Grin.

Professor Lee-Jahnke addressed my conference on issues of translation and interpretation and helped us think about the future translators and interpreters whose education at school level we are responsible for. We learned a lot. But why should you, people who are responsible for the professional education of translators and interpreters, listen in return to a talk on issues in school language education?

There are perhaps three reasons why what happens in schools concerns you: first, because the debates about language education

* Talk given at the Forum of the Conférence Internationale permanente d'Instituts Universitaires de Traducteurs et Interprètes (CIUTI), United Nations, Geneva, 25th January 2007.

in schools are reflective of wider cultural issues within a society and these issues of course impinge on your work as well; second, because what happens in schools can play a major role in shaping a society's attitudes towards language use; and, third, because of the impact of what we do in schools on the educational development of future translators and interpreters.

I shall talk about four issues in language education in schools: the teaching of the main language of instruction and/or national language; bilingual education; the choice of foreign languages to be studied and how these are taught; the maintenance of the mother tongue when this is different from the language of instruction.

First, the teaching of the main language of instruction and/or national language.

I seem to have spent a large part of my career in initiatives designed to get across the message that all teachers, whatever their subject, are responsible for developing the student's language of instruction to the highest level possible and to ensure that they are provided with the tools with which they can perform this role. I have particular memories of 1980s initiatives in the UK to promote 'language across the curriculum'. The effort is still essential to ensure that teachers of physics or of history, for example, also see themselves as teachers of language. It is sensitivity to language and to learners' needs in relation to language that is above all required. This is particularly the case in a school such as mine where a very high proportion of the students do not have the language of instruction (English or French in our case) as their mother tongue, but it is a situation that is increasingly replicated across national education systems as a consequence of mass migration. One of our initiatives at my school is to encourage our teachers to follow a course on 'English in the Mainstream', a course that was first developed in Australia, which is designed to help all teachers, and not just language teachers, work with students in their classes who do not have English as their first language.

But it isn't just a matter of the initial training and continuing professional development of teachers. It is also about the allocation of resources: the need for initial small immersion classes into which newly arrived students are placed before they join the mainstream class; the need for ongoing additional learning support for these students once they have joined the mainstream class; the pressure to reduce the size of language classes so that students are able to receive more individual attention. Investment in the core educational task of language development pays off and is known to pay off, but that still does not mean that it is easy to find the necessary resources when there are competing demands and the money is finite.

The other main issue of course is the use of the language of instruction, or the national language, as a vehicle for the transmission of the culture and cultures associated with that language. In an international school, teaching through English or French, we are very conscious of our duties with regard to the whole range of cultures associated with those two world languages. We study Shakespeare but we also study authors writing in English from Africa, India, the Caribbean, Australia and so on, and similarly with the world of *la francophonie*. In national schools there is a particular, though far from exclusive, obligation with regard to the transmission via language education of the culture of that particular country. It is here that western education finds some of its fiercest critics with accusations in English of 'dumbing down' and in French of *l'amnésie planifiée* (planned amnesia), the latter from George Steiner, the great linguist and scholar and former professor at the University of Geneva.

Although schools are often rightly criticized in this regard they face an uphill struggle in a world in which global, and in particular US-based, mass media, consumerist pressures, the dominance of the visual, and the rapidity of social and cultural change push in different directions. How we use language education in schools as a basis for the cultural development of our students is, I am sure, one of the aspects of our work that most concerns you as the educators of translators and interpreters. I would be interested in hearing whether you think schools are doing a good job and, in particular, whether you have noticed changes over time in this area. Is George Steiner right?

I should also be interested to know how many of your students have had a bilingual education as opposed to just being bilingual or multilingual. Bilingual education is my second theme and was the main focus of my school's recent education conference. The conference was opened by our local education minister (each of Switzerland's cantons has its own education minister). He talked about the issues in this area facing Switzerland, a plurilingual country with four official languages. Fierce debates are taking place here at the moment about the choice and timing of education in second and third languages, with those insisting that the second language should always be another of Switzerland's national languages, rather than English, still – happily – in the ascendant. As yet, however, the debate is mostly about second and third language instruction rather than about teaching whole parts of the curriculum in a second language (which is what I mean by bilingual education), although bilingual education in this sense does take place in some parts of the country where two national languages are spoken alongside each other. There is growing interest, however, and some experimentation, in bilingual education, for example through offering the Swiss baccalaureate *(maturité)* in French and English or in French and German. My own school, being a bilingual school, offers programmes in English, in French, and in various combinations of the two. Indeed in one of our secondary schools each subject is offered simultaneously in the two languages and students can put together an *à la carte* course using the two languages as they see fit and as is appropriate to their needs.

Elsewhere in the world there are many variants of bilingual education: early immersion in the second language, later immersion, and using varying proportions of the two languages. The message from research studies is that all of these approaches, where well taught, can be enormously successful in embedding the two languages (and sometimes three languages as some schools offer immersion in both a second and a third language). The key messages from the research are that bilingual education does not disadvantage progress in the first language, does not disadvantage progress in the subjects in which one is learning the second language, and is as appropriate for the less able as for the more able. There are advantages in starting as early as possible, but it is not essential and late immersion can also be highly successful. The cognitive advantages of a bilingual education, and of bilingualism, are also well attested, as all of you of course well know.

Where bilingual education is least developed is in countries with a dominant national language and no strong sense of an incentive to develop an equivalent competence in a second language. In my own country, the UK, for example, there is some very successful practice in teaching through both Welsh and English in Wales, but virtually no efforts at bilingual education that I know of in England despite that country's increasingly plurilingual nature. This is surprising given the enormous advantages, both to the individual and to the society, of bilingualism. There are of course huge logistical issues to do with teacher supply and mobility but given the high rewards that would come from making an effort in this area it is nonetheless surprising that bilingual education initiatives are so low on policy-makers' priority lists. We have obviously not got across sufficiently the benefits and pleasures of bilingualism and multilingualism.

Much of the debate about other languages, as in Switzerland, is therefore about which second and third (or sometimes fourth) languages should be taught, when and how. As someone who was once responsible for England's national curriculum and is the veteran of many initiatives in foreign language education my abiding feeling is one of despair at the disproportion between the time and money spent on foreign language education in schools and the outcomes in terms of students' linguistic competence. And it isn't just in England, with its traditional insularity reinforced by the rapid global expansion of a variant of its language, that people have these feelings. This is why the possibilities of bilingual immersion are so attractive as a way of breaking out of the deadlock of learning other languages for three or four periods a week over a number of years and ending up barely able to cope even when on holiday in one of the countries in which the language is spoken. Foreign language learning in schools can be an excellent basis for the small minority of students who go on to study languages at university (and maybe go on then to be translators and interpreters). It can be good for general awareness-raising of cultural and linguistic diversity. But it is often not serving its purpose of enabling significant numbers of people in a society to operate comfortably in a plurilingual context.

There are many possible ways forward, however, in this area. These include re-examining the age at which languages are taught, developing opportunities for teaching through the second language (even when fully bilingual education is not available), and making creative use of new technology.

One of the main initiatives has to be getting across the absolutely fundamental message that language learning is important and useful. We are very fortunate in Geneva where our non-francophone students have an incentive to learn French to operate successfully in discos, bars and night clubs, and to widen their choice of boyfriends and girlfriends, where our non-anglophone students need English to cope in a school that is English – rather than French – dominant, and where everyone around them moves in and out of languages all the time without too much self-consciousness. Ability in more than one language is valued, obviously useful and high status. It is not the same if you are a French student learning German in largely monolingual Toulouse or an English student learning French in largely monolingual Manchester. This does not mean, however, that these obstacles, and especially the attitudinal ones, cannot be tackled and overcome.

The other issue of course in the teaching of 'foreign' languages, i.e. those not spoken within the country in question, is which ones to choose. I will mention only two aspects of this. The first is the drift towards the selection of English as *the* first foreign language.

I was until recently a member of the *Haut Conseil de l'évaluation de l'école*, a think tank set up by the French minister of education, and we had fascinating debates about this subject following a report that was pushing heavily in the direction of *tout à l'anglais*. It is a trend to be resisted in the interests of maintaining linguistic and cultural diversity. The second is the growing interest, in the West, in the teaching of non-European languages in schools. It is a trend to be supported even if the numbers who take up the option are small and they do not reach high levels of linguistic competence in schools. It will be useful in stimulating a greater interest in studying these languages at university and it will send across messages within schools about the nature of the modern world.

The last aspect of language education that I wish to mention is that of mother tongue maintenance where the mother tongue is different from the language of instruction or the national language. Traditionally schools felt no obligation to help with this and indeed saw other languages as threatening the core task of instruction in the national language. Despite numerous initiatives, not least UNESCO's convention on cultural diversity, some of these attitudes survive. The research evidence from bilingual education that I mentioned, however, makes clear the advantages to general cognitive development of maintaining the language of the home and being helped to use it at a higher, including written, level. This is a major theme in many international schools which obviously have a particular responsibility in this area given the mobility of their populations. It is a matter for greater controversy within some national education systems. There are understandable concerns about the identity of immigrant populations should there be a huge investment in the teaching of minority languages and thus in developing bilingualism. Such an investment might well, however, pay off. Linguistically able young people, fluent in both languages (as is often not the case at the moment), might well have more satisfying identities and thus a greater sense of commitment to their countries than is sometimes the case at present. It is at least a matter for further reflection and one that will become increasingly relevant in a world of mass migration.

I have raised a number of issues in: the teaching of the national language or language of instruction; bilingual education; the teaching of other and 'foreign' languages; and the maintenance of the mother tongue. The work of schools in all these areas is important for ensuring that you continue to receive appropriately prepared candidates to be translators and interpreters. More importantly, success or otherwise in schools in these aspects of language development has major cultural, social, economic and political implications. I have touched briefly on some of these but not had time to develop them very far.

La traduction à l'ONU

Marie-Josée DE SAINT ROBERT

Les instituts universitaires de traducteurs et interprètes sont naturellement appelés à être des pépinières de traducteurs et d'interprètes. Ces instituts préparent en effet leurs étudiants à réussir les concours d'entrée aux professions linguistiques qu'organisent régulièrement les organisations internationales. C'est dans le cadre de la préparation des étudiants aux professions qu'offre l'ONU que s'appliquent les remarques ci-après formulées à l'intention des formateurs désireux de mieux connaître les besoins actuels de l'ONU en matière de traduction:

1. *Des combinaisons linguistiques* difficiles à trouver. L'ONU travaille en six langues: l'anglais, l'arabe, le chinois, l'espagnol, le français et le russe. Pour travailler efficacement dans toutes les combinaisons linguistiques et sans langues relais, il lui faut des traducteurs et des interprètes capables de travailler à partir de toutes ces langues dans leur langue principale qui doit également être une des six langues mentionnées. Or il existe une réelle pénurie de traducteurs dans les combinaisons suivantes: arabe-anglais, arabe-français, chinois-anglais, chinois-français, russe-anglais, russe-français. Les instituts relevant de la CIUTI devraient combler ces lacunes dans l'offre mondiale des langues.
2. *Une méthode de travail spécifique.* A l'ONU, le traducteur reçoit non seulement un texte à traduire mais un dossier de documents d'accompagnement dont il doit se servir dans son travail de traduction: la cohérence terminologique d'un document à l'autre, la fidélité aux précédents qui ont souvent fait l'objet de consensus de la part de la communauté internationale sont autant de critères pour juger de la qualité et de la pertinence de la traduction. En outre, le traducteur anglais et français est

amené à préparer des comptes rendus analytiques de séance qui font appel à des techniques qu'il faut enseigner et à un esprit de synthèse qu'il faut cultiver.

3. *Un esprit de collaboration très poussé.* A l'ONU, le traducteur ne travaille pas en vase clos: il doit faire appel à des référenciers pour compléter le cas échéant son information, vérifier auprès d'un auteur le sens d'un mot peu courant ou dissiper une ambiguïté, rectifier au besoin une erreur de l'auteur, apporter des commentaires et des suggestions dans les bases de données textuelles et terminologiques pour améliorer la qualité générale de la traduction.
4. *Une évolution du travail du traducteur.* Les outils informatiques et télématiques sont devenus non seulement des sources d'information indispensables mais des supports sur lesquels les traducteurs préparent leurs textes. Il ne s'agit donc plus seulement de savoir chercher l'information la plus pertinente, mais également de porter un jugement sur un texte préalablement traduit. La frontière est de plus en plus floue entre le texte fourni au traducteur sur la base de mémoires de traduction ou de corpus de textes dont la traçabilité est assurée et les textes issus d'un processus de traduction automatique. Le traducteur devient un valideur de textes et un réviseur, avant parfois d'avoir fait complètement ses preuves dans le domaine de la traduction. Il est aussi dans l'urgence appelé à s'auto-réviser et ne bénéficie plus dans la même mesure des conseils des réviseurs confirmés. Le futur traducteur de l'ONU doit apprendre à recycler des textes pour abaisser le coût de la traduction.
5. *Les principes de gestion des entreprises s'appliquent aussi aux organisations internationales.* Le traducteur de l'ONU est astreint à des normes de productivité fixées par la communauté des Etats Membres. Ainsi, il doit produire en moyenne 1650 mots par jour (davantage s'il s'auto-révise ou s'il révise un texte). La recherche de l'efficacité doit aller de pair avec la recherche de la qualité. Un mauvais traducteur aura peu de chances de faire une brillante carrière à l'ONU.

Die speziellen kommunikativen Aufgaben der Translatoren in den Sprachendiensten der Vereinten Nationen

Martin FORSTNER

1 Einleitung

Dies war nicht das erste CIUTI FORUM, das in den Räumen der Vereinten Nationen in Genf stattfand, aber es war das erste, das die Vereinten Nationen in den Mittelpunkt stellte, und zwar deren *Languages Services & Conference Services Division, UNO Geneva.* Vertreter der jeweiligen Abteilungen *(Arabic, Chinese, English, French, Russian & Spanish Translation Service)* ergriffen das Wort und legten dar, was es denn gerade bei ihnen mit dem Titel dieses CIUTI FORUMs 2007 *New Needs, New Translators* auf sich habe. Für die Translatoren (d.h. Übersetzer und Konferenzdolmetscher) ausbildenden Institute (insbesondere derjenigen, die der CIUTI angehören) war dies von besonderem Interesse, da Informationen über die Sprachendienste dazu anregen können, die Ausbildungsprogramme zu überprüfen und unter Umständen Veränderungen vorzunehmen oder neue Komponenten einzufügen. Darüber hinaus sollten die Institute erfahren, welche akademische Ausbildung bei der Rekrutierung von Translatoren bei UNO GENEVA (UNOG) vorausgesetzt werde, welche Fremdsprachenkombinationen besonders nachgefragt seien (etwa solche mit Arabisch, Chinesisch oder Russisch), und welche speziellen Fachkenntnisse (Recht, Wirtschaft, Politik) erwartet würden.

Dieses Forum bot demnach den ausbildenden Instituten Gelegenheit, sich über dieses Marktsegment, das die UNOG darstellt, zu informieren. Allerdings hatten die Vertreter der Institute stets zu bedenken, welche Teile ihrer Studiengänge sie im Interesse einer gewünschten *Translation for the United Nations* anpassen können oder sollen, denn bei aller Rücksichtnahme auf ihre Wünsche stellen die Vereinten Nationen doch nur einen kleinen Arbeitgeber dar, verglichen mit dem globalen und extrem diversifizierten Markt der Sprachendienstleistungen, auf dem Übersetzer und Dolmetscher weltweit tätig sind.

Während des FORUMs gewann man den Eindruck, als ob die Sprachendienste der Vereinten Nationen Änderungen anstrebten und Anpassungen an die modernen kommunikationstechnischen Möglichkeiten mit dem Ziel ins Auge fassten[1], die mehrsprachige Kommunikation innerhalb und außerhalb der Organisation der Vereinten Nationen nicht nur effektiver, sondern sogar effizienter zu gestalten, was angesichts der wachsenden Bedeutung der Kommunikation in der internationalen Politik gar nicht hoch genug eingeschätzt werden kann. Allerdings hat sich die Rolle der Vereinten Nationen (und ihrer Sonderorganisationen) in der Weltöffentlichkeit gewandelt und damit auch die Art und Weise der notwendigen Translationsleistungen.

1 Mit derartigen Aufgaben waren in den letzten Jahren auch die Sprachendienste der Europäischen Kommission befaßt, so etwa die Generaldirektion Übersetzung (Directorate-General for Translation) und die Generaldirektion Kommunikation (Directorate-General for Communication), die immerhin mit 23 Amtssprachen zu arbeiten haben.

2 Die Weltgesellschaft als vernetzte Kommunikationsgemeinschaft

In ihrer Habilitationsschrift *Vom Völkerrecht zum Weltrecht* (2007) hat Angelika Emmerich-Fritsche die besondere Rolle der Vereinten Nationen hervorgehoben, wobei sowohl deren bisherige Leistungen gewürdigt, als auch Veränderungen, die vorgenommen werden müßten, angeregt wurden, um dem Ziel einer Weltrechtsordnung[2] näher zu kommen. Emmerich-Fritsche unterstrich, daß eine solche Weltrechtsordnung einer Weltöffentlichkeit bedürfe, die dann, letztendlich, eine Weltcivitas wäre, was allerdings ein allgemeines Weltbürgerbewußtsein voraussetze, an dem es aber heute noch fehle. Miriam Meckel (2001: 3), die von einer Weltgemeinschaft spricht, sieht eine solche Weltöffentlichkeit noch in weiter Ferne, da eine solche eine auf Zusammengehörigkeit ausgerichtete menschliche Willensbildung voraussetze.

Die derzeitige Weltgesellschaft[3] kann als „erdumspannende Gesamtheit aller möglichen Kommunikationen" verstanden werden (so Kneer/Nassehi 1993: 155), allerdings noch nicht als Vor-

2 Fischer-Lescano 2010: 20f. zeigte, daß die Weltgesellschaft wegen ihres Bedürfnisses nach Regulierung globaler Sachverhalte von zahlreichen Rechtsregimen durchdrungen ist, seien diese nun supranationales Recht der von Staaten selbst ins Leben gerufenen internationalen Organisationen mit eigener Rechtssetzungsbefugnis (z.B. die Europäische Union) oder transnationale Rechte, die durch private Akteure mit teilweise staatlicher Beteiligung durch Verträge entstanden. Wir haben es nunmehr mit einem neuen Rechtspluralismus zu tun mit einem Zustand von Interlegalität, „in dem parallele Normsystem unterschiedlicher Herkunft sich wechselseitig anregen, gegenseitig verbinden, ineinander greifen und durchdringen, ohne zu einheitlichen Super-Ordnungen zu verschmelzen, die ihre Teile absorbieren, sondern in ihrem Nebeneinander als heterarchische Gebilde dauerhaft bestehen" (25). – Zum transnationalen Recht im Rahmen eines globalen Rechtspluralismus s. Fischer-Lescano/Teubner 2006: bes. 143f.

3 Dazu Forstner 2000.

stufe eines integrativen globalen Entwicklungsprozesses, an dessen Ende optional die „Weltgemeinschaft" aufscheint, die durch ein Weltbewusstsein als integrierte Gesamtheit aller Denkprozesse, Kommunikationen und Handlungen im globalen Kontext (so Meckel 2001: 47)[4] geprägt sei. Heute bereits von einer allgemeinen Weltöffentlichkeit sprechen zu wollen, ist also verfrüht, vielmehr gibt es eine Anzahl[5] von Teilöffentlichkeiten, die nebeneinander existieren und die erst durch die Medien hergestellt, aber auch verbunden werden. Diese wenn auch noch immer unvollständige Vernetzung läßt sich nicht mehr rückgängig machen[6]. Zwar ist die enge Verbindung von kommunikativer und ökonomischer Freiheit durch die wirtschaftliche Globalisierung und kommunikationspolitische Liberalisierung nicht immer automatisch gegeben, aber sie ist zumindest erwünscht[7], da sie als unerläßlich gilt für die

4 Nach Meckel 2001: 47f. sei damit Weltgesellschaft aus systemtheoretischer Perspektive nichts anderes und vor allem wenig mehr als das „theoretische Konstrukt der Möglichkeit von Weltgesellschaft".

5 Nach Meckel 2001: 51 haben wie es zu tun mit „einer Vielzahl von Teilöffentlichkeiten, von denen die Weltöffentlichkeit lediglich *eine* ist. Weltöffentlichkeit existiert weder als übergeordnete oder Meta-Öffentlichkeit verschiedener gesellschaftlicher Systeme, noch führt sie die unterschiedlichen Öffentlichkeiten einzelner Teilsysteme integrativ zusammen".

6 Meckel 2001: 67: Wenn Information und Wissen zu zentralen Produktionsfaktoren avancieren, wenn sich die Wirtschaftsprozesse dematerialisieren und kommunikativ vernetzen, dann ist fehlende Kommunikationsfreiheit langfristig betrachtet gleichbedeutend mit einer Abkopplung von den transnationalen Wirtschaftsnetzwerken, die benötigt werden, um auch die nationale Ökonomie auf Modernisierungskurs zu halten. Insofern impliziert die Vernetzung – nicht unmittelbar, aber langfristig konsequent – kommunikative (und damit politische) Freiheit.

7 In diesem Zusammenhang sei verwiesen auf die Neue Weltinformationsordnung, die die Zukunftskompetenzen unterstrich und die den Vernetzungsdiskurs einläutete, was letztendlich bereits 1979 aufgenommen wurde in die Mediendeklaration der UNESCO (dazu Meckel 2001: 91), in deren Artikel IX es heißt: *free flow and wider and more balanced dissemination of information* (UNESCO 1979): Declaration on Fundamental Principles concerning the Contribution of the Mass Media to Strengthening Peace and Inter-

wirtschaftliche Entwicklung eines jeden Staates, selbst wenn dann und wann versucht wird, hier manipulierend einzugreifen. Es zeigt sich, daß diese gesellschaftlich vernetzte Welt sich politisch noch immer als eine Staatengemeinschaft[8] versteht, wobei die Vereinten Nationen eine Art Rechtssetzungsorgan für diese nichtorganisierte Gemeinschaft geworden sind, selbst wenn ihr Durchsetzungsorgane fehlen (vgl. Paulus 2001: 361, 423f. und 430).

3 Die Vereinten Nationen als organisierte Staatengemeinschaft

Nicht mehr allein unter den Aspekten des Völkerrecht *(international law)* oder der Internationalen Beziehungen *(international relations)* befaßt sich die Fachliteratur mit der Organisation der Vereinten Nationen, vielmehr ist diese selbst Gegenstand eines eigenen Forschungszweigs mit durchaus unterschiedlichen theoretischen Ansätzen geworden[9]. Die realistische Schule ist der Auffassung, dass das Streben nach Macht sowie das Eigeninteresse der Staaten die wichtigsten Kategorien zum Verständnis internationaler Politik darstellen würden, weil die souveränen Nationalstaaten keiner übergeordneten Instanz mit Sanktionskompetenz unterworfen seien

national Understanding, to the Promotion of Human Rights and to Countering Racism, Apartheit and Incitement to War. Adopted by acclamation on 22nd November 1978 at the Twentieth Session of the General Conference of Unesco held in Paris). – Auch die EU verkündete auf dem EU-Sondergipfel von Lissabon (23./24. März 2000) ein „eEurope – Eine Informationsgesellschaft für alle", mit dem Ziel, ein digital mündiges Europa zu schaffen.

8 Und nicht, wie eine idealistische Vision es sieht, eine Völkergemeinschaft (dazu Paulus 2001: 289).

9 Dazu Gareis/Varwick 2006: 60ff. mit umfangreicher Fachliteratur; außerdem Barnett/Finnemore 2007: 41ff.; Gordenker/Jönsson 2007: 85ff.; Varwick 2007: 240ff.

und auch nicht sein könnten. „Die Realisten sehen deshalb in der rein intergouvernementalen Zusammenarbeit der Nationalstaaten die einzige Möglichkeit, das Gleichgewicht der Kräfte zu erhalten und damit Kriege zu verhindern und Zusammenarbeit zu fördern" (Gareis/Varwick 2006: 61), weshalb die Vereinten Nationen weiterhin ein Werkzeug der Großmächte blieben, die in einer anarchischen Welt ihre eigenen Interessen durchzusetzen suchten[10]. Demnach hinge der Einfluß der Vereinten Nationen auf die Welt davon ab, was die mächtigen Staaten gerade wollen, nicht zuletzt deshalb, weil diese sie weitgehend finanzierten[11]. Allerdings funktioniere das nicht immer, denn häufig entsprächen die Vereinten Nationen nicht dem, was eine Großmacht von ihnen erwartete[12].

Die sog. idealistische Schule der Internationalen Beziehungen stellt hingegen darauf ab, wie Anarchie zu regulieren sei, und verweist darauf, dass internationale Kooperation für alle Beteiligten Vorteile bringe, was allmählich zu einer Art universeller Gemeinschaft führe, die aus sich heraus friedensstiftend wirke (Gareis/Varwick 2006: 62). Demnach liege es, was auch die sog. rationalistische Schule betont, im Interesse der Staaten, eine Organisation wie die Vereinten Nationen zu haben und internationale Abkommen durchzusetzen, von denen die Staaten glauben, sie würden ihnen nützen (Barnett/Finnemore 2007: 45).

10 Barnett/Finnemore 2007: 44: International organizations, including the UN, exist because strong states create them and find their continued existence serves their interests.

11 Barnett/Finnemore 2007: 44: From a realistic perspective, the UN's influence in the world is dependent on what powerful states are willing to do. Without the support of strong states, the UN's ability to mediate disputes or mount a peacekeeping mission would be negligible. Without the financial contributions of strong states, the UN's ability to do any of the development assistance, human rights work, or technical assistance of specialized agencies would be hobbled. Further, strong states can stop the UN from doing anything they do not like by using the veto and/or withholding financial support.

12 The US's failure to get approval for a war against Iraq in March 2003 is only one of the most obvious and recent examples of a great power disappointed (Barnett/Finnemore 2007: 45).

Zusammenfassend ist zu sagen, daß die Vereinten Nationen auf der multilateralen[13] intergouvernementalen Zusammenarbeit der ihr angehörenden Staaten beruhen, die aber keine direkten Souveränitätsrechte an sie abgegeben haben[14], weshalb sie als internationale Organisation auch kein einheitlicher Akteur sind, sie vielmehr ein weit verzweigtes und komplexes Netzwerk von Haupt-, Neben- und Spezialorganen darstellen mit sowohl unterschiedlichen Kompetenzen und Zuständigkeitsbereichen als auch differierenden organisatorischen Strukturen (Gareis/Varwick 2006: 70). In der Hauptsache fungieren die Vereinten Nationen als Forum, in dem die verschiedenen Interessen formuliert und diskutiert werden können, wobei aber ständig Konsens gesucht wird und Kampfabstimmungen vermieden werden.

13 Varwick/Knelangen 2002: 5: Multilateralismus kann ganz allgemein als ein Politikstil verstanden werden, bei dem die Beziehungen zwischen drei oder mehr Staten auf der Basis bestimmter allgemein akzeptierter Verhaltensregeln und Prinzipien ablaufen. – Multilateralismus ist das konzeptionelle Gegenmodell zum Unilateralismus, bei dem einzelne Staaten sich vorbehalten, je nach eigener Interessenlage alleine und, wenn notwendig, auch gegen andere Staaten zu handeln. In der politischen Praxis neigen vor allem große und mächtige Staaten zu unilateralem Vorgehen, weil sie sich davon die maximale Durchsetzung ihrer eigenen Interessen versprechen.

14 Gareis/Varwick 2006: 65: Eine Ausnahme stellt der Bereich der Friedenssicherung dar, in dem es formal alle Mitgliedstaaten bindende Entscheidungen des Sicherheitsrates geben kann, die sogar durch den Einsatz militärischer Zwangsmaßnahmen durchgesetzt werden können. – Wie Rosenfeld 2009: 219 ausführte, liegt die Hauptverantwortung für die Wahrung des Weltfriedens weiterhin beim Sicherheitsrat, der in den letzten Jahrzehnten seinen Aktionsradius auch auf die Nachsorge von Konflikten erweiterte (172), so daß nunmehr neben das *ius in bello* ein *ius post bellum* getreten ist. – Diese positive Einschätzung steht im Gegensatz zu den Ausführungen Maurice Bertrands, eines hochrangigen Mitglieds der Gemeinsamen Inspektionseinheit (Joint Inspection Unit) der Vereinten Nationen, der den Beitrag des Sicherheitsrates zur Friedenserhaltung sehr skeptisch beurteilte. Daß die Welt heute sicherer geworden sei, sei der Integration Europas zu verdanken. „Die UN haben bei diesem Wandel einer kriegerischen in eine friedliche Welt keinerlei Rolle gespielt“ (Bertrand 2005: 177).

Was die Zukunft der Vereinten Nationen angeht, so wirkt sich das Spannungsverhältnis zwischen den Zielen und Grundsätzen ihrer Charta auf der einen und der politischen Realität auf der anderen Seite stark aus, denn wesentliche Grundsätze der Charta[15] werden in der Praxis der internationalen Politik immer aufs Neue relativiert, verändert oder schlichtweg systematisch missachtet[16], doch ist es unwahrscheinlich, daß die Vereinten Nationen untergehen oder keine Rolle mehr spielen werden, denn die global relevanten Problembereiche Menschenrechtsschutz, Wirtschaft, Entwicklung und Umweltschutz lassen sich kaum ohne sie effektiv behandeln. Andererseits werden sich die Vereinten Nationen sicherlich nicht zu einer Weltregierung entwickeln können, denn dann müßten sie auch Koordinations- und Sanktionsbefugnisse erhalten, was zu äußerst problematischen Machtkonzentrationen führen könnte. Vielmehr werden kleine Veränderungen vorgenommen werden können, was Gareis/Varwick 2006: 316 als *Muddling Through* bezeichnen, denn es sind die Mitgliedstaaten selbst, denen die Unfähigkeit der Vereinten Nationen, sich tiefgreifend zu reformieren, anzulasten ist (so Paschke 2005: 173). Die Vereinten Nationen bleiben „eine unvollkommene, reformbedürftige, aber doch in vielen Bereichen eminent wichtige internationale Organisation", die für die Stabilität des internationalen Systems unverzichtbar sind, da tragfähige Antworten auf die zentralen Menschheitsprobleme im 21. Jahrhundert allenfalls multi-

15 Nach Paulus 2001: 306 ist unbestritten, daß die Charta der Vereinten Nationen ein multilateraler Vertrag ist und keine Verfassung!

16 Gareis/Varwick 2006: 315 fassten wie folgt zusammen: „Der souveränen Gleichheit aller Staaten steht ein ausgeprägtes Machtgefälle, der Pflicht zur friedlichen Streitbeilegung allgegenwärtige Gewalt im internationalen System gegenüber und trotz des Allgemeinen Gewaltverbots nehmen sich die Staaten immer wieder das Recht auf unilaterale Gewaltanwendung. Zudem erzwingt die Globalisierung grundlegender Problembereiche eine Erosion staatlicher Souveränität, die aber gemäß der Charta und dem festgeschriebenen Verbot der Einmischung in die inneren Angelegenheiten der Staaten untersagt ist".

lateral zu geben seien und sie in dem Geflecht multilateraler Regime und Organisationen eine herausragende Rolle spielen, wie Gareis/Varwick 2006: 319 meinen.

Generalsekretär Kofi Annan machte dies deutlich, als er im März 2006[17] feststellte, „today's United Nations is vastly different from the Organization that emerged from the San Francisco conference more than 60 years ago", was nicht zuletzt damit zusammenhängt, daß die Vereinten Nationen mittlerweile verstärkt mit Nichtregierungsorganisationen (NGOs) zusammenarbeiten. Diese[18] sind oft nichtstaatlich und betrachten sich als Vertreter einer *global civil society*, die bei den Vereinten Nationen ihre Bühne finden (vgl. Anheier/Glasius/Kaldor 2001; Martens 2005), denn Art. 71 der Charta der Vereinten Nationen sieht dies für *nongovernmental organizations* (NGOs) auch so vor. Ihr Verhältnis ist ein solches der Gegenseitigkeit, denn die Vereinten Nationen greifen auf die NGOs zurück, um bestimmte Ziele zu erreichen[19], z.B. im Umweltschutz, bei der Förderung der Frauen, zur Durchsetzung der Menschenrechte[20], und umgekehrt bedienen sich die NGOs der

17 Kofi A. Annan: Investing in the United Nations. For a Stronger Organization Worldwide. UN Document A/60/692, 7 March 2006, 1, zitiert nach Weiss/Daws 2007: 23.

18 Weiss/Daws 2007: 6: Hence, it is no longer disputed that NGOs play a prominent role on the world stage and that we are unable to fully understand contemporary international relations without looking at such nonstate actors.

19 Wapner 2007: 262: What is essential is that the United Nations and NGOs look to each other to compensate for their own failings and work together to address global collective action problems. – Zum Verhältnis zu den supranationalen und transnationalen Organisationen s. Zürn 2010: 16.

20 Über die Menschenrechts-Konventionen, die in den 1980er Jahren verabschiedet wurden, schreiben Weiss/Daws 2007: 12: While ratification and implementation are not always correlated as closely as we would like, it nonetheless is significant that almost a hundred countries, over half of UN member states, have now ratified six of the seven major human rights instruments, each of which has a committee of experts to monitor implementation; and some of which are supplemented by optional protocols. Moreover, about three-quarters of member states have ratified the International Covenants on Civil and Political Rights and on Economic, Social and Cul-

Vereinten Nationen, um sich zu legitimieren[21]. Hervorzuheben ist, daß die Vereinten Nationen in den letzten Jahrzehnten an Ansehen gewonnen haben in Bereichen des Menschenrechtsschutzes, der Stärkung von Demokratie, der Verbesserung des weltweiten Lebensstandards, aber auch im Feld der friedenserhaltenden Operationen *(peacekeeping operations)*[22], denn diese Probleme können selbst mächtige Einzelstaaten nicht allein lösen. Umwelt, Bevölkerungsexplosion, Urbanisierung sowie Terrorismus waren Themen

---

tural Rights, and over 20 percent of countries the International Convention on the Elimination of All Forms of Racial Discrimination as well as the Convention on the Elimination of All Forms of Discrimination Against Women (CEDAW), a kind of international bill of rights for women.

21 Dazu Wapner 2007: 257 und 261: While scholars and others initially looked to NGOs as the paradigmatic expression of global civil society and thus representative of humanity as a whole, this has been changing. Since the mid-1990s, many scholars (as well as governments) have begun to question the representative character, legitimacy, integrity, public-mindedness, and accountability of civil society actors themselves. Rather than assuming that their inputs were positive, this criticism has problematized a set of questions revolving around governing authority and accountability at the global level. As their critics often point out, NGOs are unelected groups, operate free from systematic scrutiny, and at times advance self-serving interests. Furthermore, since many civil society organizations have headquarters in the global North, many observers regard civil society organizations as promoting the agenda of industrialized countries. In short, while some see civil society as representing the interests of humanity, serious questions have been raised about its ability to play this role. These criticisms of NGOs place the UN in a quandary, since it wishes to maintain its own claims to good governance and simultaneously depends on NGOs to help it establish this reputation.

22 Weiss/Daws 2007: 11: But what made the UN's design and establishment so remarkable was its broader ambitions – for human rights on a global scale, for sovereign independence and freedom and democracy in all parts of the world, for improvement in standards of living worldwide. While such lofty idealism is often derided, more of that original vision has been achieved than is often recognized. No period in human history has seen so many people benefiting from advances in life expectancy, health, education, and living standards as in the UN's lifetime. The organization cannot claim credit for all the progress that had been made, any more than it can be blamed for the lack thereof.

Globaler Konferenzen (vgl. Schechter 2005), die den gegenwärtigen Diskurs um eine Weltordnungspolitik[23] *(global governance)* stark beeinflußten.

Die Vereinten Nationen sind demnach als Organisation für die internationale Staatengemeinschaft unerläßlich, denn obwohl sie keine Durchsetzungsorgane haben, können sie neues Recht setzen und die Weltöffentlichkeit beeinflussen, was aber ein gutes Kommunikationsmanagement erforderlich macht. Gerade in diesem Bereich sind in den letzten Jahren auffallende Veränderungen zu konstatieren.

4 Mehrsprachigkeit als Kommunikationsproblem

Unter Bezugnahme auf die Menschenrechtskonventionen der Vereinten Nationen ist in der einschlägigen Fachliteratur oft von linguistischen Menschenrechten *(linguistic human rights*[24]*)* die Rede, obwohl der Begriff selbst im Internationalen Recht höchst umstritten ist[25]. Dabei wird vertreten, daß jeder Mensch das Recht habe, seine Sprache immer und überall zu verwenden[26], was durch

23 Dazu Varwick/Knelangen 2002: 6 ff.; Gareis/Varwick 2006: 74: Unter *global governance* versteht die Politikwissenschaft ein alternatives Steuerungsinstrument des internationalen Systems, das sowohl internationale Organisationen als auch informelle Regelungen und Normen umfasst. Dieses Konzept ist ausdrücklich nicht mit gelegentlich anzutreffenden Vorstellungen von einer Art Weltregierung *(global government)* zu verwechseln, sondern ist am besten mit dem Begriff „Weltordnungspolitik" zu übersetzen.

24 So Phillipson 1992: 93 ff.; dazu auch Phillipson 1999; vgl. Creech 2005: 138 ff.

25 Dazu die umfassende Untersuchung von Arzoz 2009: bes. 542, 548, 553 und 566 ff.; 573: language rights have a more disputed character than what some seem to suggest. There is no universal understanding of language rights; 574: Language rights are local, historically rooted claims, not fixed universals.

26 Dies führte dann zu neuen Problemen, etwa der Art, inwieweit dieses Individualrecht ausgedehnt werden könne und solle auf Minderheiten – also auf

die am 18. Dezember 1992 von der durch die Generalversammlung verabschiedeten *Declaration on the Rights of Persons Belonging to National or Ethnic, Religious and Linguistic Minorities* gestützt werde[27], doch ist dabei zu bedenken, dass es sich hier um *soft law* handelt, das keinesfalls für alle Staaten bindend ist[28].

Daraus, daß jeder Mensch seine Sprache verwenden dürfe, folgt noch nicht, daß er verlangen könne, seine Gesprächspartner müßten diese seine Sprache auch kennen und können. Das ihm zugestandene linguistische Individualrecht ist demnach zu trennen von der Notwendigkeit, ihm auf gemeinschaftlicher Ebene, sei sie nun lokal, regional, national oder global, die Kommunikation zu ermöglichen, denn hier geht es um kommunikative Praktikabilität, weshalb mit Emmerich-Fritsche 2007: 639 argumentiert werden könnte, daß man von allen Bürgern grundsätzlich ein Interesse für Fremdsprachen erwarten dürfe, wenn sie sich in der globalen Kommunikationsgesellschaft bewegen wollen, was ja noch lange nicht mit dem Verlust der eigenen Sprache verbunden wäre, denn das Recht auf „eigene Sprache" werde insoweit nicht berührt. Sie führte aus, daß ein Recht, ausschließlich in einer Sprache, nämlich der eigenen, kommunizieren zu dürfen, nicht erkennbar sei. Auch gebe es

---

Minderheitensprachen (vgl. dazu Varennes 1999; dazu Creech 2005: 138 f. über den Schutz von Minderheitensprachen).

27 Dazu Wright 2004: 191 f. – Diese Deklaration läßt aber zahlreiche Einschränkungen auf nationaler Ebene zu; letzten Endes hängt alles vom guten Willen des jeweiligen Staates ab (ausführlich mit Literaturangaben Creech 2005: 139). In Europa bieten The Framework Convention for the Protection of National Minorities (1995) und die European Charter for Regional or Minority Languages (1992) den am weitesten fortgeschrittenen Schutz von Minderheitensprachen (Arzoz 2009: 554 ff.; dazu auch Guskow 2009 über die Entstehungsgeschichte der Europäischen Charta der Regional- oder Minderheitensprachen).

28 Arzoz 2009: 568: Freedom of language includes the right to use one's mother tongue or any other language, both in speech and writing. Linguistic intolerance and repression of non-dominant languages is regarded to be inconsistent with fundamental rights. Freedom of language only guarantees the right to freely determine one's linguistic behaviour. Its scope is the private sphere.

kein Menschenrecht auf Ignoranz oder darauf, eine andere Sprache, auf die sich die Menschheit als Weltkommunikationssprache in globalen Angelegenheiten einige, *nicht* erlernen zu müssen, um auf Weltebene kommunikationsfähig zu sein. Ebenso wenig könne man volle Kommunikationsfähigkeit beanspruchen, wenn man sich beharrlich weigere, Sprachen zu lernen, obwohl man es könnte.

Heutzutage wird sehr selten darauf hingewiesen, daß die Mehrsprachigkeit[29] oft beträchtliche negative kommunikative Nebenwirkungen haben kann[30], behindert sie doch die transnationale zwischenmenschliche Kommunikation, oder verhindert diese sogar, wie Grucza 2003: 15 am Beispiel der Mehrsprachigkeit Mitteleuropas ausführte. „Sprachen sind einfach Faktoren, die zwar manche Menschen miteinander verbinden, andere aber voneinander trennen (können), und dies nicht nur kommunikativ, sondern auch bezüglich ihrer Identität."

Da die Lösung weder weltweit noch in der EU darin bestehen kann, daß alle Menschen alle Sprachen sprechen (was in der Europäischen Union mit ihren 23 Amtsprachen nicht einmal den Sprachgenies unter den Eurokraten in Brüssel gelingt), tendiert der weltweite Markt[31] zu einem selektiven Multilingualismus, denn es werden für

29 Nach Stickel 2005: 100 ist zu unterscheiden zwischen Plurilinguismus, worunter die individuelle Mehrsprachigkeit zu verstehen ist, und Multilingualismus, womit soziale oder territoriale Mehrsprachigkeit gemeint ist. Die beiden Arten der Mehrsprachigkeit „treffen nur teilweise zusammen: In einer mehrsprachigen Gesellschaft oder einem mehrsprachigen Land sind nicht alle Menschen mehrsprachig." – Bilingual verwenden wir bei Menschen, die zwei Sprachen beherrschen, seien diese nun „natürlich" erworben durch Herkunft und Erziehung, oder sekundär durch Erlernen einer Fremdsprache. Bei Translatoren sprechen wir von funktionaler Zweisprachigkeit; vgl. dazu Forstner 2004: 50 ff.

30 Darauf hat jüngst Schneiders 2007: 28 f. hingewiesen.

31 Die Berücksichtigung des Marktes im Zusammenhang mit Sprachen wird angegriffen von der Soziolinguistin Skutnabb-Kangas (1999: 197), nach deren Meinung dadurch nicht nur Umweltvernichtung und Vergrößerung des Abstandes zwischen Arm und Reich, sondern auch *linguistic and cultural genocide* bewirkt würden.

die Kommunikation diejenigen Sprachen verwendet, die den größten Kommunikationswirkungsgrad[32] haben, wenn es darum geht, mit Menschen, die eine andere Sprache sprechen, zu kommunizieren. Das bedeutet, daß Menschen, die weltweit miteinander kommunizieren *müssen*, sich derjenigen Sprachen bedienen, von denen sie glauben, oder von denen sie auf Grund ihrer langjährigen Erfahrung wissen, daß sie mit ihnen den größtmöglichen Erfolg erzielen bei der Verbreitung ihrer Anliegen, Wünsche, Ideen, Angebote und Interessen. Diesen größten Kommunikationswert hat nun einmal heute das Englische als Kontaktsprache im internationalen Marketing, in der Diplomatie, Wirtschaft und im digitalen Informationstransfer (Haarmann 2002b: 159) weltweit, aber auch in der Europäischen Union (vgl. de Swaan 2002: 158 und 161; Jaekel 2009: 447).

Es hat sich in den letzten Jahrzehnten gezeigt, daß „der Zugriff auf das Englische oder andere Weltsprachen eine *Conditio sine qua non* für die kommunikative Mobilität interkultureller Kontakte ist“ (Haarmann 2002a: 21). Zwar ist das Englische nicht immer vorherrschend, denn es existieren regionale Sprachenzonen, in denen Spanisch (Lateinamerika), Französisch (West- und Zentralafrika), Arabisch oder Chinesisch verwendet werden, gleichwohl können wir von einem Megatrend des sprachlichen Kosmopolitismus sprechen, der strukturiert ist als ein *national/English bilingualism*[33], der weitgehend die Forderung nach kommunikati-

32 Forstner 2000: 163; de Swaan 2002: 33: communication potential of a language.

33 Haarmann 2004: 111: The network society has produced a new pattern of communication, which I call *national-English bilingualism* (NEB). – On the other hand, we are confronted with the reality that NEB is needed for keeping us in the currents of global information exchange (115). Vgl. Haarmann 2002b: 165 f.: Die Zweitsprachenkomponente Englisch dieses Kommunikationstyps sei jeweils stabil (166). Es entstehe aber eine technologisch hochgerüstete, funktional-zweisprachige Elite von Wissensmonopolisten, die die Entwicklungsdynamik in den wirtschaftlichen, politischen und kulturellen Abläufen der Network Society kontrolliere, während die große Masse der Bevölkerung als Konsumenten vom akkumulierten Wissen der wenigen abhängig sei (167). Aber diese Elite sei durchaus offen und für jeden zugäng-

ver Effektivität und Effizienz erfüllt[34], denn die Dominanz des Englischen in der Welt ist nirgendwo eine absolute: „Überall stehen lokale Sprachen in Konkurrenz zum Englischen, dessen funktionales Spektrum sich mit den lokalen Sprachen verzahnt“ (Haarmann 2002b: 159). Zu diesen Sprachen zählen diejenigen Sprachen, denen sich die Vereinten Nationen seit ihrer Gründung bedienen. Insoweit sind sie recht gut positioniert, denn ihre Großsprachen haben ein hohes Kommunikationspotential, einen großen Kommunikationsradius und einen hohen Gebrauchswert[35].

4.1 Vorrang für die kommunikative Praktikabilität

Als die Vereinten Nationen nach dem Zweiten Weltkrieg das Fünf-Sprachen-System (seit 1973 mit Arabisch[36] das Sechs-Sprachen-System) in ihre Charta aufnahmen, entschieden sie sich, freilich

---

lich, „vorausgesetzt er versteht es, sich mit dem geforderten Know-how auszurüsten, und dazu gehören heutzutage eine Vertrautheit mit den Funktionen der digitalen Literalität sowie aktive englische Sprachkenntnisse. Wenn sich diese Requisiten noch mit einer wissenschaftlichen Fachausbildung assoziieren, dann sind eine aktive Teilhabe an und Einflussnahme auf die Wissensmonopole der Network Society gesichert“.

34 Über kommunikative Effizienz und über Phänomene des Sprachenwandels s. Roelcke 2002: 34.

35 Dazu Manz 2002: 37; Coulmas 1992: 83 ff.; vgl. auch Li 2009: 427: market value of a language.

36 Als offizielle Sprachen wurden bereits in Art 111 der Charta der VN Chinesisch, Französisch, Russisch, Englisch und Spanisch erwähnt und dann in der Resolution 2 (I) vom 1. Februar 1946 festgelegt, ehe dann 1973 noch Arabisch (Resolution 3190 (XXVIII) hinzu kam (vgl. dazu Edzard 1998: 36; Tabory 1980: 238 f. und 251 ff.; Baigorri-Jalón 2004: 30 f.). 1974, nachdem 1973 die BRD und die DDR in die Vereinten Nationen aufgenommen worden waren, erhielt Deutsch den Status eine Dokumentensprache, was bedeutet, daß die wichtigsten offiziellen Schriftstücke der Generalversammlung sowie die Resolutionen des Sicherheitsrates und des Wirtschafts- und Sozialrates ins Deutsche übersetzt werden, allerdings tragen die deutschsprachigen Staaten die Kosten dafür (dazu Paqué 1997: 63 ff.).

ohne sich dessen bewußt zu sein, für den Vorrang einer praktikablen Kommunikation, waren es doch die am meisten verbreiteten Großsprachen, selbst wenn zunächst politische Erwägungen vorrangig gewesen sein dürften.

Angesichts der Vielzahl der Sprachen[37] der Welt praktizieren die Vereinten Nationen eine *geregelte* Mehrsprachigkeit und erreichen dadurch den Großteil der Weltbevölkerung. Sie haben demnach eine gute Ausgangsposition im Wettbewerb der Kommunikationsmedien und verfügen über ein großes globales kommunikatives Funktionspotential mit Chinesisch, Englisch, Arabisch, Russisch, Spanisch und Französisch[38]. Dabei steht das Englische im Vordergrund als Motor der Globalisierung, als Symbol der Modernität und als Prestigesprache, bietet es doch den Zugang zu Wissen und Technologie und damit im Endeffekt Millionen von Bürgern, die sie als Zweitsprache erlernen, die Möglichkeit der transnationalen Teilhabe an der weltweiten Kommunikation (dazu Wright 2004: 117 und 155f.; vgl. auch Schendl/Seidlhofer/Widdowson 2003: 188f.) Dieses Sechs-Sprachenregime[39], das allerdings ergänzt wird durch weitere Sprachen in den regionalen Unterorganisationen, hat einen hohen Kommunikationswirkungsgrad und kann als weit-

37 Je nach Zählweise gibt es etwa 5000–6800 Sprachen der Welt, aber 100 Großsprachen decken gut 90 Prozent der Weltbevölkerung ab. „Diese hegemoniale Tendenz nimmt weiter zu“ (Hinnenkamp 2010: 28; Verweis auf Nettle/Romaine 2000). Man kann es nicht oft genug wiederholen: „Der weitaus größte Teil der Sprachen wird von Gruppen von weniger als einer Million Menschen gesprochen, wobei viele Sprachen über weniger als 1000 Sprecher verfügen“ (Hinnenkamp 2010: 28; vgl. dazu Haarmann 2002a: 20f.).

38 Diese Sprachen gehören neben Hindi, Malaiisch, Portugiesisch, Japanisch und Deutsch zu den sog. *central languages*, wie de Swaan 2002: 4f. darlegte, mit jeweils mehr als 100 Millionen Sprechern, wobei Englisch die *global hyper-central language* darstellt (de Swaan 2002: 6).

39 Dazu noch immer grundlegend Paqué 1980: 166 mit einem Überblick über die Verwendung der sechs Sprachen in den wichtigsten Hauptorganen der Vereinten Nationen; außerdem Baigorri-Jalón 2004 unter besonderer Berücksichtigung der Aufgaben der Dolmetscher.

gehend selektiv multilingual bezeichnet werden kann, wohingegen die Europäische Union einen egalitären Multilingualismus vertritt, der keine Rücksicht auf die Zahl der Sprecher der jeweiligen Sprache nimmt[40], vielmehr dem Prinzip einer „integralen Multilinguistik" folgt und sich damit grundlegend unterscheidet. Der Grundsatz dieser sprachlichen Gleichberechtigung geht zurück auf die europäische Integration und ist Dogma der Europäischen Union geworden, wodurch jedem EU-Bürger der unmittelbare Kontakt zu den EU-Institutionen in seiner Sprache[41] gesichert werden soll, was bei den Vereinten Nationen als Ziel gar nicht erst angestrebt worden war. Gleichwohl handelt es sich sowohl bei der Sprachenordnung der Vereinten Nationen (und ihrer Sonderorganisationen) als auch beim Sprachenregime der Europäischen Union um Systeme mit einem sog. egalitären Multilingualismus[42] *(egalitarian multilingualism)*, der von Amts wegen festgelegt worden war[43]. Allerdings waren die Motive dafür unterschiedlich. Die Europäische Union strebt einen weitgehenden „Schutz der Sprachen" an, indem sie die Sprachenvielfalt in ihrem Sprachenregime[44] verankert

40 Wenn die Europäische Union auf die Zahl der Muttersprachler einer Sprache abstellen würde, so läge Deutsch vor Englisch, Französisch und den anderen europäischen Sprachen.

41 In der Fachliteratur spricht man daher vielfach von einem „Grundrecht auf die eigene Sprache" (Pfeil 1999: 146f.). – Für die EU ist die Begründung dafür rechtlicher Art: „Der Zugang aller EU-Bürger zu den Rechtsvorschriften, Verfahren und Informationen der Union in ihrer eigenen Sprache" ist zu gewährleisten (to give all EU citizens access to the Union's legislation, procedures and information in their own language; de donner à tous les citoyens de l'Union européenne l'accès à la législation, aux procédures et aux informations européennes dans leur propre langue).

42 Zu diesem vom Verf. schon 1996 anläßlich einer Tagung in Triest verwendeten Begriff s. Forstner 1997: 167 und Forstner 1998.

43 Theme 2002: 147 schreibt, in den Europäischen Institutionen werde ein „künstliches Reservat" gleichberechtigter Sprachen aufrechterhalten.

44 Dazu Creech 2005: 13ff. mit umfassender einschlägiger Literatur; Jaekel 2009: bes. 446f.; Weber 2004: bes. 6ff.; Ross 2003: 20ff.; Theme 2002: 21ff., 145; Cillia 2003: 30ff.; Reichelt 2006: 5: integraler Multilingualismus; außerdem Manz 2002: 140ff.

hat, was zur Folge hatte, daß die jeweiligen Staatssprachen[45] der Mitgliedstaaten zu Amtssprachen *(official languages; langues officielles)* der Union geworden sind, was zur Einrichtung sehr großer und auch leistungsstarker Übersetzungs- und Dolmetschdienste geführt hat, deren Vertreter auf diesem CIUTI-FORUM 2007 gesprochen haben. Dabei wurde die Selbstverpflichtung der Europäischen Union zur *linguistic diversity* deutlich[46], die sich immer wieder konkretisiert in großen Sprachenprogrammen zur Förderung derselben und deren Begründung darauf abstellt zu zeigen, daß der Multilingualismus eine Bereicherung sei[47] und auf keinen Fall ein Hindernis darstelle, am wenigsten im Bereich der Wirtschaft (vgl. Creech 2005: 72 und 157f.).

Allerdings ist dieser multilinguale Habitus der Europäischen Union von Nachteil für die Herausbildung einer europäischen Öffentlichkeit und damit einer übernationalen Diskursfähigkeit, wie Strohmeier 2007: 28f. betonte. „Die Sprachenvielfalt verhindert somit langfristig sowohl aus quantitativen als auch aus qualitativen Gründen das Entstehen einer europäischen Kommunikationsgemeinschaft – sowie (in der Folge) das Entstehen europäischer Medien, Parteien und Verbände“, aber der Multilingualismus ist

45 Für die übrigen Sprachen Europas gilt die 1998 in Kraft getretene Europäische Charta der Regional- oder Minderheitensprachen von 1992 (dazu Pfeil 2000; Rindler Schjerve 2003: 56f.).

46 Wagner/Bech/Martínez 2002: 1: For us multilingualism is a fundamental principle with the additional meaning of „equal rights for all official languages“.

47 Dazu Creech 2005: 51: The EU offers two basic reasons for its „linguistic diversity“ programs, one cultural in nature, the other economic. Pronouncements on linguistic diversity are often made with lofty rhetoric about the humanistic value of Europe's multilingualism, but the programs that stem from them often seem to emphasize the economic value of learning another language, in particular the major commercial languages of English, French and German. The EU's programs do not acknowledge that economic and political integration is in fact inherently antagonistic to linguistic diversity.

zu einem Dogma geworden[48], das nicht hinterfragt werden darf[49]. Jüngst hat Sue Wright (2009) auf diese Ideologiegebundenheit der europäischen Sprachenpolitik aufmerksam gemacht, was natürlich nicht dazu beiträgt, eine europäische Kommunikationsgemeinschaft[50] zu schaffen, welch letztere aber an sich gebraucht würde, denn eine lingua franca würde sicherlich von Vorteil sein[51], weshalb denn auch Cogo/Jenkins 2010: 90 meinen, die Europäische Union solle Englisch als ihre lingua franca willkommen heißen.

48 Ein schönes Beispiel, wie man die Mehrsprachigkeit der EU verinnerlichen kann, bietet Athanassiou 2006: 8: These are only some of the reasons why linguistic equality is so crucial to the EU. Taken together, these reasons clearly establish that multilingualism is so intimately associated, whether historically, conceptually or legally, with the European integration project that, notwithstanding ist inevitable complications it would be difficult to imagine a genuinely united Europe without it.

49 Über die Voreingenommenheit der Wissenschaftler hinsichtlich der Mehrsprachigkeit in Europa schrieb Schreiner 2006: 140: „Es fällt auf, dass ein übergroßer Anteil der Wissenschaftler(innen), die sich mit der Sprachenpolitik der Europäischen Union befassen, zugleich Vorschläge für ein künftiges europäisches Sprachenregime unterbreiten. Noch auffälliger ist, dass die allermeisten Vorschläge die politisch gewünschte Vielsprachigkeit erhalten und individuelle Mehrsprachigkeit zur Norm machen wollen. Es ist einigermaßen schwer, den Grund für dieses Phänomen zu finden; sicherlich spielt auch die Überzeugung eine Rolle, dass einem vielsprachigen Europa ein Wert an sich zukomme." – Ein weiterer trivialer Grund könnte sein, daß Projekte, die diesem Ziel dienen, finanziell durch die EU vorrangig gefördert zu werden scheinen (z. B. die Interkomprehensionsforschung).

50 Wright 2009: 97: One might wonder why linguistic diversity should be the goal of the EU. A common political project needs a community of communication. – There is a need for a European public sphere. – ...there is as yet no discernable European community of communication.

51 Wright 2009: 114: A lingua franca allows contact and exchange across borders and permits the circulation of knowledge. A single lingua franca does this more effectively than a number of different languages shared by different constellations of groups. A lingua franca is of general benefit to Europeans.

4.2 Kulturelle Heterogenität als Kommunikationshindernis

Die Vereinten Nationen bestehen aus einem weit verzweigten und komplexen Netz von Haupt-, Neben- und Spezialorganen mit unterschiedlichen Kompetenzen, Zuständigkeitsbereichen und Strukturen, weshalb sie nicht als einheitlicher Akteur wahrgenommen werden. Sie finden die Aufmerksamkeit der Weltöffentlichkeit zumeist immer dann, wenn die Generalversammlung die Arena spektakulärer Selbstdarstellungen der Oberhäupter der Mitgliedstaaten ist, oder wenn der Sicherheitsrat als machtpolitisches Instrument weltweit Friedenssicherungsaktionen initiiert. Andererseits geraten sie aber ins Scheinwerferlicht als eigenständiger Akteur, wenn sie große Weltkonferenzen zu Themen wie Gleichstellung der Frau, Bevölkerungsexplosion, Klima- und Umweltschutz oder Global Governance in Zusammenarbeit mit bekannten NGOs ausrichten, wobei jeweils eigene Kommunikationsformen und Strategien zur Anwendung gelangen.

Andererseits wollen sich die Vereinten Nationen an die Weltöffentlichkeit wenden, um möglichst erfolgreich ihre Ziele, Projekte und Vorhaben bekannt zu machen, wie Kofi Annan als Generalsekretär immer wieder betont hatte. Hier kommt es darauf an, daß das Generalsekretariat als Meinungsführer[52] *(opinion leader)* wahrgenommen wird, was jedoch extrem heikel sein kann, da alles vom Charisma und der Überzeugungskraft der Führungspersönlichkeiten, nicht zuletzt des Generalsekretärs selbst, abhängt. Wagen sich diese zu weit vor, wie es durch eine zunehmend selbstbewußte Inanspruchnahme eines eigenen politischen Mandats im

52 Rogers 2003: 362: *Opinion leadership* is the degree to which an individual is able to influence informally other individuals'attitudes or overt behavior in a desired way with relative frequency. Opinion leaders play an important role in diffusion networks, and are often identified and utilized in diffusion programs.

letzten Jahrzehnt der Fall war[53], so erregen sie Argwohn, wenn nicht gar Eifersucht bei den führenden Staatsmännern der Mitgliedstaaten, die die Vereinten Nationen gerade nicht aufgewertet sehen wollen, wenn es um Bemühungen um eine neue Weltordnungspolitik etwa im Bereich der Finanzen oder des Klimaschutzes geht, was eine starke und handlungsfähige Weltorganisation mit einer klar erkennbaren multilateralen Strategie erforderlich macht. Aber eine solche den Anspruch auf *opinion leadership* unterstreichende Kommunikationspolitik, die sich an die gesamte Weltöffentlichkeit richten will, sieht sich nicht nur dem Problem der Sprachenvielfalt gegenüber, was ja durch die Beschränkung auf die sechs Sprachen durchaus zufriedenstellend gelöst ist, sondern auch der kulturellen Heterogenität der Weltbevölkerung.

In diesem Zusammenhang sei verwiesen auf die Forschungsergebnisse Everett Rogers (2003: 19), der zeigte[54], daß die Verbreitung und Übertragung neuer Ideen meistens dann am besten funktioniere, wenn kommunikativ interagierenden Personen hinsichtlich ihrer Werte, Sprache, Religion, Bildung und sozioökonomischer

53 Über die Funktionen des Generalsekretärs im Wandel der Zeiten und die Versuche der Amtsinhaber, politische Freiräume zu gewinnen s. Conrady 2009. Dort bes. 283 ff. über die *Commission on Global Governance*, durch die der Generalsekretär anregen, mitwirken und steuern kann.

54 Rogers 2003: 19: One of the most distinctive problems in the diffusion of innovations is that the participants are usually quite heterophilous. – An obvious principle of human communication is that the transfer of ideas occurs most frequently between two individuals who are similar, or homophilous. *Homophily* is the degree to which two or more individuals who interact are similar in certain attributes, such as beliefs, education, socioeconomic status, and the like. In a free-choice situation, when an individual can interact with any one of a number of other individuals, the tendency is to select someone who is very similar. *Heterophily*, the opposite of homophily, is defined as the degree to which two or more individuals who interact are different in certain attributes. – Rogers verwendet in diesem Zusammenhang die englischen Begriffe *heterophily* and *homophily*, was wir hier nicht übernehmen, da im deutschsprachigen Kontext damit unweigerlich eine sexuelle Konnotation gegeben ist.

Stellung gleichartig wären. Seien sie dagegen stark heterogen, so störe dies den Transfer häufig beträchtlich, nicht zuletzt deshalb, weil die Kommunikationsversuche dann kognitive Dissonanzen bewirken können[55], da die Adressaten Informationen und Botschaften ausgesetzt werden, die mit ihren Erwartungen und Werten nicht übereinstimmten (beispielsweise im Bereich der Menschenrechtsschutzes[56]), weshalb die Botschaften der Vereinten Nationen unbeachtet bleiben oder gar auf Widerstand stoßen würden. Andererseits können unter Umständen, etwa in Ländern mit autoritären Regimen, in solchen Kommunikationssituationen die Vereinten Nationen gerade deswegen zu nachgefragten *opinion leaders* werden, da sie vermehrt in den Massenmedien genannt werden, dort auftreten und sich für humanitäre Ziele einsetzen, weshalb sich dann die Unterdrückten wegen dieser kommunikativen Nähe *(communicative proximity)* auf sie berufen können.

Auf diese Weise gelang es in der Vergangenheit oft, für Programme, Vorhaben und Ziele der Vereinten Nationen so viele Anhänger zu gewinnen, daß diese bald eine kritische Masse[57] *(critical mass)* bildeten, was zur Folge hatte, daß die Verbreitung selbsttragend *(self-sustaining)* wurde. War dies erst einmal erreicht, so beschleunigte sich die Akzeptanz, wie es etwa der Fall war bei den Konventionen gegen den Rassismus *(Convention on the Elimination of All Forms of Racial Discrimination)* oder gegen Diskriminierung der Frau *(Convention on the Elimination of All Forms of Discrimination against Women)*. Den Gegnern solcher Innovatio-

55 Rogers 2003: 306: Individuals enjoy the comfort of interacting with others who are similar. Talking with those who are markedly different requires more effort to make communication effective. Heterophilous communication between dissimilar individuals may cause cognitive dissonance because an individual is exposed to messages that are inconsistent with existing beliefs, an uncomfortable psychological state.

56 Vgl. dazu Forstner 2002: 485 ff.

57 Rogers 2003: 343: The *critical mass* occurs at the point at which enough individuals in a system have adopted an innovation so that the innovation's further rate of adoption becomes self-sustaining.

nen blieb dann nichts anderes übrig, als sich – freilich unter gewissen Vorbehalten[58] – dem Mainstream anzuschließen, denn die Normen und Werte des gesamten Systems hatten sich nunmehr geändert, in unserem Fall zugunsten der Vereinten Nationen und damit der Weltbevölkerung.

Es liegt also im Interesse der Vereinten Nationen, insbesondere des Generalsekretariats, ein solcher *opinion leader* zu werden, gerade wegen der kulturellen, gesellschaftlichen und wirtschaftlichen Heterogenität der Weltöffentlichkeit, die sie auf ihre Seite ziehen wollen, weshalb das von Kofi Annan initiierte neue Kommunikationsmanagement der Vereinten Nationen ein wichtiges Instrument war, das allerdings wegen der Komplexität des Systems der Vereinten Nationen noch immer nicht leicht zu handhaben ist und das auch anfällig für Störungen bleibt.

5 Die komplexe Kommunikationssituation der Vereinten Nationen

Von Anfang an, und dann besonders in den Zeiten des Kalten Krieges und der folgenden Periode des Nord-Süd-Gegensatzes der 1980er Jahre, konnten (oder wollten) die Vereinten Nationen nicht mit einer Stimme sprechen. Die ideologischen Gegensätze wirkten sich im Generalsekretariat, der Generalversammlung und dem Sicherheitsrats insofern aus, als die veröffentlichten Texte und Dokumente einen spezifischen Stil annahmen. Dazu schreibt Wesel, daß ein ernstzunehmender Grund für die Masse papierener Rhetorik in der UNO im erwähnten Zwang zum Konsens gelegen habe, der fast die gesamte Arbeit in ihr präge, aber oft eben auch erst

58 Beispiele für Vorbehalte der islamischen Staaten im Zusammenhang mit der Religionsfreiheit s. Forstner 2002: 490 f.; Knüppel 2010: 53 ff., 62 ff. und 78 ff.

ermögliche, denn kein Staat dürfe auf Dauer ausgeschlossen bleiben und keine Regierung nachhaltig ihr Gesicht verlieren.

> Niemand darf sich mehr vom Wegbleiben als vom Mitmachen versprechen; nicht nur die mächtigen Regierungen müssen eingebunden werden, sondern gerade bei Problemen wie der Durchsetzung der Menschenrechte oder dem Umwelt- und Klimaschutz auch möglichst viele schwächerer Staaten (Wesel 2003: 610).

Dieses Verlangen, die Vereinten Nationen sollten neutral sein, machte es immer schwieriger, nach außen mit einer Stimme zu sprechen, nachdem die Zahl der Mitglieder von 25 Staaten 1946 auf 192 Staaten zu Beginn des 21. Jahrhunderts gestiegen war und im Laufe der Zeit viele Sonderorganisationen hinzugekommen waren. Ingrid Lehmann (2003: 572), dank ihrer langjährigen Tätigkeit für die Vereinten Nationen bestens vertraut mit diesem Problem, vertrat, daß diese Aufsplitterung in Generalversammlung, Sicherheitsrat, Generalsekretariat und Sonderorganisationen und die damit verbundene Organisationsvielfalt es erschwere, eine einheitliche Position in der Öffentlichkeit deutlich zu machen.

> Kaum eine Abteilung des UN-Sekretariats hat in den vergangenen sechzig Jahren so viel Kritik, Spott und Anschuldigungen über sich ergehen lassen müssen wie die Hauptabteilung für Öffentlichkeitsarbeit, das „Department of Public Information" (DPI), das bereits 1946 eingerichtet worden war und den Auftrag hatte, das „informierte Verständnis für die Arbeit und Aufgaben der Vereinten Nationen" zu fördern[59].

Hinzu komme, daß es in den letzten Jahren neuen Machtverschiebungen im Rahmen der sich etablierenden politischen Multipolarität gekommen sei, was eine enorme Themenvielfalt zur Folge gehabt habe, was es den Vereinten Nationen sehr schwer mache, öffentlichwirksam zu sein.

Nicht weniger kritisiert wurde der Umstand, daß sich die Vereinten Nationen über viele Jahre hinweg ein Netzwerk von Informa-

59 Dazu Lehmann 2006: 201 mit umfassender Literatur; vgl. auch Conrady 2003: 55.

tionsbüros auf der ganzen Welt leisteten, das in den 1970er und 1980er Jahren auf über 60 Büros angewachsen war. Wie Lehmann 2006: 212 ausführte, sollten diese *UN Information Centres* (UNICs) die Vertretung der Vereinten Nationen in möglichst vielen Ländern der Welt sein und sowohl als Kontaktstellen mit den betreffenden Öffentlichkeiten fungieren als auch Informationen über für die Vereinten Nationen wichtige Entwicklungen in diesen Ländern nach New York zurückberichten. Einige dieser Büros hätten gut funktioniert, insbesondere, wenn die jeweilige Regierung sie finanziell und ideell unterstützte, doch in vielen Fällen wären sie zu klein, bürokratisch oder ineffizient gewesen, um wirksame PR-Arbeit machen zu können. Als die Kritik in den 1990er Jahren immer lauter geworden war, wurden sie durch Regionalisierung dann zusammengelegt, was zur Schließung von 9 Zentren in Westeuropa führte.

Darüber hinaus gab Lehmann 2003: 579 zu bedenken, dass bis zum Ende der 1990er Jahre grundlegende innerorganisatorische Voraussetzungen für effektive und zeitgemäße Informationspolitik im UN-Sekretariat gefehlt hätten, wobei sie bürokratischen Defizite benannte wie mangelnde Strategie und Koordination sowie unzureichende Personal- und Finanzausstattung, und schließlich ungenügende Aufmerksamkeit für die Wichtigkeit der weltweiten Kommunikation überhaupt auf der Führungsebene. Es war erst Generalsekretär Kofi Annan, der die Bedeutung einer effektiven Kommunikationsarbeit für die *Public Information*[60] der Vereinten Nationen erkannte und eine Gruppe von Kommunikations-

60 *Public information* im Sinne der VN läßt sich nach Lehmann 1999: 9 beschreiben als: Public information refers to the policy and practices of the United Nations and other international organizations to disseminate their information materials (print, audio, visual) worldwide, through media contacts, direct mailing and a system of information centres in key capitals, as well as the field headquarters of peacekeeping missions. The information products are usually couched in neutral, objective language, which meet the strict UN criteria of impartiality.

spezialisten unter der Leitung von Mark Malloch Brown, damals Vize-Präsident der Weltbank für externe Beziehungen, beauftragte, eine Studie über die Kommunikationsprobleme der Organisation zu erstellen, die später unter dem Titel *Global Vision – Local Voice* 1997 veröffentlicht wurde.

In der Folgezeit wurde das *Department of Public Information (DPI)* umorganisiert unter Shashi Tharoor, dem Under-Secretary-General for Communication and Public Information (dazu Crossette 2007: 282; vgl. Fröhlich 2005: 48 und 50), der am 4. Dezember 2002 seine Reformpläne vorstellte und damit die Kommunikationsthematik in allen neuen, öffentlichkeitsrelevanten Programmen planmäßig einbezogen sehen wollte (Lehmann 2006: 210), was die Vereinten Nationen in die Lage versetzen sollte, im weltweiten Informationsfluß mitzuhalten[61]. Dem DPI oblag es nunmehr, die Medien weltweit mit Nachrichten in den sechs offiziellen Sprachen zu versorgen, ganz zu schweigen von den regionalen Sonderorganisationen, die in weiteren Sprachen veröffentlichen (dazu Crossette 2007: 278).

Dieses neue Kommunikationsmanagement nutzte modernste Kommunikationstechnologie und ermöglichte eine Koordination der Öffentlichkeitsarbeit der Vereinten Nationen. Die Kommunikationsstruktur bezog nunmehr alle bei der Planung neuer Programme Beteiligten ein, was die bereits genannte Expertin und Kennerin der Vereinten Nationen, Ingrid Lehmann, als die von Kofi Annan 1997 ins Leben gerufene ‚Kultur der Kommunikation' bezeichnete. Aber dazu brauchte es, fuhr sie fort, vor allem professionelle Kommunikatoren im Sekretariat, also Mitarbeiter, die in den modernsten Techniken der Informationsaufnahme und -vermittlung geschult und geistig offen wären für die Anforderungen der globalen Informationsgesellschaft. Die Bedeutung des gesamten Kommunikationssektors werde nunmehr von der Leitung

61 Mittlerweile ist die UN-Webseite www.un.org eine der am meisten konsultierten internationalen Internetadressen und in allen sechs offiziellen Sprachen der Vereinten Nationen abrufbar (Lehmann 2006: 209).

des Sekretariats prioritär gesehen. Damit gehe die UNO gestärkt in das neue Millennium und sei in einer besseren Ausgangsposition, um ihre strategische Position in der Zukunft auszubauen (so Lehmann 2003: 589). Doch seien, worauf Ingrid Lehman auch hinwies, noch viele strukturelle Hindernisse gegeben, nicht zuletzt bedingt durch die Vielschichtigkeit der Kommunikationsebenen der Vereinten Nationen und ihrer Sonderorganisationen. Schnelle Änderungen könnten hier nicht erreicht werden, vielmehr komme es darauf an, den internen Kommunikationsfluß zu stärken und die Mitarbeiter professionell zu schulen. Dies betreffe alle Sektionen und Abteilungen der Vereinten Nationen, also die gesamte internationale Beamtenschaft *(international civil service)* im Allgemeinen und auch die Sprachendienste im Besonderen, die dafür zu sorgen haben, daß alle Dokumente und Veröffentlichungen in der angemessenen sprachlichen Form und rechtzeitig produziert werden.

6 Die Struktur der Vereinten Nationen unter kommunikativen Aspekten

Die Vereinten Nationen müssen sich in einer Weltöffentlichkeit behaupten, die wegen der Heterogenität ihrer Bürger keineswegs eine homogene Kommunikationsgemeinschaft darstellt, selbst wenn durch das Internet und zahllose weltweite Netzwerke der Eindruck von Homogenität hervorrufen wird. Doch ist dies nur ein Oberflächenphänomen, denn in der Praxis existieren regionale Kommunikationsgemeinschaften unterschiedlicher Ausdehnung. Während die Vereinten Nationen weltweit agieren, ist dies in diesem Ausmaß und dieser Intensität nicht der Fall bei einem Gebilde wie der Europäischen Union, den ASEAN-Staaten, der Arabischen Liga oder der NATO, um nur einige Beispiele zu nennen, die spezielles

Wissen nutzen, produzieren sowie verbreiten und dabei jeweils eigene Akzente setzen. Die europäische Kommunikationsgemeinschaft pflegt einen anderen Stil als die nordamerikanische oder südostasiatische oder arabische, weshalb jeweils verschiedene Kommunikationskulturen[62] mit speziellen Kommunikationsformen nebeneinander existieren.

Das System der Vereinten Nationen ist dafür ein gutes Beispiel, wobei zu unterscheiden ist zwischen dem Hauptsitz in New York (United Nations Office New York, UNONY) sowie den weiteren Büros in Genf (United Nations Office Geneva, UNOG), Wien (United Nations Office Vienna, UNOV) und Nairobi (United Nations Office Nairobi, UNON) und den zahlreichen Sonderorganisationen (ILO, FAO, UNESCO, WHO, UNIDO etc.), ganz zu schweigen von den Spezialorganen (wie UNRWA, UNICEF, UNCTAD), nicht zu vergessen die Menschenrechtsgremien wie CERD, CEDAW, CAT, CRC und die Friedensmissionen[63].

Es handelt sich also um ein riesiges Gebilde mit über den Globus verteilten Zweigstellen und Sonderorganisationen, das sich in der Vergangenheit nicht gerade als effizientes Kommunikationssystem zu präsentieren wußte. Nachdem der Ruf nach einer Aufhebung der kommunikativen Monokulturen, die sich in den letzten Jahrzehnten herausbildet hatten, laut geworden war, gelang es durch die Kommunikationsreform Kofi Annans, zumindest am Hauptsitz in New York Änderungen herbeizuführen. Gleichwohl sind die Vereinten Nationen weiterhin stark differenziert, zum einen segmentär (d.h. regional und weltweit) mit relativ autonomen Einheiten in Form von Unterorganisationen, zum anderen stratifiziert, da sie als Bürokratien in sich hierarchisch organisiert sind, und schließlich funktional nach politischen, wirtschaftlichen, und gesellschaftlichen Aufgabengebieten, darunter auch die Konferenzdienste mit ihren Übersetzungs- und Dolmetschabteilungen, die uns, die wir Übersetzer und Dolmetscher ausbilden, besonders interessieren.

62 Dazu Erich Prunč in diesem Band.

63 Der neueste Stand findet sich jeweils auf der Website der Vereinten Nationen.

Unter Rückgriff auf das von Giesecke 2002: 410 vorgelegte allgemeine Modell für Kommunikationskulturen kann das System der Vereinten Nationen als Ergebnis der Interaktion dreier Kommunikationsformen erklärt werden. Zum einen gibt es eine *hierarchische* Organisationskommunikation, die sich verkörpert in einer umfangreichen Bürokratie; zum anderen deren *rückkopplungsintensive* face-to-face Interaktion, die durch Gespräche der Beteiligten gleichwohl Effektivität und Effizienz entwickeln kann, und schließlich die in der Organisation zu findende und verwendete Informations- und Kommunikationstechnologie, die aber, falls falsch eingesetzt, gerade interaktionsarme Verhältnisse etablieren kann. Ungleichgewichte dieser drei Komponenten können die an sich angestrebte Vernetzung der Beteiligten beschneiden oder vereinseitigen, oder gar zu Einschränkungen führen, wohingegen stark rückkopplungsintensive Interaktionssysteme sich günstig auswirken (soweit Giesecke 2002).

Es fällt auf, daß in einem der Hauptorgane der Vereinten Nationen, dem Sekretariat, über Jahrzehnte hinweg eine hierarchische Organisationskommunikation mit einem linearen, möglichst einkanaligen Informationsfluß in den wirtschaftlichen, juristischen, politischen Abteilungen, und auch in den Konferenzdiensten mit ihren Sprachenabteilungen, bevorzugt worden war, die der Bürokratie, den einzelnen Abteilungen und ihren Chefs zugute kam und die deshalb noch immer aufrecht erhalten wird.

Wenn man, wie in der Betriebswirtschaftslehre üblich, in der Kommunikation die Gesamtheit aller Kommunikationsinstrumente und -maßnahmen eines Unternehmens sieht, die eingesetzt werden, um das Unternehmen und seine Leistungen bei den relevanten Zielgruppen darzustellen (so Meier 2000: 11), dann bedarf es eines perfekten Zusammenspiels

> in Form einer integrierten Kommunikation, worunter ein Prozess der Planung und Organisation verstanden wird, der darauf ausgerichtet ist, aus den unterschiedlichen Instrumenten der Internen und Externen Kommunikation eine Einheit herzustellen (Meier 2000: 29).

Dies verlangt eine organisatorische Kommunikationskultur[64] mit akzeptiertem Informationsverhalten aller Beteiligten, deren Bezugspunkt eine strategische Führung ist, die fähig ist zur Abstimmung übergreifender Aufgaben und zur Schaffung eines einheitlichen Unternehmensbildes, wobei die Mitarbeiter aller hierarchischen Ebenen in den Nachrichtenstrom einzubinden sind. Auch die Vereinten Nationen sind wie jedes große Unternehmen mit der Aufgabe konfrontiert, einen weltweiten externen Kommunikationsaustausch zu organisieren, gleichzeitig aber für eine effiziente interne Kommunikation zu sorgen, die die gesamte Beamtenschaft vor allzu großem Leerlauf bewahrt. Dabei gilt es vor allen Dingen, Parallelkommunikation und damit Reibungsverluste zu vermeiden, was letztendlich das Ziel der Anstrengungen des Generalsekretariats unter Kofi Annan vor einigen Jahren war, in der Hauptorganisation der Vereinten Nationen ein neues Kommunikationsmanagement einzurichten, was aber angesichts der Zusammensetzung der Bedienstetenschaft der Vereinten Nationen ein schwieriges Unterfangen war.

7 Die Rolle der Internationalen Beamtenschaft der Vereinten Nationen

Die Vereinten Nationen und ihre zahlreichen Sonderorganisationen und Spezialorgane sind durch ein breites Spektrum allgemeiner Regeln und Verfahren gekennzeichnet, durch welches sie sich nicht nur selbst als Organisationssystem aufrecht erhalten, sondern gleichzeitig ihre eigene soziale Welt konstruieren, wie es Gareis/

64 Dazu ausführlich Semling 2005: bes. 15 ff. – Zu betonen ist, daß eine erfolgreiche Organisationskultur auch gekennzeichnet ist durch ein akzeptiertes Konfliktverhalten, was wiederum von der Führung ein antizipierendes Krisenmanagement verlangt.

Varwick 2006: 67 beschreiben[65]. Ihre internationale Beamtenschaft kann als autonomer Akteur der Weltpolitik betrachtet werden, die über beträchtlichen Einfluß verfügt, versteht sie es doch, die sozialen Realitäten und damit auch die Interessen der Staaten zu beeinflussen, ja diese zielgerichtet zu manipulieren. Dies bringt es mit sich, daß sich eine internationale Organisation wie die Vereinten Nationen eigenständig, und unter Umständen ungeachtet der Präferenzen ihrer Mitgliedstaaten, wandeln kann, wie es gerade in den letzten Jahren unter Generalsekretär Kofi Annan geschehen war, wenn auch in bescheidenem Maße.

Dabei waren, entsprechend dem von Barnett/Finnemore 2005 vorgelegten Ansatz, vier Faktoren ausschlaggebend, die einer Beamtenschaft so großes Gewicht verleihen, was allerdings außenstehenden und mit dem System nicht vertrauten Betrachtern häufig nicht klar ist. Die Beamtenschaft der Vereinten Nationen verfügt über eine *abgeleitete Autorität* mit speziellen Kompetenzen, die von den Mitgliedstaaten auf die Gemeinschaftsorgane übertragen worden sind. Diese offizielle Autorität, die als der exogene Anteil der bürokratischen Macht der Vereinten Nationen bezeichnet werden kann, wird ergänzt durch einen endogenen Anteil, bestehend aus einem mehr oder weniger komplexen Regelwerk, das den Mitgliedern in festgelegten Bereichen Verhaltensweisen verbindlich vorschreibt, woraus der Organisation ihre *rational-legale Autorität* erwächst. Hinzu kommt eine *moralische Autorität* der Vereinten Nationen als neutraler und unparteiischer Akteur, da sie als Organisation überstaatliche Interessen jenseits der auf den eigenen Nutzen abstellenden Mitgliedstaaten verfolgen. Schließlich ist noch die *auf Expertenwissen beruhende Autorität* zu nennen, denn in vielen Fällen verfügt keine andere nationale Behörde über ein vergleichbar umfangreiches Wissen wie die Beamtenschaft der Vereinten Nationen, die infolgedessen einen uneinholbaren Wissensvorsprung hat (so sie denn davon Gebrauch macht).

65 Das Folgende nach Gareis/Varwick 2006: 67, die vor allem dem von Barnett/Finnemore (2005) vertretenen konstruktivistischen Ansatz folgen.

Diese vier Faktoren erzeugen allerdings, wie Gareis/Varwick 2006: 68 unter Bezugnahme auf Barnett/Finnemore darlegen, nicht zwangsläufig einheitliche Entscheidungen, vielmehr komme es gleichwohl vor, daß man sich nicht einigen könne, was auf *cultural contestation* innerhalb der Beamtenschaft zurückzuführen sei und deshalb zu Dysfunktionen führe, da der Einfluß der Staaten, aus denen die Beamten stammen, niemals ganz auszuschalten sei, was Barnett/Finnemore 2005: 39–41 als Pathologien internationaler Bürokratien bezeichnen[66].

- Mit *irrationality of rationalization* bezeichnet man das weit verbreitete Symptom, dass die allgemeinen Regeln und Prozeduren mit der Zeit zum Selbstzweck erhoben werden, wodurch die Bürokratie zunehmend schwerfällig und inflexibel wird.
- Verstärkt wird dies dann durch einen *bureaucratic universalism*, was heißt, daß die Regeln derartig verabsolutiert werden, dass die Dominanz des Regelwerks die Möglichkeiten der Anpassung an spezielle Situationen unterdrückt.
- Andererseits kann es zur *normalization of deviance* kommen, wodurch nun wiederum die Ausnahme zur Regel erhoben und das vorhandene einheitliche Regelwerk stellenweise ausgehöhlt wird.
- Zuletzt besteht die Gefahr einer *insulation*, womit die Tendenz einer professionellen Einrichtung gemeint ist, sich zunehmend zu isolieren und sich nicht ausreichend empfänglich für das notwendige Feedback von außen zu erhalten.

Die Gefahr, daß solche Dysfunktionalitäten auftreten, besteht bei allen internationalen Organisation, nicht nur bei den Vereinten Nationen und ihren Sonderorganisationen, sondern auch bei der Europäischen Union, bei den NGOs, ja sogar bei viel kleineren *associations internationales*, also auch – sit venia verbo – bei der CIUTI.

66 Das Folgende zitiert nach Gareis/Varwick 2006: 67.

Eine besondere Anfälligkeit für solche Funktionsstörungen bei den Vereinten Nationen kann ihre Ursachen in der besonderen Art der Rekrutierung ihrer multinationalen Beamtenschaft haben. Im Prinzip ist nur Art. 101 Abs. 3 der Charta der VN heranzuziehen, der besagt, daß bei der Personalauswahl höchste Maßstäbe an Leistungsfähigkeit, Sachkenntnis und Integrität angelegt werden sollen, gleichwohl sei auch eine geographische Mischung zu beachten. Dazu meint Paschke[67] (1994–1995 Untergeneralsekretär für das Interne Aufsichtswesen der Vereinten Nationen), daß in der Realität der Weltorganisation die ‚geographische Ausgewogenheit' des Personalkörpers über die Jahre hinweg aber immer mehr Gewicht gewonnen habe. Auch würden die Mitgliedstaaten regelmäßig so großen Druck auf den Generalsekretär und die Verwaltungs- und Personalabteilung ausüben[68], Kandidaten aus unterrepräsentierten Staaten den Zuschlag zu geben, dass dabei fachlich deutlich besser qualifizierte Konkurrenten nicht selten auf der Strecke blieben, nur weil sie nicht die ‚richtige' Staatsangehörigkeit hätten[69].

In diesem Zusammenhang muß berücksichtigt werden, daß in der Bürokratie der Vereinten Nationen mehr als 150 Nationalitäten vertreten sind, wie Paschke 2003: 555 ausführte, wobei jeder Bedienstete sein eigenes Wertsystem, seine Gewohnheiten und Praktiken, seine anerzogenen Umgangsformen, seine Auffassungen von

67 Dazu Paschke 2003: 554.

68 Über den steigenden Einfluß der Generalversammlung auf die Personalentwicklung des Generalsekretariats s. Conrady 2003: 262ff.

69 Bertrand 1995: 91f., der als langjähriger Vorsitzender der *Joint Inspective Unit* (eingerichtet 1976; vgl. Conrady 2003: 264 und 271) die Bürokratie der Vereinten Nationen sehr genau kannte, verstieg sich zu der Bemerkung, daß die durchschnittliche akademische Qualifikation sämtlicher UNO-Bediensteter gerade wegen dieser geographischen Orientierung völlig unzureichend sei. Auch die 2005 vom Generalsekretär dem UN-Weltgipfel unter großem medialen Aufwand vorgelegten Reformvorshcläge zeitigten kaum konkrete Maßnahmen, da keinerlei Konsens über eine echte Strukturreform erreicht werden konnte, unter anderem auch nicht im Bereich der Einstellungspolitik der Vereinten Nationen (so Bertrand 2005: 175).

Autorität und Hierarchie, sein Verständnis vom öffentlichen Dienst mitbringe. Nach einigen Jahren der Zugehörigkeit mag er die Praktiken, Arbeitsabläufe, Prozeduren und Regeln der UNO verinnerlicht haben; oft erfolge die Sozialisation am Arbeitsplatz sogar viel rascher, weil Bewerber für den internationalen Dienst im Allgemeinen eine besonders hohe Bereitschaft zur Assimilierung und auch die erforderliche mentale Flexibilität mitbrächten, dennoch blieben die nationale Herkunft und die daraus resultierenden Wertvorstellungen und Verhaltensmuster des einzelnen Bediensteten erhalten; wahrscheinlich träten sie im multikulturellen Umfeld der Weltorganisation sogar noch stärker ins Bewusstsein des Einzelnen. Paschke betonte auch, daß der Personalkörper der Vereinten Nationen gerade nicht aus uniformen, in Denken und Verhalten nivellierten Staatenlosen bestehe.

> Im Gegenteil: diese Bedienstetenschaft ist kosmopolitisch farbenreich und kreativ, anregend in ihrer ethnischen Vielfalt, stark motiviert für den internationalen Dienst, aber nicht sehr formiert, eher etwas chaotisch, immer zu haben für politische Rabulistik, weniger empfänglich für moderne Managementanliegen wie Effizienz oder Kostenbewusstsein. Die UN-Bürokratie ist tatsächlich ein Spiegelbild unserer Welt mit allen ihren Farben und Kontrasten, und das ist gut so; jedes Mitgliedsland kann sich in dieser bunten Truppe wiederfinden, im Sekretariat ebenso wie in den Sonder- und Unterorganisationen (Paschke 2003: 556).

Für die interne Kommunikation, die das Räderwerk der Hauptorganisation mit ihren über den ganzen Globus verteilten Sonderorganisationen am Laufen hält, verwendet diese internationale Beamtenschaft eine Institutionensprache[70], also eine Fachsprache, die

70 Im Bereich der Fachsprachen kann man unterscheiden die reinen Theoriensprachen der Wissenschaften, die Techniksprachen (in der über die Technik der Gerätschaften und deren Einsatz kommuniziert wird) und die Institutionensprachen. Unter letzteren sind zu verstehen Fachsprachen, „die innerhalb von so etwas wie (öffentlichen oder nichtöffentlichen) Organisationen, die eine festgelegte Struktur zeigen und einen bestimmten Zweck verfolgen, verwendet werden" (Roelcke 1999).

der genaueren und schnelleren Verständigung dienen soll und die durch Explizitheit, Standardisierung und Formalisierung gekennzeichnet ist. Dies wird allerdings erschwert durch die Mehrsprachigkeit in der tagtäglichen Kommunikation, selbst wenn sich das Englische als Dachsprache[71] weitgehend hat durchsetzen können, während sich das Französische (insbesondere am Standort Genf) noch mit Mühe behauptet, das Spanische, Russische und Chinesische nicht weiter auffallen, doch läßt sich nach Paschke (2003: 562) feststellen, daß es, was die interne Kommunikation der Vereinten Nationen anlangt, auf den Standort ankomme. So kommunizieren die Bediensteten am Standort New York fast ausschließlich auf Englisch, sowohl bei ihren dienstlichen Verrichtungen[72] als auch im privaten Umgang miteinander, was seine Ursache auch darin habe, daß die meisten Angehörigen des administrativen Unterbaus, die Sekretärinnen, Boten, Sicherheitskräfte, Haushandwerker *locally hired staff*, also Ortskräfte, seien, deren allgemeiner Lebensmittelpunkt der Großraum New York ist. Was den Standort Genf anlange, so stellte Paschke 2003: 562 fest, daß hier das französischsprachige Umfeld prägend wirke; das Arbeitstempo sei langsamer, der Umgang förmlicher. Für Genf sei außerdem charakteristisch, daß die Präsenz zahlreicher Sonderorganisationen mit sehr unterschiedlichen Inhalten den Vereinten Nationen ein Ge-

71 Dabei handelt es sich nach Baigorri-Jalón 2004: 147 oft um ein simplifiziertes Englisch „of a technocratic nature, and in addition, it has the self-censorship of the ‚political correct' phenomenon (espacially regarding the female sex, blacks, non-heterosexual groups) which often ends up as a mess of empty euphemisms (as the aim is only to keep up puritan appearances of facts which refute the supposed neutrality of the terms)".

72 Nach Paschke (2003: 562) wirkt hat auch die US-Verwaltungspraxis stilbildend gewirkt. „Wer je mit amerikanischen Behörden zu tun gehabt hat, wird vermutlich meinen Eindruck teilen, dass sich das UN-Sekretariat dabei nicht unbedingt an ‚best practices' orientiert. Amerikanische administrative Kultur ist nämlich äußerst personalextensiv, nicht sehr entscheidungsfreudig und von starkem Zuständigkeitsdenken geprägt. In der UNO habe ich die gleichen Beobachtungen machen konnen".

sicht mit vielen Facetten verleihe, da jede Sonderorganisation eifersüchtig über ihre Eigenständigkeit wache, weshalb das Gesamtbild in der ‚internationalen Metropole' der Schweiz nicht einheitlich sei. Paschke betonte den Umstand, daß sich der Multinationalismus hier in realistischer Weise zeige: diffus, in zahlreiche Kästchen und Mini-Biotope aufgefächert, mit deutlichen Defiziten in der horizontalen Kommunikation.

Was die anderen Standorte anlangt[73], so werden sie von den großen Sonderorganisationen geprägt, in Wien von der Internationalen Atomenergie-Organisation *(International Atomic Energy Agency)* und der Organisation für industrielle Entwicklung *(United Nations Industrial Development Organization)*, während sich Nairobi auf Umweltfragen *(United Nations Environment Programme)* und Programme des Wohn- und Siedlungswesens *(United Nations Centre for Human Settlements)* konzentriert.

Da die Staatenvertreter offiziell darauf bestehen, daß die Sprachenvielfalt in den Vereinten Nationen zu bewahren sei[74], werden die Publikationen und Presseerklärungen usw. in allen sechs offiziellen Sprachen erstellt, was in Zeiten des budgetären Nullwachstums die Handlungsfähigkeit des Sekretariats enorm einschränkt, wie Lehmann 2003: 570 ausführte, denn das Beharren einiger Länder auf Sprachenparität bedeutet für das *Department of Public Information*, daß unter Einsatz Hunderter von Übersetzern und Dolmetschern weiterhin sehr arbeitsintensiv und ausgabenrestriktiv produziert werden muß.

73 Da sich Vertreter der Standorte Wien (UNOV) und Nairobi (UNON) bei diesem CIUTI FORUM nicht zu Wort meldeten, bleiben sie bei den weiteren Ausführungen unberücksichtigt.

74 So deutlich geworden in der Resolution 50/11 vom 2. November 1995 (abgedruckt in Vereinte Nationen 1997: 76), die die strikte Aufrechterhaltung des Sechs-Sprachenregimes wiederholt. Vgl. dazu die aufschlußreiche Darstellung der Hintergründe bei Paqué 1997: 66ff.

In diesem Zusammenhang kommt dann den Sprachen- und Konferenzdiensten[75] des Generalsekretariats am Hauptsitz New York und am Nebensitz Genf große Bedeutung nicht nur in der internen, sondern auch externen Kommunikation zu, wenn es gilt die Weltöffentlichkeit zu informieren. Wurde doch im Bericht *Global Vision – Local View 1997* dargelegt, daß die Vereinten Nationen zwar bei vielen Menschen hohes Ansehen genössen, doch das reiche nicht aus, vielmehr komme es darauf an, die Weltöffentlichkeit für die Durchsetzung der Ziele zu gewinnen, denn die ‚core agenda' der Vereinten Nationen mit ihren Themen Kampf gegen Kriminalität, Drogen und Krankheit, Stärkung des Arbeitsmarktes, Förderung von Bildung und sozialer Dienste, Umweltschutz und Menschenrechte betreffe die Menschen in allen Ländern direkt. Das große Potenzial der Vereinten Nationen liege in ihrem Internationalismus, ihrer weltweiten Präsenz und ihrer Agenda, die die Menschen überall auf der Welt dazu bewegen sollten, sie als eine unverzichtbare Institution zu sehen, wie Lehmann 2003: 580 schrieb. Unter den Empfehlungen des genannten Berichts sei eine besonders hervorgehoben:

> The UN is principally a forum for the exchange of ideas. We argue that in some senses the UN can be thought of as a global communications agency. A culture of communications must therefore pervade the entire organization, with responsibility for public diplomacy borne by all senior officials, ambassadors and the larger UN family.

75 Zur Hauptabteilung Konferenzdienste *(Department of Conference Services)* gehören jeweils die Übersetzerabteilung *(Translation Division)* und der Dolmetschdienst *(Intepretation Service)*, aber auch die Abteilung Redaktion und Offizielles Protokoll *(Editorial and Official Records Division)* und die Verlagsabteilung *(Publishing Division)*. Die Übersetzungsabteilung und der Dolmetschdienst haben jeweils Dienste *(services)* für die sechs Sprachen, sowie eine Dokumentations- und Terminologiesektion und eine Stelle für die Vergabe von freiberuflichen Übersetzungen *(contractual translation)*.

8 Übersetzen in der Öffentlichkeitsarbeit der Vereinten Nationen

Diesem Auftrage entsprechend richten sich die Vereinten Nationen sowohl an hochentwickelte Industrienationen, die bereits auf dem Weg zu wissensbasierten Gesellschaften *(knowledge-based societies)* sind, als auch an Nationen, die noch weit davon entfernt sind, was bei der Produktion der sechs-sprachigen Informationsmaterialien, die sich zwischen extremer Fachlichkeit einerseits und reinen auf allgemeine Verständlichkeit abstellenden Informationstexten andererseits bewegen, berücksichtigt werden muß.

Bekanntlich erweist sich bereits innerhalb einer monolingualen Sprachgemeinschaft der Unterschied zwischen Fach- und Laienkommunikation als großes Hindernis, wie Roelcke 2002: 35 ff. dargelegt hat, denn die sprachlichen Fähigkeiten der Laien reichen in der Regel oft nicht aus für eine Kommunikation mit den Fachleuten, was dann sehr oft dazu führt, daß Laien die Texte derselben nicht verstehen[76], selbst wenn letztere überzeugt sind, sich klar und deutlich ausgedrückt zu haben. Die Folge ist eine Kommunikationsbeeinträchtigung dergestalt, daß der „Normalbürger" den Arzt, den Anwalt oder den Vermögensberater nicht vollständig versteht, wenn diese in ihrer jeweiligen Fachsprache mit ihm sprechen. Weichen im Rahmen fachkommunikativer Produktion oder Rezeption die Fähigkeiten, sich zu verstehen, mehr oder weniger deutlich voneinander ab, „so droht eine fachsprachliche Kluft im Sinne kommunikativer Ineffektivität oder Ineffizienz, die sich unter Umständen als ausgesprochen problematisch erweisen kann", wie Roelcke 2002: 36 darlegte und dies am Beispiel der deutschen Sprachgemeinschaft erklärte. Der deutsche Sprachgebrauch in Wissenschaft, Technik und Institutionen zeichne sich gegenüber demjenigen in Alltag und Bildung durch eine ganze Reihe an lexi-

76 Beispiele wären die deutschen Formulare zur Einkommensteuererklärung oder die oft schwer verständlichen Gebrauchsanleitungen für Geräte.

kalischen, grammatischen und textuellen Besonderheiten aus, welche die Kommunikation innerhalb dieser Fachbereiche insbesondere in symbolfunktionaler (aber auch in symptom- und appellfunktionaler Hinsicht) unterstützen würden, die dem Laien aber fremd seien, denn diese fachsprachlichen Besonderheiten würden von ihm entsprechende Fähigkeiten zu fachsprachlicher Kommunikation erfordern. Diese würden durch sein allgemein- oder bildungssprachliches Vermögen nur zum Teil erreicht, so dass (stark vereinfacht) bei thematisch vergleichbarer Kommunikation unter Experten oder unter (interessierten bzw. vorgebildeten) Laien jeweils verschiedene Ausprägungen an fachsprachlichen Besonderheiten und fachsprachlichen Fähigkeiten anzunehmen seien (Roelcke 2002: 35).

Dieses Problem wird noch gravierender[77] bei einer Kommunikation in sechs Sprachen wie innerhalb der Einrichtungen der Vereinten Nationen, oder zwischen den Vereinten Nationen und der Außenwelt. Gerade bei den an die Weltöffentlichkeit gerichteten Aktionen lassen sich als Kommunikationsmodi eine zielgerichtete *Kommunikation für Experten* und eine *für Laien* unterscheiden, wobei allerdings nicht immer genau abgegrenzt werden kann, denn hier kommt ins Spiel, was als Adressatenbezogenheit zu bezeichnen ist, nämlich der Umstand, daß zahlreiche Texte sowohl an Fachleute als auch an Laien gerichtet sind, wobei, wenn der globale Aspekt zu berücksichtigen ist, noch zu unterscheiden ist zwischen informierten Laien und absoluten Laien[78], welch letztere

77 Daß in solchen Fällen auch in der Europäischen Union beträchtliche Schwierigkeiten auftreten, zeigen die Versuche der Europäischen Kommission, mit ihren Bürgern besser zu kommunizieren. 2006 wurde zu diesem Zweck eine eigene Generaldirektion Kommunikation (Directorate General Communication) eingerichtet (vgl. Fassbender 2007: bes. 118), denn die Veröffentlichungen der Europäischen Union richten sich einerseits an Experten, andererseits an den Bürger, weshalb sie für den „Mann von der Straße" in dessen Sprache kommunikativ aufbereitet werden müssen. Daß dies nicht immer gelingt, zeigt sich daran, daß die Bürger eine ziemlich distanzierte Haltung zu Brüssel entwickelt zu haben scheinen.

78 Dazu in der Kommunikationsforschung Wichter 1994: 42ff., der zeigte, daß sich Kommunikationsschwierigkeiten wegen des Unterschieds der Wis-

bisher über keinerlei Kenntnisse bezüglich der Aufgaben und Ziele der Vereinten Nationen hatten (Müller 2010: 15). Zahlreiche Veröffentlichungen der Vereinten Nationen sind politischer, rechtlicher oder ökonomischer Natur, die sich an Experten in den Regierungen, Ministerien, wirtschaftlichen Vereinigungen, internationalen Organisationen usw. richten, weshalb hier dann eine reine Fachkommunikation mit Experten vorliegt. Daneben gibt es dann aber eine nicht minder große Zahl von Veröffentlichungen, die an „alle Menschen“ gleich welchen Bildungsstandes gerichtet sind, also an die „Laien“. Diese zwangsläufige Mehrfachadressierung der Texte der Vereinten Nationen stellt deshalb eine Schwierigkeit für die Übersetzungsdienste dar, da oft nicht klar ist, ob sich die Texte ausschließlich an Fachleute oder auch an Nichtfachleute richten, wovon aber letztendlich abhängt, ob die Allgemeinsprache oder eine für Fachleute in ihrer Diskursgemeinschaft übliche Fachsprache zu verwenden ist. Die Sprachendienste der Vereinten Nationen müssen beides kombinieren, weshalb bei der Produktion des Ausgangstextes bereits derartige Entscheidungen getroffen werden, was dann aber gleichwohl wegen kultureller Unterschiede bei den weltweit anzusprechenden Rezipienten hohe Anforderungen an die Übersetzer stellt, müssen sie doch vertraut sein mit den Eigenarten der speziellen Institutionensprache der Vereinten Nationen und der Art, wie diese dann zu redigieren sind[79], um rezipienten- oder funktionenorientiert zu wirken. Die Aufgabe besteht also auch darin, die Weltgesellschaft kommunikativ zu beeinflussen im Sin-

---

sensniveaus der Experten und Laien ergeben können (47). In heutigen Gesellschaften könne eine Person durchaus Experte in einem Fachgebiet sein, gleichzeitig aber Laie in der Fachaußenwelt auf anderen anderen Gebieten (50).

79 Das Generalsekretariat erläßt regelmäßig Direktiven, wie die Texte zu gestalten sind. Vgl. dazu Guenot-Hovnanian 2009: 378 und 384: L'un des problèmes que rencontre l'éditeur onusien tient au fait que les auteurs n'écrivent pas toujours dans la langue qu'ils dominent le mieux et il faut parfois s'efforcer de penser dans la langue principale de l'auteur pour comprendre ce qu'il écrit en anglais – il importe de noter que plus de 80 % des rapports soumis à l'édition le sont dans cette langue.

ne der Ziel der Charta der Vereinten Nationen, weshalb dann letztendlich ihre durch die Printmedien (aber auch das Internet) verbreiteten Informationen prinzipiell dementsprechend selektiert und inszeniert werden, damit sie ihre Wirkung im gewünschten Sinne entfalten[80].

8.1 Textproduktion in kontaktintensiven Prozessen

Im Gegensatz zu den Sprachendienstleistungen in der Europäischen Union, bei denen sich die Übersetzungen – jedenfalls bisher – in einem gemeinsamen europäischen Kulturrahmen bewegen, ist dies bei den Vereinten Nationen viel schwieriger, da hier, etwa bei Übersetzungen ins oder aus dem Chinesischen oder Arabischen, die kulturellen Unterschiede deutlich werden, was es dann sehr schwierig macht, jeweils adressaten- und zielkulturorientiert zu kommunizieren.

Auf den ersten Blick scheint das recht gut zu gelingen, denn Monat für Monat werden zahllose Dokumente in sechs Sprachen ausgeliefert, was auf eine gut koordinierte Zusammenarbeit in den und zwischen den jeweiligen Sprachensektionen – Arabisch, Chinesisch, Englisch, Französisch, Russisch und Spanisch – hindeutet. Dies allein ist schon eine beeindruckende Leistung, denn das kooperative Bearbeiten von eingehenden Informationen und deren Umwandlung in mehrsprachige Texte will gelernt sein, ganz zu schweigen von der Schwierigkeit, die entsprechende Fachterminologie in allen sechs Sprachen zu finden, aber auch konsequent zu verwenden. Von den Fachübersetzern der Vereinten Nationen

80 Dazu die aufschlußreichen Ausführungen bei Krotz 2001: 48 und 79 über Kommunikation als soziales Handeln der Menschen und als spezifische Form der Interaktion mit beabsichtigter Übertragung von Information. Dabei diene die Kommunikation dazu, beim anderen eine positive Rezeption auszulösen und bestimmte Handlungsweisen zu fördern, wie es heute weitgehend durch die Medien (Presse, TV, Internet) erfolge.

wird neben ihren translatorischen Kompetenzen deshalb auch die individuelle Fähigkeit zur Kooperation mit den Kollegen erwartet, um Effektivität und Effizienz bei der mehrsprachigen Textproduktion zur Realisierung eines weltweiten Informationstransfers zu gewährleisten, wobei es darum geht, Fachlichkeit mit Verständlichkeit zu verbinden.

Effektivität (engl. *effectiveness*; franz. *efficacité*) bedeutet in diesem Zusammenhang, daß durch die Übersetzungen *(Translate)* in sechs Sprachen die Weltöffentlichkeit über die Aktivitäten der Vereinten Nationen und ihrer Sonderorganisationen erfolgreich informiert wird. Die für die weltweite Verbreitung zu erstellenden Zieltexte sind in der Regel Übersetzungen eines „Urtextes“ in eine der sechs Sprachen (zumeist englisch). Ob diese Übersetzungen effektiv sind im Sinne von gut oder schlecht, oder optimal oder suboptimal, ist ein Problem, mit dem sich Generationen von Übersetzern und Translatologen befaßt haben, ohne eine allseits befriedigende Antwort gefunden zu haben (falls es eine solche überhaupt geben kann), denn es kommt hier die Qualität der Übersetzungen ins Spiel und nach welchen Maßstäben diese wohl zu beurteilen oder gar sicherzustellen sei[81]. Es soll hier dahingestellt bleiben, ob und wie innerhalb der Sektionen der Sprachendienste die anzulegenden Maßstäbe genau festgelegt werden, gleichwohl wird die Frage nach der Qualität der Übersetzungen immer wieder aufgeworfen, nicht zuletzt in den Vereinten Nationen selbst, wie etwa im Bericht[82] von 1999, der von Qualitätssicherung spricht: „*The maintenance of staffing levels in the translation services [...] allowing the organization to place more emphasis on the improvement of the quality of the translation of documents into the six official languages*“. In den letzten Jahren haben denn auch die Sprachendienste selbst umfangreiche Maßnahmen zur Sicherung der Qualität ergriffen (vgl. über die Lage am UNOG de Saint-Robert 2009).

81 Vgl. dazu Thelen 2009: bes. 211 ff.; Stejskal 2009: bes. 296.
82 A/54/478 Multilingualism – Report of the Secretary-General.

Nicht weniger wichtig ist die Frage, ob die Übersetzungsleistungen in den Sprachensektionen auch *effizient* erbracht werden. Während es bei der Effektivität darum geht, das „Richtige" zu tun, also „gute" Translate zu produzieren, wird bei der Effizienz (engl. *efficiency*; franz. *efficence*) darauf abgestellt, dies in „richtiger" Weise zu tun, wobei Aufwand an Personal, Zeit und Geld und Ergebnis in einem angemessenen, gerechtfertigten und vertretbaren Verhältnis stehen sollen[83]. Die Sprachendienste müssen beide Forderungen – Effektivität und Effizienz – erfüllen, denn es ist ihre Aufgabe, Zieltexte rechtzeitig vorzulegen. Schon vor Jahren war bemängelt worden, daß die für die Generalversammlung und andere wichtigen Gremien notwendigen Texte und Arbeitspapiere nicht immer zeitgleich in allen Sprachen vorlägen; zwar wären die englische und die französische Fassung in der Regel vorhanden, aber die anderen ließen auf sich warten, wie in mehreren Resolutionen (1966; 1981; 1999) kritisch festgestellt worden war[84].

Ob in diesem Zusammenhang die hierarchische Organisation der Sprachendienste unter Umständen eine negative Rolle spielt, kann von uns nicht beurteilt werden. Es wäre denkbar, daß dies

83 Wenn es um den sprachlichem Aufwand und das sprachlichem Ergebnis geht, so wäre nach Roelcke 2002: 34 noch Folgendes zu unterscheiden: „Doch bereits im Hinblick auf eine nähere Bestimmung dieses Verhältnisses sind hier erhebliche Unterschiede festzustellen, indem zahlreiche Definitionen an einem vorwissenschaftlichen Mini/Max-Prinzip (Maximierung des Ergebnisses bei Minimierung des Aufwands) ansetzen, während andere Definitionen wissenschaftliche Effizienzvorstellungen aufgreifen und insbesondere Aufwandeffizienz (Minimierung des Aufwands bei einem bestimmten Ergebnis) diskutieren und Ergebniseffizienz (Maximierung des Ergebnisses bei einem bestimmten Aufwand) problematisieren."

84 In der Resolution 2247 (XXI) vom 20. Dezember 1966 stellte die Generalversammlung fest, daß die Dokumente nicht rechtzeitig in allen Sprachen zur Verfügung stehen würden; in der Resolution 36/117B vom 10. Dezember 1981 wurde gefordert wird, die Dokumente sollten in allen 6 Sprachen zeitgleich vorliegen. Auch am 19. Oktober 1999 wird im Bericht über die Mehrsprachigkeit *(A/54/478 Multilingualism – Report of the Secretary General)* wieder einmal festgestellt, daß die Übersetzungen nicht rechtzeitig erfolgten.

der Fall sein könnte, wenn die Hierarchie nicht gemildert würde durch rückkopplungsintensive face-to-face Interaktionen zwischen den einzelnen Übersetzern in den und zwischen den Sprachensektionen. Diese hierarchische Struktur ist allerdings formell vorgeschrieben und dauerhaft, was Auswirkungen haben kann dergestalt, daß in den Sprachensektionen asymmetrische Verhältnisse entstehen[85], so daß sich auch zwischen hierarchisch gleichgestellten Mitarbeitern Abhängigkeiten ergeben und sich Netzwerke gegenseitiger Verpflichtungen einstellen, was sich nachteilig auf die Kommunikation und Kooperation auswirken kann, sind doch die Übersetzer zur Erfüllung ihrer Aufgaben auf die Mit- oder wenigstens Zuarbeit aus den jeweils benachbarten Sprachsektionen angewiesen, wie es nun einmal die Aufgabe der sechssprachigen Textproduktion verlangt. Gerade zur Vermeidung einer Dysfunktionalität in Gestalt einer *insulation*, wie sie sich bei professionellen Abteilungen wie den Sprachensektionen als Isolation einstellen kann, sollte alles getan werden, die Kooperation zwischen den Sprachensektionen noch mehr zu stärken.

8.2 *Rekrutierungsprobleme*

In den letzten Jahren sehen sich die Konferenz- und Sprachendienste in New York und Genf mit der Tatsache konfrontiert, daß sie für ihre Sektionen Chinesisch, Arabisch und Russisch nicht genügend qualifizierte Übersetzer und Konferenzdolmetscher[86] finden[87],

85 Aus der Betriebswirtschaftslehre ist bekannt, daß Vorgesetzte wichtige Informationen vorenthalten und verdrehen, oder umgekehrt, was nicht weniger schädlich ist, ihre Mitarbeiter mit Informationen überhäufen können. Auf diese Weise können sie die Informationsweitergabe in großem Umfang manipulativ-strategisch gestalten (dazu Meier 2000: 16).

86 Dazu vor allem Baigorri-Jalón 2004: 147f., der feststellte, daß in der Chinesischen bzw. Arabischen Kabine sowohl aus der als auch in die Fremdsprache gedolmetscht werden muß.

87 Anläßlich der Diskussion um die Beibehaltung der Mehrsprachigkeit in den Vereinten Nationen wurde in Resolution 50/11 vom 2. November 1995 der

weshalb sie im Verlauf des CIUTI-FORUMs 2007 versuchten[88], den ausbildenden Hochschulen nahe zu bringen, diese sollten ihr Augenmerk bei der Ausbildung von Fachübersetzern und Konferenzdolmetschern auf solche Sprachenkombinationen richten, die aus der Sicht der Vereinten Nationen zur Zeit und im kommenden Jahrzehnt besonders nachgefragt seien[89], nämlich auf Kombinationen mit Arabisch, Chinesisch und Russisch.

Aus der Sicht der ausbildenden Hochschulen wäre darauf zu antworten, daß die in Europa lokalisierten Institute bis auf wenige Ausnahmen voll und ganz damit ausgelastet seien, die Nachfrage der Institutionen der Europäischen Union nach Übersetzern und Dolmetschern in den 23 offiziellen Sprachen zu erfüllen. Schon deshalb werden die von den Vereinten Nationen dringend gesuchten Kombinationen von Englisch, Französisch und Spanisch einerseits mit Chinesisch, Arabisch und Russisch andererseits kaum ins Zentrum der Ausbildung an den europäischen Hochschulen rücken können, nicht einmal in Wien oder in Genf, deren Institute wegen ihrer Nähe zu Einrichtungen der Vereinten Nationen vor allem in Frage kämen. Obwohl die Hochschulinstitute nicht gezielt für die spezifischen Bedürfnisse der Vereinten Nationen ausbilden, wie Baigorri-Jalón 2004: 126 zeigte, haben doch viele Dolmetscher der Vereinten Nationen der letzten Generation einen solchen Abschluß.

Auch der Umstand, daß im europäischen Hochschulraum im letzten Jahrzehnt als Folge des Bologna-Prozesses mit der Umstellung auf Bachelor- und Master-Abschlüsse starke Veränderungen erfolgten, ändert daran nichts. In den seltensten Fällen gehen die

---

Generalsekretär ersucht, dafür zu sorgen „daß insbesondere durch die Ausbildung und Einstellung von Fachleuten sichergestellt werden muß, daß die erforderlichen Ressourcen verfügbar sind, um die richtige und rechtzeitige Übersetzung von Dokumenten in die verschiedenen Amtssprachen der Vereinten Nationen zu gewährleisten“ (Beschlußziffer 5). Auch wird er daran erinnert, „daß die gleichzeitige Verteilung dieser Dokumente in den Amtssprachen sichergestellt werden muß“ (Beschlußziffer 6).

88 Vgl. den Beitrag von Marie-Josée de Saint-Robert in diesem Band.

89 Zu dieser seit Jahren bestehenden Nachfrage s. Baigorri-Jalón 2004: 148 ff.

Angebote über einen Sprachunterricht Chinesisch hinaus auf die höhere Ebene der Ausbildung von Fachübersetzern (Technik, Recht, Wirtschaft) oder Konferenzdolmetschern. Auch für Arabisch sind die Ausbildungsstätten, die eine Translatorenausbildung auf diesem Niveau anbieten, selten.

Unter diesen Umständen wäre es vielmehr eine Aufgabe der Hochschulen in der Arabischen Welt, in China und Russland, für die Sprachendienste der Vereinten Nationen diese gesuchten Sprachenkombinationen abzudecken. In der Sowjetunion waren einst Übersetzer und Dolmetscher für Tätigkeiten in den Vereinten Nationen am ehemaligen Maurice-Thorez-Institut in Moskau ausgebildet worden (dazu Paqué 1980: 168; vgl. Baigorri-Jalón 2004: 97f., 100 und 122), wohingegen heute in Rußland eine solche Ausbildung an mehreren Universitäten, oft in Zusammenarbeit und mit Unterstützung des Sprachendienstes UNONY, angeboten wird. Was China anlangt, so konzentrierte sich die Zusammenarbeit mit den Vereinten Nationen nach dem Zweiten Weltkrieg auf einige wenige Universitäten (darunter die Beijing Foreign Studies University[90]). Nunmehr, nachdem durch die chinesische Regierung nach jahrelangen Vorarbeiten 2007 die Studienprogramme[91] *Master in Translation and Interpretation* eingeführt worden sind, werden an zahlreichen Universitäten Übersetzer und Dolmetscher auch für Kombinationen mit Spanisch, Arabisch und Russisch ausgebildet. An den Hochschulen der Arabischen Welt scheint allerdings bis jetzt Chinesisch kaum über das Stadium eines Sprachunterrichts hinausgekommen zu sein.

Angesichts des Umstandes, daß wirklich hochqualifizierte Übersetzer und Dolmetscher für Kombinationen mit Arabisch und Chinesisch auf dem Markt nicht häufig anzutreffen sind, scheint noch hinzu zu kommen, daß diese Spezialisten nicht immer bereit sind,

90 Über die enge Verbindung der Beijing Foreign Studies University seit den 1970er Jahren mit den Vereinten Nationen im Bereich der Ausbildung von Übersetzern und Dolmetschern s. Wang 2009: 214.

91 Dazu Zhang 2009: 219.

sich dem etwas strikten Verwaltungsregime der Vereinten Nationen mit ihrer Bürokratie zu unterwerfen und sie dort höchstens als freie Mitarbeiter tätig werden wollen, ganz abgesehen davon, daß die Sparmaßnahmen der Vereinten Nationen auch hier die Konkurrenzfähigkeit der Sprachendienste im Rekrutierungssektor zu beeinträchtigen scheinen.

8.3 International Translation and Interpretation *als Module für Masterstudiengänge?*

Da für die Sprachendienste der Vereinten Nationen in New York und Genf das Problem darin zu bestehen scheint, daß eine qualifizierende Ausbildung weltweit nicht in vergleichbarer Weise angeboten wird und sie deshalb bei der Rekrutierung von Übersetzern (und Dolmetschern) ihren Bedarf nicht oder nicht ausreichend decken können, wurde im Verlauf des CIUTI-FORUMs 2007 vorgeschlagen (s. den Beitrag von Mohammed Didaoui), die Hochschulen sollten einen *Master in International Translation* einführen, der der Ausbildung von Übersetzern und Dolmetschern für die Vereinten Nationen und ihren Sonderorganisationen gewidmet wäre. Nach Meinung der Vertreter der Hochschulen wäre ein solches Vorhaben doch etwas zu hoch angesetzt, da allenfalls die Sprachendienste der Vereinten Nationen als Arbeitgeber in Frage kämen, die zwar wichtige, aber insgesamt doch eher bescheidene Marktteilnehmer darstellen. Vielmehr würde es wohl genügen, an den Hochschulen jeweils Module einzuführen, die die notwendige auf die Vereinten Nationen sich beziehende Internationale Dimension enthielten, was für die ausbildenden Institute keine große zusätzliche Belastung wäre, für die Studierenden aber durchaus nützlich sein könnte, wenn für diejenigen unter ihnen, die sich auf eine Tätigkeit bei den Vereinten Nationen kaprizieren, dadurch die Chancen signifikant verbessern würden.

Ein solches Modul *International Translation (and Interpretation)* müßte dann spezielle Kenntnisse bezüglich des gesamten System der Vereinten Nationen und ihrer Strukturen vermitteln, aber auch ein besonderes Training enthalten hinsichtlich der in ihr gepflegten Institutionensprache und der oft extrem fachsprachlichen Texte. Fachsprachenkompetenzen vermitteln die ausbildenden Institute bereits jetzt, allerdings nicht speziell auf die Bedürfnisse der Vereinten Nationen zugeschnitten[92]. Was jedoch weniger häufig geübt wird, ist, hochgradig fachsprachliche Inhalte in allgemeinsprachlichen – also für Laien verständlichen – Texten wiederzugeben.

In diesem Zusammenhang wäre den Studierenden die spezielle Sprache der Vereinten Nationen zu erläutern, denn in der Generalversammlung, im Sicherheitsrat und in den wichtigsten Ausschüssen – abgesehen von gelegentlichen Ausrutschern im Kalten

92 Vgl. Baigorri-Jalón 2004: 126, der auch auf die Ausbildung von Konferenzdolmetschern an einigen bekannten Hochschulinstituten einging, dabei die bekannte Frage anschneidend, ob die Ausbilder erfahrene Dolmetscher sein sollten oder nicht, wie es auch Pearl 1995: 162 getan hatte: „Teachers, who may or may not be experienced interpreters, and interpreters, who may or may not be good teachers". Baigorri-Jalón meint: „So, international prestige as an interpreter is no guarantee that this person will be able to transmit pedagogically his skill and a good interpreterwith good teaching qualities offers no guarantee of self-sacrificing dedication to teaching" (129). Hinzu kommt, daß aktive Konferenzdolmetscher oft ihre Lehrverpflichtung nicht ernst nehmen (oder gar on-line oder nur noch virtuell ausbilden wollen) und oft genug ihre Stunden ausfallen lassen, worauf die erfolgreiche Dolmetscherin der Vereinten Nationen in Genf, Paula Faraone, schon vor Jahren hingewiesen hatte: „What I noticed about my interpreting teachers is that they were not teachers, but interpreters. We were taught by interpreters who had to fulfil their interpreting commitments and would often disappear, leaving us with a substitute teacher. The number of classes they taught depended on the number of contracts they had. What I mean is that 90 % of them preferred interpreting to teaching. They didn't teach by choice, it was simply a means of working. I don't know if it had anything to do with how good they were or not. I mean, I don't know whether they didn't have more interpreting work because they were not so good. Anyway, there were some good teachers, but they were good intuitively, not because they have had any teacher training or experience" (zitiert bei Baigorri-Jalón 2004: 128).

Krieg oder im Zusammenhang mit dem Nahost-Problem – wird ein diplomatischer Stil gepflegt, der, wie Wesel 2003: 600 ihn beschrieben hat, naturgemäß weniger von Präzision geprägt ist, sondern u.a. von dem Bemühen, sich zur Wahrung des eigenen Spielraums möglichst wenig festzulegen und doch das Gespräch aufrechtzuerhalten. An vielen Beispielen zeigte Wesel, wie die Sprache verschleiernd ablenken kann, möglicherweise schon allein dadurch, dass sie von der Lektüre abschreckt[93]. „Die an die ‚Weltöffentlichkeit' gerichtete Sprache (z.B. Hauptreden in der Generalversammlung und auf ‚Welt-Konferenzen' und ‚Welt-Gipfeln') liefert meist nur zu nichts verpflichtende Erklärungen, oft pathetische Beschwörungen, Appelle an alle und niemanden, generell Absichts- und Bereitschaftserklärungen und Gutwilligkeitsversicherungen, ‚Wir'-Weltgemeinschafts-Anrufungen usw. Zumal in den feierlichen Abschlusserklärungen von Welt- und Gipfelkonferenzen und in den seltenen ‚Deklarationen' ist die Häufung von ‚Hochwertwörtern' und Edelfloskeln so stark, dass man sich manchmal nicht des Eindruckes erwehren kann, eine Parodie auf Sakralsprache zu lesen."

Angesichts des Umstandes, daß die Vereinten Nationen als Forum für alle dienen sollen, auf dem selbst Staaten im Gespräch bleiben können, deren Interessen völlig unterschiedlich sind, haben diese sich durch Inhaltslosigkeit auszeichnenden und die wahren Gegensätze oft verschleiernden Äußerungen dann ihren Sinn, wenn Konkretes zu sagen nicht möglich oder angebracht ist, was unter den Bedingungen der Arbeit im Rahmen der Vereinten Nationen aus guten Gründen der Normalfall sein dürfte. Die Sprache der „Leerformeln"[94] hat jedenfalls ihre politische Funktion. Wichtige Prämisse der UN-Textproduktion ist es, die Kultur der

93 Wesel 2003: 600 Fn. 23: Die offiziellen Dokumente sind zudem durch Spezifika diplomatischer bzw. völkerrechtlicher Sprachregelungen geprägt, die Außenstehenden meist unzugänglich sind. Vgl. dazu noch immer Rudolf 1972.

94 Dazu Bertrand 1995: 74.

Organisation zu respektieren: Alles geht nur auf der Basis des *Konsens*. Oft kann nur die strikteste Einhaltung des Prinzips des kleinsten gemeinsamen Nenners multilaterale Verhandlungssituationen aufrecht erhalten; dies gilt besonders in selbst für UN-Verhältnisse delikaten Fällen, in denen es beispielsweise um die Bestandsaufnahme von Menschenrechtsverletzungen geht: Auch die Vertreter von Regierungen, in deren Verantwortungsbereich diese Verletzungen geschehen, müssen die Texte absegnen können (soweit Wesel 2003).

Seit Bestehen der Vereinten Nationen sind es diese Sprachkunststücke, wie Wesel 2003: 601 es bezeichnete, die in ihren feierlichen Reden von Staatsoberhäuptern und Regierungschefs oder wenigstens Außenministern vor der UNO gehalten werden, etwa bei der Eröffnung der jährlichen Sitzungsperiode der UN-Generalversammlung oder auf „world summits". Offizielle Reden vor Gremien der Vereinten Nationen seien schon so etwas wie ein eigenes Genre. Kulturspezifische Eigenarten seien festzustellen, aber auf fast allen Arbeitsebenen und wenigstens in den formellen Sitzungen folgen sie bestimmten ungeschriebenen Regeln, von denen abzuweichen oder die gar zu verletzen, meist selbst eine Botschaft bedeute.

Diese nivellierende Sprache ist auch zu finden in den Veröffentlichungen der Vereinten Nationen, die an die Weltöffentlichkeit gerichtet sind, wobei, wie es Paqué 1980: 167 treffend beschreibt, die verschiedensten Themen und Sachgebiete angesprochen werden, freilich so, daß Anspielungen oder Zitate aus einzelnen Kulturbereichen oder Religionen, die vielleicht nicht von allen verstanden würden oder bei einzelnen Mitgliedstaaten Anstoß erregen könnten, schon bei den Originalfassungen bzw. der Endredaktion dieser Fassungen bewußt vermieden würden[95]. Die Einheitlichkeit (manchmal auch Eintönigkeit) der zudem zu etwa 90 Prozent in

95 Gleichwohl traten schon immer was das Arabische anlangt zahlreiche kulturbedingte Probleme bei den Übersetzungen auf, wie Edzard 1998: 115 ff. zeigte.

Englisch verfaßten Texte sei daher größer, als man dies bei der Vielfalt der in den Vereinten Nationen vertretenen Länder und Kulturen zunächst erwarten würde.

Darüber hinaus müßte bei einer auf die Tätigkeit bei den Vereinten Nationen abstellenden Ausbildung besonders geübt werden, was als *précis-writing* (Protokollierung) bezeichnet wird, nämlich die Herstellung von Kurzprotokollen *(summary records)* der Beiträge in den Ausschüssen der Organe der Vereinten Nationen. Der Anteil dieser Kurzprotokolle sei etwa 35–40 Prozent der Übersetzungsarbeit eines Jahres, weswegen alle Bewerber des englischen, französischen und spanischen Dienstes bei der Einstellung auch in dieser Fertigkeit geprüft würden und die offizielle Funktionsbezeichnung dafür nicht „Translator", sondern „Translator/Précis-writer" (etwa: Übersetzer/Protokollant) sei (Paqué 1980: 168).

Letztendlich ist noch zu bedenken, daß die Hochschulen in ihren Studienprogrammen zumeist die Vermittlung der Translationskompetenz im Sinne der Effektivität der Kommunikation zum Ziel haben, weshalb Fragen der Effizienz zumeist zurücktreten, wohingegen die Berufswelt von professionell ausgebildeten Translatoren immer eine Verbindung von Effektivität und Effizienz in Form einer Translatorenkompetenz *(translator's competence)* erwartet. Zwar ist nunmehr in der Ausbildung in Europa festzustellen, daß die Translatorenkompetenz (wozu dann auch der effiziente Einsatz von *translation tools* gehört) in den Mittelpunkt gerückt ist[96], doch besteht weiterhin ein großer Unterschied, wie es Thelen 2009: 208 treffend beschrieben hat:

> Thus far, there are two seemingly separate systems for QM (i.e. Quality Management) for Translation: That in use in the professional world and that applied in translator training. Despite the fact that both sectors are interdependent not only vis-à-vis each other but also vis-à-vis society/clients, their QM systems still seem to operate independently.

96 Vgl. dazu Lee-Jahnke 2009: 162 ff. und 169.

Wenn das Angebot an effektiv *und* effizient arbeitenden Übersetzern, die für die kommunikativen Aufgaben der Vereinten Nationen einsetzbar wären, zu gering erscheint, und wenn gleichzeitig behauptet wird, daß die Qualitätsmaßstäbe, die ausbildenden Institute und die professionellen Übersetzer (und Dolmetscher) anlegen, zu unterschiedlich wären, dann wäre es höchste Zeit, daß beide Seiten kooperierten, um den Mißstand zu beseitigen. Dies könnte vorzugsweise dadurch geschehen, wie Thelen 2009: 208 f. ausführte[97], daß die Sprachendienste der Vereinten Nationen Praktika für die Studierenden oder Unterstützung in der Ausbildung anböten, um den Hochschulen die Einführung eines Moduls *International Translation (and Interpreting)* zu erleichtern.

8.4 Kooperation – aber in welcher Form?

Nun weiß man aber aus Erfahrung, daß es sehr leicht ist, Kooperation zu verlangen, daß es aber ungleich schwerer ist, eine solche auch zu praktizieren, wenn die Interessen und Erwartungen der Beteiligten recht unterschiedlich sind.

Die europäischen Hochschulen sind in der Regel hinsichtlich ihrer Studiengänge extrem differenziert und dezentralisiert, auch haben einige von ihnen jahrzehntelange Erfahrung in der Ausbildung von Translatoren (Übersetzern und Konferenzdolmetschern), was mit der zunehmenden Integration Europas und letztendlich mit der heutigen Europäischen Union und ihrem Sprachenregime zusammenhängt. Diese Institute bieten vergleichbare qualitativ hochstehende Studienprogramme an, damit ihre Absolventen den Anforderungen der Sprachendienste der Europäischen Kommis-

97 Marcel Thelen 2009: 208 f.: „Translator training trains students to become professional translators that in their turn (should) want to satisfy the translation needs of clients in the execution of their profession. For this training, translator training relies on the professional world for placements and other forms of direct assistance and support".

sion und des Europäischen Parlaments genügen können, und damit in der Regel auch der Vereinten Nationen, solange es die Sprachen Englisch, Französisch und Spanisch sind.

Den Vereinten Nationen, in der ja alle Staaten dieser Welt vertreten sind, muß aber daran gelegen sein, daß sich ihre Sprachendienste in ihren Zusammenarbeitsangeboten nicht nur auf die europäischen Hochschulen konzentrieren, selbst wenn diese in der Vergangenheit ihre Expertise im Bereich der Ausbildung von Translatoren unter Beweis gestellt haben. Vielmehr müssen die Vereinten Nationen danach streben, auch Ausbildungsinstitute außerhalb Europas heranzuziehen und sie für ein zu bildendes Netzwerk mit einem multilateralen Ansatz zur Implementierung des genannten Moduls *International Translation and Interpretation* zu gewinnen.

Wie das erreicht werden kann, ist noch unklar, da die Einzelinstitute, die sich beteiligen werden, wahrscheinlich eine bilaterale Zusammenarbeit mit den Sprachendiensten in New York oder Genf einem übergreifenden multilateralen System vorziehen werden. Andererseits dürfte es aber im Interesse der Vereinten Nationen sein, wenn sich eine Zusammenarbeit der ausbildenden Institute mit den Sprachendiensten weltweit auf multilateraler Basis etablieren ließe, da auf diese Weise Monopolbildungen vermieden werden könnten. Eine solche übergreifende Zusammenarbeit in Form eines *collaborative academic training and research* wäre für alle von Nutzen, wenn durch diese Vernetzung eine fachkommunikative Ausbildung im internationalen Bereich unter besonderer Berücksichtigung der Institutionensprache der Vereinten Nationen und ihrer spezifischen Terminologie als Modul *International Translation and Interpretation* in die bestehenden Studienprogramme eingebaut werden könnte. Den Sprachendiensten in New York und Genf, aber auch in Wien und Nairobi käme hier die Aufgabe einer anwendungsorientierten Ausbildungs- und Forschungsförderung zu, indem sie transektorale Vernetzungen *(cross-sectoral linkages)* einer fachkommunikativen Ausbildung in den vor allen gesuchten Kombinationen mit Chinesisch, Arabisch und Russisch organisierten.

Eine Schnittstellenoptimierung könnte dabei erreicht werden durch wohlüberlegte Anreizsetzungen zur Förderung der Mobilität von Studierenden, durch Angebote von Praktika in den Standorten New York, Genf und Wien, aber auch durch Unterstützung einschlägiger gemeinsamer Forschungsprojekte. Dabei könnte die CIUTI, die ja als NGO in Genf zugelassen ist, gute Dienste leisten als Schnittstelle *(interface)* zwischen den Sprachendiensten der Vereinten Nationen und den ausbildenden Hochschulen, um solche Module *International Translation and Interpretation* zu propagieren.

Bibliographie

Anheier, Helmut/Glasius, Marlies/Kaldor, Mary (eds) (2001): *Global Civil Society*. Oxford: Oxford University Press.

Athanassiou, Phoebus (2006): *The application of multilingualism in the European Union context*. Frankfurt: European Central Bank. Legal Working Paper Series No. 2. March 2006.

Baigorri-Jalón, Jesús (2004): *Interpreters at the United Nations. A History*. Salamanca: Universidad de Salamanca.

Barnett, Michael/Finnemore, Martha (2005): *Rules for the World: International Institutions in Global Politics*. Ithaca, NY: Cornell University Press.

Barnett, Michael/Finnemore, Martha (2007): Political approach. In: Weiss, Thomas G. / Daws, Sam (eds.): *The Oxford Handbook on the United Nations*. Oxford: Oxford University Press. 41–57.

Bertrand, Maurice (1995): *UNO. Geschichte und Bilanz*. Frankfurt am Main: Fischer Taschenbuch Verlag.

Bertrand, Maurice (2005): Lehren aus einer gescheiterten Reform. Das Problem der „politischen Globalisierung“. In: *Vereinte Nationen* 5/2005. 174–179.

Cillia, Rudolf de (2003): Tendenzen und Prinzipien europäischer Sprachpolitik. In: Krumm, Hans-Jürgen (Hrsg.): *Sprachenvielfalt. Babylonische Sprachverwirrung oder Mehrsprachigkeit als Chance?* Innsbruck: Studienverlag. 27–40.

Cogo, Alessia/Jenkins, Jennifer (2010): English as a lingua franca in Europe. A mismatch between policy and practice. In: *European Journal of Language Policy* 2.2 (2010). 271–294.

Conrady, Jan (2009): *Wandel der Funktionen des UN-Generalsekretärs*. Berlin: Duncker & Humblot.

Coulmas, Florian (1992): *Die Wirtschaft mit der Sprache. Eine sprachsoziologische Studie*. Frankfurt am Main: Suhrkamp.

Creech, Richard L. (2005): *Law and Language in the European Union. The Paradox of a Babel „United in Diversity"*. Groningen: Europa Law Publishing.

Crosette, Barbara (2007): Media. In: Weiss, Thomas G. / Daws, Sam (eds.): *The Oxford Handbook on the United Nations*. Oxford: Oxford University Press. 275–284.

de Saint-Robert, Marie-Josée (2009): Assessing Quality in Translation and Terminology at the United Nations. In: Forstner, Martin / Lee-Jahnke, Hannelore / Schmitt, Peter A. (Hrsg.): *CIUTI-Forum 2008. Enhancing Translation Quality: Ways, Means, Methods*. Bern: Peter Lang. 385–392.

de Swaan, Abram (2001): *Words of the World. The Global Language System*. Cambridge: Polity Press.

Edzard, Lutz (1998): *Language as a Medium of Legal Norms. Implications of the Use of Arabic as a Language in the United Nations Systems*. Berlin: Duncker & Humblot.

Emmerich-Fritsche, Angelika (2007): *Vom Völkerrecht zum Weltrecht*. Berlin: Duncker & Humblot.

Fassbender, Dirk (2007): Europa vermitteln. Die Kommunikationspolitik der Europäischen Union. In: Schmitt, Peter A. / Jüngst, Heike E. (Hrsg.): *Translationsqualität*. Frankfurt am Main: Peter Lang. 118–123.

Fischer-Lescano, Andreas / Teubner, Gunther (2006): *Regime-Kollisionen. Zur Fragmentierung des globalen Rechts*. Frankfurt am Main: Suhrkamp.

Fischer-Lescano, Andreas / Viellechner, Lars (2010): *Globaler Rechtspluralismus*. In: *Aus Politik und Zeitgeschichte 34–35/2010*. 20–26.

Forstner, Martin (1997): Translation and Interpreting Studies and the Challenge of the Official Multilingualism of the European Union, in: *Le Plurilinguisme dans la Société de l'Information. Mulilingualism in an Information Society. UNESCO, 4–5–6 – XII – 1997*. Paris 1997: Forum International des Sciences Humaines. 167–174.

Forstner, Martin (1998): Über den europäischen Multilingualismus im allgemeinen und in Osteuropa im besonderen, oder: Können und sollen wir uns ein multilinguales Europa überhaupt leisten? In: *Atti del Convegno Verso un' Unione Europea allargata ad Est: Quale ruolo per la traduzione? (Trieste, 27–28 maggio 1996). Quaderni di Libri e Riviste d'Italia* 37 (1998). 189–201.

Forstner, Martin (2000): Zwischen globalisierter Kommunikation und kultureller Fragmentierung – zur Rolle der Translatoren in der neuen Informations- und Kommunikations-Welt. In: Wilss, Wolfram (Hrsg.): *Weltgesellschaft, Weltverkehrssprache, Weltkultur. Globalisierung versus Fragmentierung*. Tübingen: Stauffenberg. 139–183.

Forstner, Martin (2002): Menschenrechte zwischen Geltungsuniversalität und Inhaltspartikularität – ein Problem für den Islam in Europa? In: Pahud de Mortanges, René / Tanner, Erwin (Hrsg): *Muslime und schweizerische Rechtsordnung*. Freiburg (Schweiz): Universitätsverlag. 2002. 479–528.

Forstner, Martin (2004): Muss der Translator bikulturell sein? Überlegungen zur interkulturellen Kompetenz. In: *Translation Studies in the New Millennium. An International Journal of Translation and Interpreting* (Bilkent University, Ankara) 2 (2004). 43–83.

Fröhlich, Manuel (2005): Zwischen Verwaltung und Politik: Die Arbeit des UN-Sekretariats. In: Dicke, Klaus / Fröhlich, Manuel (Hrsg.): *Wege multilateraler Diplomatie. Politik, Handlungsmöglichkeiten und Entscheidungsstrukturen im UN-System*. Baden-Baden: Nomos. 41–63.

Gareis, Sven Bernhard / Varwick, Johannes (2006): *Die Vereinten Nationen. Aufgaben, Instrumente und Reformen*. Opladen: Barbara Budrich.

Giesecke, Michael (2002): *Von den Mythen der Buchkultur zu den Visionen der Informationsgesellschaft. Trendforschungen zur kulturellen Medienökologie*. Frankfurt am Main: Suhrkamp.

Gordenker, Leon / Jönsson, Christer (2007): Evolution in knowledge. In: Weiss, Thomas G. / Daws, Sam (eds.): *The Oxford Handbook on the United Nations*. Oxford: Oxford University Press. 84–94.

Grucza, Franciszek (2003): Mehrsprachigkeit in Mitteleuropa und der Europäischen Union. Traditionen – Gefahren – Ausblicke. In: Besters-Dilger, Juliane et al.: *Mehrsprachigkeit in der erweiterten Europäischen Union. Multilingualism in the enlarged European Union. Multilinguisme dans l'Union Européenne élargie*. Klagenfurt: Drava Verlag. 15–17.

Guenot-Hovnanian, Marianne (2009): La pré-édition à l'ONU. In: Forstner, Martin / Lee-Jahnke, Hannelore / Schmitt, Peter A. (Hrsg.): *CIUTI-Forum 2008. Enhancing Translation Quality: Ways, Means, Methods*. Bern: Peter Lang. 377–384.

Guskow, Meike (2009): *Entstehung und Geschichte der Europäischen Charta der Regional- und Minderheitensprachen*. Frankfurt: Peter Lang.

Haarmann, Harald (2002): Parameter europäischer Sprachenpolitik in der Ära der Network Society. In: Kelz, Heinrich P. (Hrsg.) (2002): *Die sprachliche Zukunft Europas. Mehrsprachigkeit und Sprachenpolitik*. Baden-Baden: Nomos. 77–93.

Haarmann, Harald (2002a): Sprachenvielfalt im Globalisierungsprozess. In: Hoberg, Rudolf (Hrsg.): *Deutsch – Englisch – Europäisch. Impulse für eine neue Sprachpolitik*. Mannheim: Dudenverlag. 9–29.

Haarmann, Harald (2002b): Englisch, Network Society und europäische Identität: Eine sprachökologische Standortbestimmung. In: Hoberg, Rudolf (Hrsg.): *Deutsch – Englisch – Europäisch. Impulse für eine neue Sprachpolitik*. Mannheim: Dudenverlag. 152–170.

Haarmann, Harald (2004): Evolution, language, and the construction of culture. In: Wuketits, Franz M. / Antweiler, Christoph (eds.): *Handbook of evolution, vol. 1: The evolution of human societies and cultures*. Weinheim: Wiley-VGH Verlag. 77–119.

Hinnenkamp, Volker (2010): Vom Umgang mit Mehrsprachigkeiten. In: *Aus Politik und Zeitgeschichte* 8/2010. 27–32.

Jaekel, Natalia Anna (2009): Das EU-Sprachenregime – Hemmschuh oder Schlüssel der europäischen Identität. Die Vision einer multilingualen Europäischen Union. In: *Verwaltungsblätter für Baden-Württemberg* 12/2009. 445–449.

Kneer, Georg / Nassehi, Armin (1993): *Niklas Luhmanns Theorie sozialer Systeme. Eine Einführung*. München: Fink.

Knüppel, Katharina (2010): *Religionsfreiheit und Apostasie in islamisch geprägten Staaten*. Frankfurt am Main: Peter Lang.

Krotz, Friedrich (2001): *Die Mediatisierung kommunikativen Handelns. Der Wandel von Alltag und sozialen Beziehungen, Kultur und Gesellschaft durch die Medien*. Wiesbaden: Westdeutscher Verlag.

Lee Jahnke, Hannelore (2009): Doppelter Praxisbezug und Kompetenzvermittlung als Problem der Qualitätssicherung translatorischer Studiengänge. In: Forstner, Martin / Lee-Jahnke, Hannelore / Schmitt, Peter A. (Hrsg.): *CIUTI-Forum 2008. Enhancing Translation Quality: Ways, Means, Methods*. Bern: Peter Lang. 133–193.

Lehmann, Ingrid A. (1999): *Peacekeeping and Public Information. Caught in the Crossfire*. London: Frank Cass.

Lehmann, Ingrid A. (2003): Öffentlichkeitsarbeit der Vereinten Nationen – vom Sündenbock zur strategischen Kommunikation. In: Schorlemer, Sabine von (Hrsg.): *Praxishandbuch UNO. Die Vereinten Nationen im Lichte globaler Herausforderungen*. Berlin: Springer. 569–589.

Lehmann, Ingrid A. (2006): Kommunikationsmanagement in den Vereinten Nationen. In: Schorlemer, Sabine von (Hrsg.): *Globale Probleme und Zukunftsaufgaben der Vereinten Nationen* (Zeitschrift für Politik. Sonderband 1). Baden-Baden: Nomos. 201–217.

Li, David C.S. (2009): Multilingualism and commerce. In: Auer, Peter / Wei, Li (eds.) (2009): *Handbook of Multilingualism and multilingual communication*. Berlin: Mouton de Gruyter. 423–443.

Manz, Viviane (2002): *Sprachenvielfalt und europäische Union. Sprachenrecht im Spannungsfeld von Wirtschaft, Politik und Kultur*. Zürich/Basel/Genf: Schulthess Juristische Medien & Stämpfli Verlag Bern.

Martens, Kerstin (2005): *NGOs and the United Nations: Institutionalization, Professionalization and Adaptation*. Houndsmill, Basingstoke, UK: Palgrave Macmillan.

Meckel, Miriam (2001): *Die globale Agenda. Kommunikation und Globalisierung*. Wiesbaden: Westdeutscher Verlag.

Meier, Philip (2000): *Interne Kommunikation von Unternehmen. Theoretische und empirische Aspekte zur Organisation und Sprache der Internen Kommunikation grosser Unternehmen in der Schweiz.* Zürich (Diss.).

Müller, Elke (2010): *Sprache – Recht – Übersetzen: Betrachtungen zur juristischen Fachkommunikation. Mit einer Darstellung am Beispiel von deutschen und spanischen Strafurteilen.* Hamburg: Kovač.

Nettle, Daniel / Romaine, Suzanne: *Vanishing voices. The extinction of the world's languages.* Oxford: Oxford University Press.

Paqué, Ruprecht (1980): Sprachen und Sprachendienste der Vereinten Nationen. In: *Vereinte Nationen* 1980. 165–171.

Paqué, Ruprecht (1997): Vielsprachigkeit, Mehrsprachigkeit, Einsprachigkeit. Zu den Sprachen der Vereinten Nationen und zur Resolution 50/11 der Generalversammlung über „Multilingualismus". In: *Vereinte Nationen* 1992. 61–75.

Paschke, Karl Theodor (2003): UNO von innen – die Besonderheiten einer multinationalen Bürokratie. In: Schorlemer, Sabine von (Hrsg.): *Praxishandbuch UNO. Die Vereinten Nationen im Lichte globaler Herausforderungen.* Berlin: Springer. 553–567.

Paschke, Karl Theodor (2005): UN-Reform – die unendliche Geschichte. In: *Vereinte Nationen* 5/2005. 170–173.

Paulus, Andreas L. (2001): *Die Internationale Gemeinschaft im Völkerrecht. Eine Untersuchung zur Entwicklung des Völkerrechts im Zeitalter der Globalisierung.* München: C.H. Beck.

Pearl, Stephen (1995): Lacuna, myth and shibboleth in the teaching of simultaneous interpreting. In: *Perspectives: Studies in Translatology* 1995. 161–190.

Pfeil, Beate Sibylle (2000): Die Erhaltung von Minderheitensprachen in Europa und das aktuelle Europarat-Instrumentarioum. In: *Europa ethnica* (Wien) 57/1 (2000). 1–18.

Pfeil, Werner (1999): Ein Grundrecht auf die eigene Rechtssprache im Gemeinschaftsrecht? In: Groot, Gerard-René de / Schulze, Reiner (Hrsg.): *Recht und Übersetzen.* Baden-Baden: Nomos. 125–147.

Philippson, Robert (1992): *Linguistic Imperialism.* Oxford: Oxford University Press.

Philippson, Robert (1999): International Languages and International Human Rights. In: Kontra, Miklós / Philippson, Robert / Skutnabb-Kongas, Tove / Várady, Tibor (eds): *Language: A Right and a Resource. Approaching Linguistic Human Rights.* Budapest / New York: Central European University Press. 25–46.

Reichelt, Gerte (2006): Sprachliche Gleichberechtigung und ihre Grenzen in der Europäischen Union. In: Reichelt, Gerte (Hrsg.): *Sprache und Recht, unter besonderer Berücksichtigung des Europäischen Gemeinschaftsrechts.* Wien: Manzsche Verlags- und Universitätsbuchhandlung. 1–10.

Rindler-Schjerve, Rosita (2003): Europäische Sprachenpolitik und Minderheiten. In: Krumm, Hans-Jürgen (Hrsg.): *Sprachenvielfalt. Babylonische Sprachverwirrung oder Mehrsprachigkeit als Chance?* Innsbruck: Studienverlag. 49–60.

Roelcke, Thorsten (1999): *Fachsprachen*. Berlin: Erich Schmidt.

Roelcke, Thorsten (2002): *Kommunikative Effizienz. Eine Modellskizze*. Heidelberg: C. Winter.

Rogers, Everett M. (2003): *Diffusion of innovations*. 5th ed. New York: Free Press.

Rosenfeld, Friedrich (2009): *Die humanitäre Besatzung. Ein Dilemma des ius post bellum*. Baden-Baden: Nomos.

Ross, Andreas (2003): *Europäische Einheit in babylonischer Vielfalt. Die Reform des Sprachenregimes der Europäischen Union im Spannungsfeld von Demokratie und Effizienz*. Frankfurt: Peter Lang.

Rudolf, Walter (1972): *Die Sprache in der Diplomatie und internationalen Verträgen*. Frankfurt am Main: Athenäum.

Schechter, Michael G. (2005): *United Nations Global Conferences*. London: Routledge.

Schendl, Herbert / Seidlhofer, Barbara / Widdenson, Henry (2003): Weltsprache Englisch – Bedrohung oder Chance? In: Krumm, Hans-Jürgen (Hrsg.): *Sprachenvielfalt. Babylonische Sprachverwirrung oder Mehrsprachigkeit als Chance?* Innsbruck: Studienverlag. 181–198.

Schneiders, Hans-Wolfgang (2007): *Allgemeine Übersetzungstheorie. Verstehen und Wiedergeben*. Bonn: Romanistischer Verlag.

Schreiner, Patrick (2006): *Staat und Sprache in Europa. Nationalstaatliche Einsprachigkeit und Mehrsprachenpolitik der Europäischen Union*. Frankfurt am Main: Peter Lang.

Semling, Corinna (2005): Information und Kommunikation in Organisationen – eine Facette der Organisationskultur: Ein verhaltensorientierter Ansatz zur Analyse der Kultur in Organisationen. In: Crijns, Rogier / Janich, Nina (Hrsg.): *Interne Kommunikation von Unternehmen. Psychologische, kommunikationswissenschaftliche und kulturvergleichende Studien*. Wiesbaden: Deutscher Universitäts-Verlag. 7–38.

Skutnabb-Kangas, Tove (1999): Linguistic diversity, human rights and free market. In: Kontra, Miklós, et al. (eds): *Language. A right and a resource*. Budapest: CEU Press. 187–222.

Stejskal, Jiri (2009): Quality Assessment in Translation. In: Forstner, Martin / Lee-Jahnke, Hannelore / Schmitt, Peter A. (Hrsg.): *CIUTI-Forum 2008. Enhancing Translation Quality: Ways, Means, Methods*. Bern: Peter Lang. 291–300.

Stickel, Gerhard (2005): Plurilinguismus und Übersetzen: Investition in Europas Zukunft. In: Nies, Fritz (Hrsg.): *Europa denkt mehrsprachig. Exemplarisch: deutsche und französische Kulturwissenschaften*. Tübingen: Narr. 97–105.

Strohmeier, Gerd (2007): Die EU zwischen Legitimität und Effektivität. In: *Aus Politik und Zeitgeschichte* 10/2007: 24–30.

Tabory, Mala (1980): Multilingualism in International Law and Institutions. *Alphen aan den Rijn (The Netherlands) / Rockville (Maryland, USA).*

Thelen, Marcel (2009): Quality Management for Translation. In: Forstner, Martin / Lee-Jahnke, Hannelore / Schmitt, Peter A. (Hrsg.): *CIUTI-Forum 2008. Enhancing Translation Quality: Ways, Means, Methods.* Bern: Peter Lang. 195–212.

Theme, Anne (2002): *Sprache und Gesetzgeber. Grenzen sprachgesetzlicher Regelungen in Deutschland und Frankreich nach dem EG-Vertrag und nationalem Verfassungsrecht.* Berlin: Duncker & Humblot.

Varennes, Fernand de (1999): The Existing Rights of Minorities in International Rights. In: Kontra, Miklós / Philippson, Robert / Skutnabb-Kongas, Tove / Várady, Tibor (eds): *Language: A Right and a Resource. Approaching Linguistic Human Rights.* Budapest/New York: Central European University Press. 117–146.

Varwick, Johannes (2007): „Die Reform der Reform": Der UN-Weltgipfel und seine Folgen. In: Schorlemer, Sabine von (Hrsg.): *Globale Probleme und Zukunftsaufgaben der Vereinten Nationen* (Zeitschrift für Politik. Sonderband 1). Baden-Baden: Nomos. 238–254.

Varwick, Johannes / Knelangen, Wilhelm (2002): Die Rolle der Vereinten Nationen in der internationalen Politik. In: *Aus Politik und Zeitgeschichte* B 27–28/ 2002. 3–10.

Wagner, Emma / Bech, Svend / Martínez, Jesús M. (2002): *Translating for the European Union Institutions.* Manchester: St. Jerome.

Wang, Lidi (2009): Quality Assurance for Quality Training. In: Forstner, Martin / Lee-Jahnke, Hannelore / Schmitt, Peter A. (Hrsg.): *CIUTI-Forum 2008. Enhancing Translation Quality: Ways, Means, Methods.* Bern: Peter Lang. 213–216.

Wapner, Paul (2007): Civil society. In: Weiss, Thomas G. / Daws, Sam (eds.): *The Oxford Handbook on the United Nations.* Oxford: Oxford University Press. 254–263.

Weber, Peter J. (2004): Bildungspolitik und Sprachenpluralismus in der Europäischen Union. Notwendigkeiten einer transnationalen und plurizentrischen Bildungspolitik. In: *Bildung und Erziehung* 57 (2004). 5–25.

Weiss, Thomas G. / Daws, Sam (2007): World politics. Continuity and change since 1945. In: Weiss, Thomas G. / Daws, Sam (eds.): *The Oxford Handbook on the United Nations.* Oxford: Oxford University Press. 3–38.

Wesel, Reinhard (2003): Die symbolischen Vereinten Nationen. In: Schorlemer, Sabine von (Hrsg.): *Praxishandbuch UNO. Die Vereinten Nationen im Lichte globaler Herausforderungen.* Berlin: Springer. 591–613.

Wichter, Sigurd (1994): *Experten- und Laienwortschätze. Umriss einer Lexikologie der Vertikalität*. Tübingen: Niemeyer.
Wright, Sue (2004): *Language Policy and Language Planning. From Nationalism to Globalisation*. Houndmills, Basingstoke/New York: Palgrave Macmillan.
Wright, Sue (2009): The elephant in the room. Language issues in the European Union. In: *European Journal of Language Policy* 1.2 (2009). 93–120.
Zhang, Wen (2009): Language Proficiency and Translation Quality: The predicament in Chinese University Translator / Interpreter Training. In: Forstner, Martin / Lee-Jahnke, Hannelore / Schmitt, Peter A. (Hrsg.): *CIUTI-Forum 2008. Enhancing Translation Quality: Ways, Means, Methods*. Bern: Peter Lang. 217–227.
Zürn, Michael (2010): Internationale Institutionen und nichtstaatliche Akteure. In: *Aus Politik und Zeitgeschichte* 34–35/2010. 14–20.

Sprache und Macht

Erich PRUNČ

Kaum jemand hätte noch geglaubt, dass nach den Erfahrungen des Holocaust und nach der Zeit der Post-Moderne, die das Ende der großen Narrative angekündigt hatte, am Ende des 20. und zu Beginn des 21. Jahrhunderts prämoderne Atavismen mit ungeheurer Gewalt ausbrechen, ganze Regionen wie den Balkan in Mitleidenschaft ziehen oder gar einen globalen Konflikt abzeichnen könnten. In diesen Kontext haben Zeichensysteme, Sprache und Sprachen auch in Europa plötzlich wieder ihren essentialistischen Fetischcharakter erhalten, den man in europäischen Denkschulen am Ausgang des 20. Jahrhunderts erfolgreich dekonstruiert zu haben glaubte.

Wenn wir von der Macht der Sprache und der Sprachen sprechen, sollten wir uns zunächst vergegenwärtigen, dass auch diese Macht – wie jede Macht eben – nicht den Phänomen, Institutionen und Personen inhärent ist, sondern ihnen von den jeweiligen Gesellschaften und Individuen zugeschrieben wird. Es sind also die Machtzuschreibungen, die wir in einem ersten Denkschritt zu hinterfragen haben.

Es kann zunächst die Macht der Sprachen sein, die aus der kulturellen, politischen, wirtschaftlichen und militärischen Macht der jeweiligen Sprachgemeinschaften resultiert. Im hegemonialen Machtdiskurs zwischen den Sprachen scheint die Regel zu herrschen, dass den Sprachen der starken Sprachgemeinschaften dabei noch mehr Macht zugeschrieben wird, während die schwachen noch stärker marginalisiert werden. Denn die jeweils Schwächeren müssen sich, wenn sie gehört werden wollen, der mächtigen Sprachen bedienen. Das dadurch zugeführte symbolische Kapital zieht eine Spirale neuer Machtzuschreibungen nach sich und übt einen exponentiell steigenden strukturellen Druck auf Spracherwerb und Sprachwahl aus, der auch durch sprachpolitische Maßnahmen kaum auszugleichen ist. In diesem Prozess hat sich das Englische als Sprache der einzigen übrig gebliebenen militärischen Supermacht mit bald einer Milliarde Sprechern eindeutig in die Spitzenposition der Weltsprachenhierarchie gehievt. Das Französische, das sich nach Angaben des *British council* noch 2000 die Spitzenposition mit dem Englischen teilte, muss sich zusehends mit Nischenfunktionen, wie etwa als Relaissprache im Konsekrationsmechanismus der *République mondiale des lettres* (Casanova 1999) zufrieden geben. Auch die Bemühungen, das Deutsche aufgrund der historischen Beziehungen in den neuen Demokratien als *lingua franca* zu etablieren, konnten dem strukturellen Druck des Englischen kaum standhalten.

Doch die Spirale von Machtzuschreibungen ist mit zwei gegenläufigen Tendenzen konfrontiert. Die *Weltsprache Englisch* beginnt dem Besitz ihrer Sprachgemeinschaften zu entgleiten und verliert, indirektproportional zur geographischen und funktionalen Ausbreitung an sinnlicher Tiefe und Differenzierungskraft (Crystal 2003). Das *global english* oder *international english* kann seine Funktionalität nur in relativ neutralen, kulturell nicht markierten Kontexten der suprakulturellen Kommunikation entfalten, während die virulenten kulturellen Unterschiede bei sensibleren Interaktionen unter die Oberfläche gekehrt werden (vgl. Snell-Hornby 1997). Das konkrete Sprechen wird so zum Vehikel einer emotionell verarmten Scheinkommunikation, die Identität der Wörter zur Scheinidentität degradiert, hinter der die Gemeinsamkeit der Sprache als eigentlich trennende Chimäre lauert.

Wie das Latein des Mittelalters steht auch die Weltsprache Englisch ohnmächtig vor den Prozessen der Regionalisierung, Hybridisierung und Kreolisierung, aufgrund derer neue Sprachvarietäten entstehen, die sich ihrerseits als identitätsstiftende Projektionsflächen für neue Machtzuschreibungen als Amts- Staat- und Nationalsprachen anbieten.

Die mythische Folie der Zuschreibung einer Einheitssprache zu einem Volk und einem Reich ist in der großen Erzählung der Bibel in die Geschichte vom Turmbau zu Babel, diesen *„Mythos vom Ursprung des Mythos"*, wie ihn Derrida (1997: 119) nennt, eingeschrieben. In diesem Mythos projiziert der patriarchalische Erzähler seine Vorstellung von der Gestaltung einer uniformen und deshalb mächtigen Gesellschaft in einen totalitären Gott, der neben sich keine anderen Götter und keine anderen Wahrheiten duldet. Was Gott in dieser Erzählung zum Handeln herausfordert, ist die Koordinationsfähigkeit der Menschen durch eine Einheitssprache, die ihrem Handeln keine Grenzen setzt: „Siehe, sie sind ein Volk und sprechen eine Sprache. Das ist erst der Anfang ihres Tuns. Fortan wird für sie *nichts mehr unausführbar sein, was immer sie zu tun ersinnen*" heißt es in Kapitel 11 der Genesis (Bibel 1966: 9, Hervorhebg. v. u.). In der Derridaschen Paraphrase des Mythos fordern die Menschen den Zorn der Gottheit heraus, „weil sie sich einen Namen machen wollen [...] einen Namen in der einer universalen Sprache" (Derrida 1997: 123), um nicht als Namenlose über die ganze Welt zerstreut zu werden. Das Recht, den Dingen, den Anderen und sich selbst Namen zu geben und damit in die Welt des Seins zu erwecken, hat der Gott der Totalität nur sich selbst vorbehalten. Er allein bestimmt, was einen Namen, eine Bezeichnung hat, und deshalb in der ontologischen Ordnung sein darf. Der Verlust der Einheitssprache, der dem Menschen die Fähigkeit zur Kooperation rauben soll, macht als Strafe nur in einem Weltkonzept einen Sinn, in dem die Verbindung zwischen Sprache und Realität eine essentiell vorgegebene ist.

Das Scheitern des Turmprojektes zu Babel symbolisiert nach Derrida die Unmöglichkeit des menschlichen Vollendens und Totalisierens. Babel ist die Metapher für die Aufgabe der ideologisch verkürzten Einheit von Welt und Wort. Der Babylonische Glücksfall entkleidet die Sprache ihrer Totalität und ihrer Macht als Hort der Wahrheit und setzt an ihre Stelle die Kontingenz und deshalb Aushandelbarkeit der Beziehung von Wörtern und Worten zu Welten und Werten, von Sätzen zu Wahrheiten. In den Symphonien und Kakophonien des postbabylonischen Sprachengewirrs ist der Mensch nicht mehr zum einfältigen Gleichschritt der Totalität verdammt, sondern der beängstigenden und beglückenden Vielfalt der Freiheit preisgegeben. Die graue Scheinobjektivität einer erträumten und ideologisierten Einheitssprache muss in der „irreduktiblen Vielfalt der Sprachen", um wieder Derrida (a.a.O. 119) zu zitieren, der kreativ-chaotischen Mannigfaltigkeit von Sichtweisen weichen, die in Sprachen ausgedrückt und durch Sprachen konstruiert werden. Babels *felix culpa* liegt schließlich auch darin, die Menschen auf ihre Sprachen als unerschöpfliche Quelle der Kreativität verwiesen zu haben. Im aktuellen kulturellen Kontext manifestiert sich die Botschaft von Babel in der Unlust, im Einheitsgrau einer verflachten und nivellierenden Weltsprache zu paradieren oder sich vom Einheitsbrei des Eurospeak zu ernähren, in der Lust, das Anderssein der anderen zu verspüren, ihre Sprach- und Denkwelten zu erschließen und sie als Vermittlungsinstanz zum Sein und zu den Sinnkonstruktionen der Anderen stets von Neuem zu entdecken, ja, in der Wollust, in ihren Laut- und Bilderwelten zu baden,

Das vorbabylonische[1] Konzept einer (zwangs)beglückenden Einheitssprache findet im europäischen Kontext des 19. Jahrhundert vor allem in den kulturellen Konstrukten von Nationalsprachen, Nationalkulturen und Nationalstaaten seine säkularisierte Reinkarnation. Die daraus resultierenden Machtzuschreibungen im interethnischen und internationalen Diskurs ist die zweite Quelle, aus der Sprache ihre janusköpfige Macht schöpft. Der positive Impetus, der von dieser Zuschreibung ausging, war imstande, Kreativkräfte zu mobilisieren und Integrationsprozesse zu initiieren, führte jedoch aufgrund ihrer inneren Logik auch zur Tilgung der innersprachlichen Vielfalt zu Gunsten nationaler Standards, die von den jeweils herrschenden Eliten geformt wurden. Gleichzeitig führe der ethnozentrische Abgrenzungsdiskurs auf der *inner*staat-

1 „Vorbabylonisch" ist in diesem Kontext nicht historisch sondern metaphorisch gemeint.

lichen Ebene zu einer, meist mit struktureller, nicht selten auch mit realer Gewalt verbundenen Marginalisierung, Stigmatisierung, Assimilation und Vertreibung von Minderheiten und schlug sich auf der zwischenstaatlichen Ebene in den Grenzkonflikten der Nationalstaaten nieder, die im Zweiten Weltkrieg kulminierten.

Trotz dieser negativen historischen Erfahrung bleibt die Dekonstruktion des Nationalsprachen- und Nationalstaatenprinzips aufgrund der vorherrschenden Ethnozentrismen noch immer im Reich der intellektuellen Utopien angesiedelt. Im Gegenteil, der grausam griffige Begriff *der ethnischen Säuberung* ist eine Erfindung, die im unmittelbaren europäischen Umfeld in den Balkankriegen zu Beginn der 1990-er Jahre geboren wurde. Gerade in diesem Kontext lässt sich auch die Zirkelhaftigkeit der Machtzuschreibungen zu Sprachen als Nationalsprachen am Zerfall des Serbokroatischen in drei Sprachen, nämlich das Bosnische, Kroatische und Serbische, anschaulich demonstrieren: Im Bestreben, sich von den rivalisierenden Sozietäten auf dem Balkan abzugrenzen, wurde das so genannte Wiener Abkommen aus dem Jahre 1849, das auf eine Konvergenz der standardsprachlichen Varietäten abzielte, aufgekündigt und die Varietäten selbst zu Nationalsprachen erhoben. Dabei wurden nicht nur Unterschiede in Phonologie, Lexik und Syntax zu Symbolen der nationalen Identität hochstilisiert, sondern gleichzeitig durch sprachpolitische Maßnahmen vor allem im Bereich der Lexik ein Prozess des systematischen Ausbaus der Unterschiede zwischen den neu entstehenden Sprachen vorangetrieben, um so neue Sprachhürden zwischen den Sozietäten aufzubauen und den Differenzierungsprozess irreversibel zu machen.

Das dritte und wesentliche Machtpotential der Sprache und der Sprachen liegt in ihrer Struktureigenschaft als Medium der Wirklichkeitskonstruktion. Diese Funktion hat die Totalitarismen aller Zeiten und unterschiedlichster ideologischer Herkunft dazu verleitet, das ideologische Konstrukt der nicht hinterfragbaren Einheit von Sprache und Welt zu dekretieren und durch entsprechende Lenkungs- und Kontrollmassanahmen abzusichern, um so den Zugriff zur Gestaltung sozialer Wirklichkeiten zu sichern. Indem

Wahrheit an einer Sprache festgemacht und Symbole mit Realitäten und Realitätskonstrukten essentialistisch gleichgesetzt werden, konnte ideologische und politische Kontrolle als Sprachkontrolle realisiert und Sprache zum Träger der geistigen und politischen Zwangsbeglückung, Nivellierung und Be-mächtigung der Anderen instrumentalisiert werden.

Aber abgesehen von dieser dekretierten Dysfunktion, die in Orwells *New Speach* ihre literarische Metapher gefunden hat, sind Sprachen das Ergebnis individueller und kollektiver Aushandlungsprozesse. Sie finden als Palimpseste von Träumen, Erfahrungen und Geschichten, aber auch als Häuser der Phantasie und als Steinbrüche, aus denen in Dichtung und Wissenschaft das Material für neue Formen und Figuren gebrochen wird, ihren sinnlich wahrnehmbaren Niederschlag. Durch Sprachen und mit Sprache werden soziale Ordnungen geschaffen, durch Sprachbilder und Metaphern soziale Realitäten diskursiv konstruiert und bewertet (vgl. z.B. Berger/Luckmann 1980, Gergen 2002). Durch unterschiedliche An- und Abwesenheit von Ausdrucksmöglichkeiten in Wort-Schätzen und Sprachstrukturen werden unterschiedlichen Kosmen und Ontologien gestaltet, werden Weltschein und Scheinwelten durch Wortsein und Wortwelten erzeugt.

Durch Sprachen wird – um mit einem neutralen Beispiel zu beginnen – die scheinbare Realität aufgesplittet, wie etwa die Realität des zweiten Planeten im Sonnensystem unter Bezug auf die jeweilige Lebenswelt in die Sinneinheiten *Morgenstern, Abendstern* und *Venus* gespalten wird. Durch die Wahl von Bezeichnungen, den Ausbau oder die Reduktion von grammatischen Strukturen werden – um mit einem vieldiskutierten Thema fortzusetzen – Frauen in Texten nach Belieben sichtbar und unsichtbar gemacht. Durch Sprachen werden in subtiler Form Identifikationsraster angeboten, die zunächst diffuse gesellschaftliche Konstellationen durch ihre treffende Bildhaftigkeit kognitiv salient und dadurch wirksam werden lassen. So wird durch die Patchworkmetapher nicht nur die Nomadisierung und Fragmentierung des globalisierten Menschen widergespiegelt, sondern mit Wortschöpfungen wie

Patchworkfamilie, Patchworkbeziehungen und *Patchworkidentität* auch soziale Identifikations- und Ordnungsmodelle gestiftet. Kreationen wie *LebensabschnittspartnerIn* – um ein letztes Beispiel anzuführen – signalisieren nicht nur den Zerfall der Institution Ehe als Reproduktionsgemeinschaft und Partnerschaft auf Lebenszeit, sondern legitimieren auch eine lebensweltliche Realität als erstrebenswerten und in Partnerschaftsannoncen durchaus zu vermarktenden Zustand.

Konkrete Sachverhalte können nicht nur unterschiedlich codiert und klassifiziert, sondern durch ihre Benennung überhaupt erst konstituiert werden. Handlungen heben sich erst dann als Straftaten, Vergehen oder Verbrechen von den übrigen Handlungsgefügen ab, wenn sie als solche definiert und mit einem rechtsprachlichen Terminus benannt werden. Ein *Ladendiebstahl* wird nicht zum Ladendiebstahl, weil er in einem Laden begangen wurde, sondern weil es im Gesetzbuch den Strafbestand und den Terminus des Ladendiebstahls gibt. Psychosomatische Zustände werden erst zu Krankheiten, wenn sie sprachlich und kulturell als solche gefasst und benannt werden. Erst durch die sprachliche Klassifikation als *Mord – Totschlag – Freitod – aktive und passive Sterbehilfe – Unfalltod – (natürlicher) Tod* wird das Kontinuum von Sterbearten in gesellschaftlich, weil juristisch relevante Kategorien eingeteilt. Es liegt allerdings in diesen Fällen nicht an der Sprache, sondern an der sozialen Durchsetzbarkeit der Definitionsmächtigen, die – im Konsens oder Dissens mit der jeweiligen Sozietät – neue Ontologien schaffen oder Seiendes durch Nicht-Benennen und Ver-schweigen aus der gesellschaftlichen Realität ver-bannen.

Die Sicht auf die geworteten Sachverhalte wird durch die aus den Morphemen ablesbare Motivation der Wörter, durch einzelne Wortmetaphern oder durch frame-gestützte oder in Narrative eingebettete Metaphernreihen bestimmt. Die Bezeichnungen *Freitod* und *Selbstmord* grenzen diese spezifische Form des Todes nicht nur von allen anderen Todesarten ab, sondern eröffnen durch die unterschiedlich motivierte Benennung auch zwei unterschiedliche emotive und moralische Perspektiven auf diese Handlung.

Als Sedimente des aktuellen oder verdrängten kollektiven Gedächtnisses sind in die Sprachzeichen die Spuren ihrer historischen Kontexte mit ihren Sonn- und Schattenseiten eingeschrieben. So ist in deutschen Wörtern wie *ausradieren, artfremd* und *arttreu, gottgläubig*, *Rasse* und *Volkswohlfahrt, Arbeitsbeschaffung* und *Aussiedlung* unauslöschbar, wie die Tätowierungen auf den Armen der KZ-Häftlinge, das Kainszeichen des Rassen- und Volkswahns eingeprägt, haftet Phrasen wie *durch den Rost fallen* und *Arbeit macht frei* der Geruch von KZ-s und Krematorien an.

Die realitätsstiftende Macht lässt Sprache als strukturierende Struktur – wie aus den angeführten Beispielen ersichtlich gewesen sein dürfte – zum Vehikel der Emanzipation der Schwachen und Marginalisierten, aber auch zur willfährigen Komplizin und Hetäre der Mächtigen werden. Durch die manipulative Formung und Zuschreibung von Signifikanten werden Klassen und Hierarchien von Menschen, Freund- und Feindbilder erzeugt: *Asylwerber* stehen *Asylanten, Arbeitslose Sozialschmarotzern* und *kritische Bürger Nestbeschmutzern* gegenüber. Durch Sprache werden soziale Randgruppen wie Behinderte und Minderheiten stereotypisiert und als *Gehörlose, Volksgruppen, Migranten* und *Saisonarbeitskräfte* in die Gesellschaft einbezogen, als *Taubstumme, Tschuschen, Zigeuner* und *Katzerlmacher* ausgegrenzt. Durch Sätze und Setzungen werden normabweichende Verhaltensweisen wie die Homosexualität als alternativ akzeptiert, als Deviation bezeichnet oder als monströse psychische Abnormalität verteufelt. Allein durch den inflationären und unreflektierten Gebrauch von Kampf- und Kriegsmetaphern in Syntagmen wie *Krieg der Worte*, *Krieg der Geschlechter, Krieg der Kulturen* und *Karikaturenkrieg*, wird die gesellschaftliche Resistenz gegen das Gewaltphänomen Krieg verringert und in den Bereich des Alltäglichen gezogen.

Es liegt in der Verantwortung der Sprach- und Definitionsmächtigen in jeder Gemeinschaft, mit Hilfe von Sprache in intra- und intersozietären Beziehungen Wertekonflikte zu schaffen, zuzuspitzen oder diskursiv auszuhandeln. *Helden* und *Freiheitskämpfer*, *Kriegsverbrecher* und *Terroristen* repräsentieren unterschiedliche ideologische und politische Wertsichten auf identische Akteure im historischen und aktuellen politischen Geschehen. Die Wertsysteme, die solchen Polarisierungen zugrunde liegen, werden zwar nicht durch Sprache, sondern durch die gesellschaftlichen Verhältnisse und politische Interessen generiert. Sie können allerdings – abgesehen von direkter physischer Gewalt – nur durch Sprache vermittelt und dadurch gesellschaftlich relevant gemacht werden. Zur sozialen und politischen Aushandelbarkeit von Wertkonflikten über Sprach-, Kultur- und ideologische Grenzen hinweg ist es also notwendig, die Kontingenz der sprachlichen Codierungen zu erkennen, gleichzeitig jedoch ihre gesellschaftlichen Wurzeln und ihre Eigendynamik freizulegen, um so den Zirkel zwischen sprachlich codierten Wertzuschreibungen und habitualisierten Werten, von sprachlichen Handlungsmodellen und Handlungen zu durchbrechen. Auch wenn die These der Sprachrelativisten, dass das Denken durch Sprache bestimmt wer de, in dieser klassischen Formulierung nicht mehr haltbar ist, so bieten doch Worte und grammatische Strukturen, die ihrerseits Produkte lebensweltlich bedingter und deshalb habitualisierter Benennungsbedürfnisse sind, vorgeprägte Handlungsmuster an, deren Suggestivkraft sich die Handelnden nur durch Reflexion entziehen können.

Auf die Verführungsmacht der Sprache, derer sich allenthalben die Rhetoren, Volkstribunen und Populisten bedienen, kann ich leider aus Zeitgründen nicht näher eingehen. Sie baut im Wesentlichen auf dem gezielten Einsatz und der Emotionalisierung der realitätsstiftenden Kraft der Sprache und die Einbettung von Fakten in kleine und große Narrative auf, blieb jedoch bis zur Erfindung und weltweitern Verbreitung der elektronischen Medien im Wesentlichen auf sozial und regional bestimmbare Zielgruppen beschränkt. In einer global entgrenzten und digitalisierten Medienwelt sind nicht nur die gesellschaftlichen und regionalen Hürden gefallen, sondern ist auch die Zeit der Übermittlung von Kommunikationsakten so sehr geschrumpft, dass die im Mediengeschäft führenden Sprachen in diesem global entgrenzten Raum auf den ersten Blick die totalitären Dimensionen vorbabylonischer Einheitssprachen zu gewinnen scheinen. In der Realität jedoch drohen ihre

Wirklichkeitskonstruktionen – und das ist das Dialektische an ihrer Allgegenwart – aufgrund der multiplen Sinnzuschreibungen vor dem Hintergrund unterschiedlichen Sprach- und Lebenswelten zum Konfliktherd zwischen den Sprachen und Kulturen zu werden: Da aufgrund der Medialität der Kommunikation der direkte Rückgriff auf die jeweils geschilderte Realität kaum möglich ist, sondern diese in erster Linie durch Sprache und Bilder konstruiert wird, entwickeln die vermittelten Sprachbilder, Metaphern und ihre Verknotungen mit Geschichten eine Eigendynamik, durch die sie aufgrund der hohen Repetivität im Trommelfeuer der Medien zu divergierenden Welten verfestigt werden. Zudem entstehen aufgrund der Transformationen durch die Sprachbilder, Metaphern und Wertsysteme der in den Mediationsprozess einbezogenen Sprachen und Kulturen nicht minder wirksame und miteinander kaum noch oder überhaupt nicht mehr kompatible Gegenwelten. Die ontologischen Klüfte, die zwischen diesen Wert- und Weltkonstruktionen durch Sprache herrschen, können eine Spirale von Missverständnissen auslösen oder gar zu irreparablen Konflikten eskalieren.

Die Rückbesinnung auf den konstruktiven Charakter der Zuordnung von Sprache zu Welt und von Welt zu Sprache, gleichzeitig aber auch die Verstärkung der Sensibilität für die Macht der Sprache, die Fähigkeit, hinter und durch die Sprachen und Sprachbilder zu blicken, um ihr heilendes und zerstörerisches Potential zu erkennen, scheint uns ein mögliches wenn auch nicht das Allheilmittel gegen die um sich greifenden Atavismen zu sein. Die Deeskalation in den Köpfen und Herzen der Menschen wird nur dann möglich sein, wenn ihr eine kooperative Dekonstruktion der Worte, Bilder, Metaphern und Symbole vorangeht, wenn vor allem die Metaphern des Krieges und des Kampfes durch Metaphern des Friedens, der Begegnung und des Aushandelns ersetzt werden, um einen nachhaltigen Dialog zwischen den Sprachen und den Menschen, die sich in den bunten sprachgeformten Häusern ihres Seins niedergelassen haben, zu ermöglichen.

Das Überbrücken der ontologischen Klüfte zwischen den soziokognitiv oder medial konstruierten Welten und Gegenwelten wird allerdings nur möglich sein, wenn die betroffenen Sozietäten auch bereit sind, die Relativität der eigenen Welt- und Wertkonstruktionen durch Sprache zu erkennen, die Leitern der Sprachen, auf denen sie durch Sprache zur Welt geklettert sind – um eine Metapher Ludwig Wittgensteins (2003: 111) zu verwenden – nicht einfach zu negieren oder wegzuwerfen, sondern sie zu Pyramiden zusammenzustellen, von denen aus sich ein kreativer Blick auf die weiten Landschaften der Kulturen, ihre Differenzen und Diskontinuitäten eröffnet. Dieser weite Blick scheint mir in einer Zeit, in der sowohl im nationalen als auch im internationalen Rahmen die Götzen der Totalität den Krieg der Kulturen schüren, geradezu unabdingbar zu sein.

Literatur

Bibel (1996): *Die Bibel. Die heilige Schrift des Alten und Neuen Bundes. Vollständige Deutsche Ausgabe.* Zweite Auflage. Freiburg-Basel-Wien: Herder.

Casanova, Pascale (1999): *La république mondiale des lettres.* Paris: Editions du Seuil.

Derrida, Jacques (1997): „Babylonische Türme. Wege, Umwege, Abwege“, in: Hirsch, Alfred ed., *Übersetzung und Dekonstruktion.* Frankfurt am Main: Suhrkamp (Aesthetica), 119–181.

Berger, Peter L. / Luckmann, Thomas (1980): *Die gesellschaftliche Konstruktion der Wirklichkeit.* Frankfurt a. M.: Fischer.

Crystal, David (2003): *English as a Global Language.* Second Edition. Cambridge: Cambridge University Press.

Gergen, Kenneth J. (2002): *Konstruierte Wirklichkeiten. Eine Hinführung zum sozialen Konstruktivismus.* Stuttgart: Kohlhammer.

Snell-Hornby, Mary (1997): „‚Jack McWorld, M. A.‘: Translatoren um die Jahrtausendwende“, in: Grbić, Nadja / Wolf, Michaela (eds.), *Text – Kultur – Kommunikation. Translation als Forschungsaufgabe.* Tübingen: Stauffenberg (Studien zur Translation 4).

Wittgenstein, Ludwig (2003): *Logisch-philosophische Abhandlung. Tractatus logico-philosophicus. Dem Andenken meines Freundes David H. Pinsent gewidmet.* Mit einem Nachwort von Joachim Schulte. Frankfurt am Main: Suhrkamp.

2. *Practical Experiences*

Translator and Interpreter Training: A Chinese Perspective

WANG Lidi

It is a great honor for us to come to the CIUTI Forum held at the UN Office in Geneva to discuss translator and interpreter training and its relevance to language service for international organizations. I would like to thank Professor Hannelore Lee-Jahnke for inviting us to this event and also thank the UN Office for providing the venue for this meeting.

As you probably know, the Translator and Interpreter Training Program at Beijing Foreign Studies University was initially sponsored by the UN Organization. From 1979 through 1994, more than 200 talented young people graduated from our training program and started their careers as professional interpreters and translators at various posts of the UN Organization. Many of them have long become seasoned language professionals or are carrying other responsibilities within the organization. Our blood relations with the UN was not severed, even when the UN sponsorship for the program was suspended in the Mid-1990s, as evidenced by the number of new recruits for UN translators and interpreters in recent years. In 2006, the UN Human Resources Department started a new round of recruitment of Chinese language translators, editors and verbatim reporters through competitive examination worldwide. Nearly half of the 19 finalists are graduates of our program.

The UN-sponsored translator and interpreter training program at BFSU, now renamed the Graduate School of Translation and Interpretation, each year produces around 50 professionally-trained interpreters and translators, who join government offices, universities or multinational companies. The UN sponsored program has sowed the seeds for quality training, now it is time for bounty harvest. So, once again, our thanks to the people at the UN who helped us to set up the training program in the first place.

Now with China's fast economic growth and increased contact with the rest of the world, the demand for translation and interpreting service is soaring. Let me just quote some statistics here. It is estimated that the current market for translation in China comes to 20 billion *yuan* RMB, (that is, about 2 billion euros), which is 10% of the world total. There are more than 800 registered translation companies in Beijing alone, as against 109 companies in 1988. This does not include those who provide such services under various disguise, which are in the thousands. Quality service and competent translators/interpreters are much sought after these days.

To regulate the service, China has drafted and put into effect a series of national standards in recent years, based on the experience of other countries. These include *Translation Service Standard: Part I on Written Translation* (GB/T19363.1–2003), *Text Quality Requirements for Translation Service* (GB/T19682–2005) and *Translation Service Standard: Part II on Interpretation* (GB/T19363.2–2006). In addition, BFSU designed the first national aptitude test for professional translators and interpreters in 2001, which created quite a stir in the local training market and was widely covered by the media at that time. That test, now carried out in collaboration with the Testing Center of the Ministry of Education, has been up and running for 5 years and it is generally recognized for its professional worth. However, the problem with the test, as we have discovered over the years, is that it has not been very well targeted at the right population. As it turned out, most of those who sit for the test are not professionally trained and the rate of success, understandably, remains very low. We have decided this year to re-target the tests to students from professional training programs in order to keep our professional standards and at the same time to lift up the rate of success with this group of new test takers. There is another nationally held translator and interpreter accreditation test under the auspices of the

Ministry of Human Resources, whose mandate is to manage the civil service of the country.

The boom in the translation service has also spurred higher education in foreign language teaching to re-orient themselves more closely to the market needs. Traditionally, translation and interpreting are taught in the senior years of university education as part of foreign language learning, but such exposure falls far short of professional requirements or market expectations. There are at least a dozen universities in Mainland China that have set up schools, departments or programs at the postgraduate level offering professional training in translation and interpreting. In 2006, the Ministry of Education gave permission to 3 universities to launch translation studies at the undergraduate level. More universities are expected to jump on the bandwagon, as 56 universities have submitted their application this year. Frankly, I am quite concerned with this speed of development. But like many other aspects of life in China, things happen at exploding speed. A decade ago, the roads in Beijing were nearly empty except for public transport; in less than ten year's time, they are filled with 3 million private cars. It is now one of the most congested cities in the world. The local residents have nicknamed the city Las Vegas, for in Chinese the phrase *du cheng* is a homophone meaning either a "congested city" or a "gambling city".

As for our own MA program, we offer a two-year postgraduate study program in translation and interpreting. Each year, we recruit up to 50 students out of nearly 1000 applicants in the English/Chinese pair. They are divided into 4 smaller classes for most of their teaching and learning activities. It is mostly skill-based training with lots of practice both inside and outside the classroom and some moderate exposure to translation and interpreting theories. They are also expected to write a short dissertation to fulfill their degree requirements. Besides skill development, the teaching emphasizes on expanding the breadth of knowledge of the learners. Topics of teaching range from international relations to domestic issues such as the reform of the banking sector in

China, from the fight again drug-trafficking to the prevention of spread of aids. Care is also given to the development of independent learning skills of the students so that they are able to constantly update their knowledge in real practice.

We have also started last autumn to recruit students who have majored in other foreign languages such as Russian, French and German, and with good English, in their undergraduate studies. Hopefully, they will turn out to be professionals with 3 language combinations; some are already in very good shape. Besides local students, we have also taken on students from Canada, France, Russia, Italy, South Korea, Singapore and exchange students from Taiwan and Macao.

With vast expansion of translation and interpreting programs in China, there comes an acute shortage of qualified teachers. To be a good teacher, one has to have both the knowledge and experience of practitioners and know how to teach. Unfortunately, universities currently have difficulties in finding and keeping competent professionals and making them concentrate on teaching and research. It is true that practical skills are indispensable for our profession, but research into the complexity of issues we are faced with in everyday teaching is equally important. Without scientific observation and research, we are blind and there is no hope of making any progress. Our Ph.D. program recruits students with teaching and work experience and their studies are much more theory-driven. They are expected to do some in-depth research on translation and interpreting from different theoretical standings. In the long run, our profession will benefit immensely from research and theoretical exploration. But now we are starting from a relatively low base and we need to make sure that our teachers and research students can have access to the relevant information they want. We are building up a library for translation studies, collecting books and journals and other publications on the subject produced both abroad and at home.

We are aware of the efforts made in the EU countries to encourage graduate students to stay in another country for a period of their study and the benefits will be obvious. We would hope to be able to establish closer ties with sister institutions in Europe and other parts of the world so that we could share our thoughts and resources and in so doing benefit our younger generation. We are eager to learn from your experience in teaching and research, to establish joint research projects and to launch student exchange programs.

We are also keen on keeping good relations with organizations such as the UN and the EU translation service to listen to your needs and advice. I am very pleased to have learned from Mr. Stephen Sekel, the head of the Documentation Division (DGACM) of UN on his recent visit to BFSU, that the organization is reaching out to universities in an effort to recognize and establish "best practices" for training professionals. We are also ready to discuss arrangement for re-training of practicing professionals, if we can be of help in such areas.

Kurzer Überblick über die erste Fremdsprachenuniversität Peking

YUAN Jianhua

1. Zur geschichtlichen Entwicklung der Universität

Die Fremdsprachenuniversität Peking (vorheriger Name: Fremdsprachenhochschule Peking) ist eine der „Schwerpunkt-Hochschulen“, die direkt dem chinesischen Bildungsministerium unterstehen. Ihre Vorläuferin, die Fremdsprachenschule Yan'an, wurde 1941 in der Zeit des antijapanischen Krieges gegründet. Sie war die erste akademische Institution Chinas, die sich auf Fremdsprachenstudien spezialisierte. In der Anfangsphase der Schule wurde aufgrund der engen Beziehung zur Sowjetunion ausschliesslich Russisch als Studiengang angeboten, 1944 wurde zusätzlich ein Studiengang für Englisch eingerichtet. Bis zur Gründung der VR China im Oktober 1949 unterstand die Fremdsprachenschule dem Militärausschuss und dem auswärtigen Ausschuss des Zentralkomitees der KP China.

Die Fremdsprachenschule Yan'an wurde von Anfang an als „Wiege der Diplomaten“ konzipiert, deshalb war es nicht verwunderlich, dass die Schule im November 1949, nach der Gründung der Volksregierung der VR China, von Shan'xi nach Peking verlegt und dem Aussenministerium unterstellt wurde. Seit 1954 befindet sich die Schule auf dem heutigen Campus. Die Fremdsprachenschule entwickelte sich in der Zeit nach dem Umzug sehr rasch. 1950 wurde das Studienangebot um Deutsch und Französisch erweitert, 1952 kam Spanisch hinzu. In dieser Zeit hat die Schule eine Reihe von international renommierten Sprach- und

Literaturwissenschaftlern wie den Anglisten Prof. Zhuoliang WANG und Guozhang XU gewinnen können. Zahlreiche ausländische Lektoren waren als Lehrkräfte tätig. 1954 wurde die Fremdsprachenschule in die Fremdsprachenhochschule umgewandelt. 5 Jahre später, im Februar 1959, wurde das Russisch-College, das im Oktober 1949 in Peking gegründet und dem Übersetzungsbüro des Zentralkomitees der KP China unterstellt worden war, der Fremdsprachenhochschule angegliedert. Dadurch wurde die Palette der angebotenen Fremdsprachen um Polnisch, Tschechisch und Rumänisch erweitert. Bereits 1965 konnten 27 B.A.-Fremdsprachenstudiengänge angeboten werden. Neben etablierten Sprachen wie Englisch und Russisch kamen Arabisch, Italienisch, Schwedisch, Portugiesisch, Ungarisch, Bulgarisch, Serbisch, Albanisch, Thailändisch, Vietnamesisch, Indonesisch, Malaiisch, Suaheli, Singhalesisch, Laotisch, Birmanisch und Kambodschanisch hinzu (vgl. Naifang CHEN 2001: 3ff.), bis 2006 insgesamt 43 Fremdsprachen.

Sprachvermittlung ist ein traditioneller Schwerpunkt der Fremdsprachenhochschule Peking. Der Bildung einer soliden Fremdsprachenkompetenz wird ein grosser Stellenwert eingeräumt. Zu dieser Kompetenz gehört zum einen die Beherrschung der ersten und der zweiten Fremdsprache. Darum wird eine bilinguale Unterrichtsform praktiziert. Die Studierenden müssen gleichzeitig zwei Fremdsprachen erlernen. So lernt der Anglist fakultativ entweder noch Deutsch, Französisch, Spanisch oder Japanisch, und umgekehrt muss der Germanist fakultativ zusätzlich Englisch belegen. Zum zweiten geht es um die Kulturkompetenz in der jeweiligen Arbeitssprache. Die Fremdsprachenhochschule Peking ist ein traditioneller Standort für die Übersetzer- und Dolmetscherausbildung. Ihre führende Stellung bei der akademischen Übersetzer- und Dolmetscherausbildung an universitären Ausbildungseinrichtungen wurde mit der Gründung des Instituts für Übersetzen und Dolmetschen im Jahr 1984 noch weiter gefestigt, das mit der Ausbildung professioneller Übersetzer und Konferenzdolmetscher für den Sprachendienst der UNO beauftragt wurde.

1994 wurde die Fremdsprachenhochschule Peking in Fremdsprachenuniversität Peking (Beijing Foreign Studies University) umbenannt. Mit der Namensänderung ist auch eine Profiländerung der früheren Hochschule verbunden: die Fremdsprachenphilologie soll um zusätzliche Diszipline erweitert werden. Die früher vor allem fremdsprachenphilologie-orientierten Studiengänge sollen um weitere Sachfächer ergänzt, die Fremdsprachenphilologen mit Zusatzqualifikationen ausgestattet werden.

Heute unterstehen der BFSU 9 Colleges (Englisch-College, Russisch-College, College for Translation, College für Erwachsenenbildung, International Business School, ChaF-College, College für E-Learning und Fernstudien, College für Jura, und College für Internationale Politik) und 7 Fakultäten (Deutsch-Fakultät, Französisch-Fakultät, Arabisch-Fakultät, Spanisch-Fakultät, Japanisch-Fakultät, Fakultät für Asiatische und Afrikanische Sprachen, Fakultät für Europäische Sprachen). Ausserdem beheimatet sie eine Reihe von Forschungszentren (Forschungsinstitut für Foreign Studies, Nationales Forschungszentrum für Zweitsprachenerwerb, Nationales Forschungszentrum für Japanologie), die das Lehr- und Forschungsangebot der Universität ergänzen. 43 Fremdsprachen werden im Rahmen eines B.A.-Studiengangs an der Universität vermittelt, außer den obengenannten Sprachen noch Kroatisch, Finnisch, Niederländisch, Ukrainisch, Slowakisch. Neben dem B.A.-Studiengang werden M.A.-Studiengänge in 13 Fachrichtungen angeboten. In 9 Fachrichtungen ist ein Promotionsstudium möglich. Studierende, die bei der Zwischenprüfung überdurchschnittlich abschneiden, dürfen ein Double Degree-Studium aufnehmen, das ihnen bei erfolgreichem Abschluss einen Doppelabschluss ermöglicht (Sprachstudium in Kombination mit einem Fachstudium wie VWL an der International Business School).

Für das akademische Jahr 2006–2007 sind 8000 Studierende immatrikuliert. Der Lehrkörper umfasst insgesamt 576 Personen (Stand 2006), darunter 113 Univ.-Professoren, 177 ausserordentliche Professoren. Ausserdem unterrichten 122 ausländische Lektoren.

Die BFSU pflegt Partnerschaften mit 187 Universitäten aus 50 Staaten. Sie hat das landesweit grösste Verlagshaus für Fremdsprachenvermittlung, das pro Jahr über 700 neue Titel herausgibt und 1,3 Milliarden RMB absetzt.

Die BFSU verfügt über einen hochkarätigen Alumni-Kreis, zu dem über ca. hundert Minister und 350 Botschafter gehören (vgl. Hong ZHU 2005: 4–5).

2. Zur geschichtlichen Entwicklung der Deutsch-Fakultät

Die Deutsch-Fakultät hat eine Geschichte von mehr als 50 Jahren. Am Anfang stand im März 1950 die deutsche Fachrichtung, die der Fremdsprachenschule zugeordnet war. Sie bildete zusammen mit der französischen und spanischen Fachrichtung eine gemeinsame Abteilung. In der Startphase gab es nur 14 Studenten, die von 2 Dozenten betreut wurden. 1956 wurde die deutsche Fachrichtung ausgegliedert, und die Deutsch-Fakultät wurde gegründet. Die Studentenzahl erhöhte sich auf ca. 100. Von 1962 an gehörte die Deutsch-Fakultät zur Fakultät für Osteuropäische Sprachen angegliedert. Erst 20 Jahre später (1981) löste sie sich aus dieser Fakultät heraus und wurde wieder zu einer selbständigen Fakultät aufgewertet (vgl. Naifang CHEN 2001: 533ff.).

Die Deutsch-Fakultät ist nach den Anglisten die zweitgrösste Fakultät an der BFSU und die grösste Deutsch-Fakultät in China. Sie hat einen Lehrkörper von 42 Personen, darunter 10 Univ.-Professoren und 11 ausserordentliche Professoren. Sie werden unterstützt von 2 DAAD-Lektoren. 7 Fachrichtungen sind an der Deutsch-Fakultät vertreten: Literaturwissenschaft, Sprachwissenschaft, Deutschlandstudien, Wirtschaft, Politologie, Translatologie und DaF-Didaktik/Methodik.

Die Deutsch-Fakultät ist die einzige Fakultät, die im Jahr 2002 von der chinesischen Regierung als Schwerpunkt-Fakultät für Germanistik identifiziert und gefördert wird. An der Deutsch-Fakultät ist auch das Büro des Chinesischen Germanistenverbandes untergebracht, und das Zentrum für Deutsche Kulturen.

Vom chinesischen Bildungsministerium wurde die Deutsch-Fakultät mit der Leitung der Arbeitsgruppe Deutsch der Nationalen Kommission für Fremdsprachenvermittlung an Universitäten betraut. Bei der Erstellung des Rahmencurriculums für das Grundstudium und das Hauptstudium im Fach Deutsch war sie federführend. Sie führt auch Forschungsaufträge durch. Ein wichtiger Forschungsauftrag war die Erhebung über die Stellung von Deutsch in China, der vom chinesischen Bildungsministerium erteilt wurde. Die Ergebnisse der Erhebung waren eine vielbeachtete Grundlage für die Gestaltung der chinesischen Sprachenpolitik (vgl. Tongsheng YIN 2004: 20f.).

Ein traditioneller Forschungsschwerpunkt an der Deutsch-Fakultät ist die Lexikographie. Das ‚Neue Chinesisch-Deutsche Wörterbuch' (Zhenmin XU 1985), bisher das grösste Chinesisch-Deutsche Wörterbuch mit ca. 80.000 Einträgen, geniesst international hohes Ansehen und wurde seit 1984 mehrmals aufgelegt. Zur Zeit wird es von einem Lexikographenteam überarbeitet. Mit der völlig überarbeiteten Version ist in absehbarer Zeit zu rechnen. Ein weiteres Highlight ist das ‚Chinesisch-Deutsche Wörterbuch nach Sachgebieten', das seit der ersten Auflage 1989 mehrmals nachgedruckt wurde und eine Auflage von mehreren tausend Exemplaren erreicht hat. Eine völlig überarbeitete Version (Guangxi DONG 2005) ist seit Mai 2005 im Buchhandel erhältlich. Weitere Wörterbücher sind das ‚Langenscheidts Grosswörterbuch Deutsch als Fremdsprache Deutsch-Chinesisch' (Bendu YE 2000) mit 66.000 Einträgen sowie das ‚Moderne Wörterbuch Deutsch-Chinesisch/Chinesisch-Deutsch' (Xuefu DOU 2003) mit 50.000 Einträgen. Es werden auch Fachwörterbücher erstellt, u.a. das ‚Deutsch-Chinesische Wörterbuch für Finanz- und Bankwesen' (Shanjun HU 2001).

Die Deutsch-Fakultät sucht den internationalen Wissenschaftsaustausch. 1985 wurde die erste Deutsch-Chinesische Germanistentagung veranstaltet, danach folgten die Chinesisch-Japanische Germanistentagung (1990) und die erste Asiatische Germanistentagung (1994). Auf Initiative der Chinesischen, Japanischen und Koreanischen Gesellschaften für Germanistik ist die Asiatische Germanistentagung inzwischen eine feste Institution. Sie hat sich als Forum für den Austausch zwischen Wissenschaftlern aus dem Bereich der Germanistik und der deutschen Sprachvermittlung etabliert. Turnusmässig alle drei Jahre ist eines der 3 Länder Gastgeber des Forums. Die letzte Tagung im Jahr 2002 mit 120 Teilnehmern wurde von der Deutschen Fakultät in Peking ausgerichtet.

Die Deutsch-Fakultät gibt seit 1979 die Sprachenzeitschrift „Wir lernen Deutsch" heraus (jedes Jahr 6 Ausgaben), deren Auflage 3.000 beträgt. Sie ist die einzige Zeitschrift in China, die sich mit dem Erwerb der deutschen Sprache befasst.

Der Lehr- und Wissenschaftsbetrieb an der Deutsch-Fakultät wird durch eine eigene Seminarbibliothek (Präsenzbibliothek) unterstützt, die über einen Bücherbestand von 13.000 verfügt. Die Bücherspenden des Ex-Bundespräsidenten Carl Castens (DM 100.000) und der Gottlieb Daimler- und Karl Benz-Stiftung (DM 20.000) waren eine grosse Hilfe bei der Ergänzung des Bücherbestandes mit neuesten Titeln.

An der Deutsch-Fakultät sind 372 B.A.-Studierende, 62 M.A.-Studierende und 21 Promovenden eingeschrieben (Stand Ende 2006).

3. B.A.-Studiengänge

Voraussetzung für die Aufnahme eines B.A.-Studiums an der Deutsch-Fakultät ist eine erfolgreiche Hochschulaufnahmeprüfung mit überdurchschnittlichen Leistungen. Die Regelstudienzeit für einen B.A.-Studiengang beträgt 8 Semester. Die B.A.-Studiengänge gliedern sich in Grundstudium und ein darauf aufbauendes Hauptstudium. Die ersten beiden Studienjahre gelten als Grundstudium, sie sind ausschliesslich dem Erwerb der für das weitere Studium notwendigen Sprach- und allgemeinen Kulturkenntnisse gewidmet (Fremdsprachen A und B sowie dazu gehörigen Kompetenzen: Hör- und Leseverständnis, Sprech- und Schreibfertigkeit, translatorische Kompetenz). Vom 5. Semester an (Hauptstudium) ist eine Schwerpunktbildung in folgenden Fachrichtungen möglich: Literaturwissenschaft, Sprachwissenschaft, Deutschlandstudien, Translatologie und DaF-Didaktik/Methodik.

Mit dem Angebot der Sachfächer für die Spezialisierung soll a) der Horizont der Studierenden neben Sprachwissen um Sachwissen erweitert werden; b) sollen die Studierenden durch den grösseren Praxisbezug der Sachfächer auf ihr künftiges Berufsleben vorbereitet werden. Die Sachfächer werden neben Lehrveranstaltungen zur Erweiterung der sprachlichen und kulturellen Kompetenz (B- und C-Sprache) in Form von Modulen angeboten, die frei wählbar sind. Der Studienplan für die Fachrichtung Translatologie umfasst z.B. folgende Module: Einführung in die Translatologie, Methodische Grundlagen des Dolmetschens, Dolmetschen I (aus B-Sprache in A-Sprache), Dolmetschen II (aus A-Sprache in B-Sprache), Übersetzen I (aus B-Sprache in A-Sprache), Übersetzen II (aus A-Sprache in B-Sprache), wobei sowohl Übersetzen als auch Dolmetschen fachthemenbezogen sind (Übersetzen und Dolmetschen im Rechtsbereich, Übersetzen und Dolmetschen im Wirtschaftsbereich).

4. M.A.-Studiengänge

M.A.-Studiengänge werden in folgenden Fachrichtungen angeboten: Germanistische Literaturwissenschaft, Germanistische Linguistik, Translatologie, Deutschlandstudien und DaF-Didaktik/Methodik. Die Regelstudienzeit beträgt 2,5 Jahre, wobei anderthalb Jahre für Lehrveranstaltungen, 1 Jahr für die Anfertigung der Magisterarbeit vorgesehen sind.

5. Promotionsstudium

Die Deutsch-Fakultät bietet Promotionsmöglichkeiten in den Fachrichtungen Germanistische Literaturwissenschaft, Germanistische Linguistik und Deutschlandstudien an. Die Regelstudienzeit beträgt 3 Jahre.

6. Deutsch-Intensivkurse

Neben der akademischen Ausbildung bietet die Deutsch-Fakultät Deutsch-Intensivkurse für Interessierte in Zusammenarbeit mit dem Institut für Weiterbildung an der Hochschule an. Das Ausbildungsspektrum erstreckt sich von Deutsch-Grundstufe, Deutsch-Mittelstufe, Dolmetschkurs (Chi/D, D/Chi) bis zu den Vorbereitungskursen für die DSH Prüfung, die im Rahmen der Partnerschaft mit der Universität Heidelberg jedes Jahr zweimal mit Heidelberger Kollegen gemeinsam durchgeführt wird. Für das Sommersemester 2006 belegen ca. 300 Kursteilnehmer die angebotenen Kurse.

7. Akademische Vernetzungen

Die Deutsch-Fakultät unterhält Partnerschaften mit einer Reihe namhafter Universitäten im deutschsprachigen Raum. Die älteste

Partnerschaft hat sie mit der Universität Heidelberg, deren Anfang bis in die 80er Jahre des letzten Jahrhunderts zurückreicht. Weitere Partner sind die Universität Mainz, mit der sie gemeinsam Dolmetschkurse anbietet, die Universität Göttingen, mit der sie einen gemeinsamen Double Degree Magisterstudiengang Interkulturelle Germanisitik im Rahmen des EU-Asia-Link Programms entwickelt, sowie das Landesspracheninstitut Nordrhein-Westfalen (Sinicum, Bochum), die Universitäten Wien und Salzburg. Die Formen der Zusammenarbeit sind sehr vielfältig. Neben regelmässigem Dozentenaustausch zu Kurzzeitdozenturen wird die gemeinsame Entwicklung von Studiengängen und die gemeinsame Abwicklung von Forschungsprojekten immer wichtiger.

8. Literaturhinweise

CHEN, Naifang (Hg. 2001): *Annalen der Fremdsprachenuniversität Beijing*. Beijing: Foreign Language Teaching and Research Press.

DONG, Guangxi (Hg. 2005): *Das Chinesisch-Deutsche Wörterbuch nach Sachgebieten*. Beijing: Foreign Language Teaching and Research Press.

DOU, Xuefu (Hg. 2003): *Das Moderne Wörterbuch Deutsch-Chinesisch/Chinesisch-Deutsch*. Beijing: Foreign Language Teaching and Research Press.

HU, Shanjun (Hg. 2001): *Das Deutsch-Chinesische Wörterbuch für Finanz- und Bankwesen*. Beijing: Foreign Language Teaching and Research Press.

XU, Zhenmin (Hg. 1985): *Das Neue Chinesisch-Deutsche Wörterbuch*. Beijing: Commercial Press.

YE, Bendu (Hg. 2000): *Langenscheidts Grosswörterbuch Deutsch als Fremdsprache Deutsch-Chinesisch*. Beijing: Foreign Language Teaching and Research Press.

YIN, Tongsheng (2004): Chinesische Germanistik im Zeichen der Globalisierung. In Wang, Jianbin (Hg. 2004): *Neues Jahrhundert, neue Herausforderungen – Germanistik im Zeitalter der Globalisierung*. Tagungsband Asiatische Germanistentagung 2002. Beijing: Foreign Language Teaching and Research Press, 15–27.

ZHU, Hong (Hg. 2005): *Studienplane für B.A.-Studiengänge an der BFSU*. Beijing: Foreign Language Teaching and Research Press.

Introduction to China Accreditation Test for Translators and Interpreters (CATTI)

LU Min

1. Reasons for Holding CATTI

Since China implemented the policy of reform and opening up, our contacts with other countries have increased considerably. There is a great demand for translators and interpreters. Various translation companies are established. The translation market expands rapidly, and there are many achievements in the translation industry. But the levels of translators and interpreters vary because of lack of uniform translation and interpretation qualification appraisal standards. Some unqualified translators and interpreters also enter the translation market. Consequently, there are many mistranslations in directions for industrial products and other publications. This causes losses to the state, enterprises, companies and individuals and even produces a negative impact.

In the 1980s, the Chinese government implemented the professional title appraisal system to encourage professional and technical personnel. There are four professional titles in the translation profession. They are assistant translator, translator, associate professor of translation and professor of translation. These professional titles are obtained only through appraisal. For over 20 years since the implementation of the translation professional title appraisal system, many translators and interpreters have been selected to meet the needs of social and economic development, but there are some defects in this system. These defects result from human factors, including favoritism, interpersonal relationships, etc.

The main reason for the above-mentioned issues is lack of effective appraisal and supervision mechanism for translators and interpreters. There is an urgent need for the state to organize a national translation test with a view to appraising the competence of translators and interpreters objectively and fairly, establishing the national translator and interpreter appraisal system and standards, raising their professional competence and improving the quality of translations.

2. Process of CATTI's Development

In 2003, the Ministry of Human Resources and Social Security of the People's Republic of China held CATTI's English Translation and Interpretation Test of Levels 2 and 3 in Beijing, Shanghai and Guangzhou on a trial basis for the first time. A total of 1,682 examinees in more than 200 specialities took the test. In 2004, French and Japanese Translation and Interpretation Tests of Levels 2 and 3 were held on a trial basis. In the first half of 2006, Arabic Translation and Interpretation Test of Levels 2 and 3 was held. In the second half of 2006, Russian, German and Spanish Translation and Interpretation Tests of Levels 2 and 3 were held on a trial basis.

So far, we have held nine English translation and interpretation tests, three English simultaneous interpretation tests, four French and Japanese translation and interpretation tests, and two Arabic, Russian, German and Spanish translation and interpretation tests. In 2005, the total number of examinees exceeded 10,000. In 2006, the total number of examinees came to more than 18,000. In 2007, the total number of examinees amounted to 21,000. From 2003 to the end of 2007, the total number of examinees amounted to over 56,000. About 8,000 examinees passed the translation and interpretation tests and obtained the translation and interpretation qualification certificates.

China Accreditation Test for Translators and Interpreters (CATTI) is the most authoritative translation and interpretation proficiency qualification accreditation test which is implemented throughout the country according to uniform standards and in compliance with the national system of professional qualification certificates and which meets social needs. It is designed to meet the needs of a socialist market economy and China's accession to WTO, build a large contingent of translators and interpreters in our country, appraise their proficiency and competence scientifically, objectively and fairly and better serve the opening up. It is an authoritative accreditation test for examinees' bilingual translation or interpretation proficiency.

3. Organs Responsible for CATTI's Operation

CATTI is a project of the Ministry of Human Resources and Social Security of the People's Republic of China. The Personnel Testing Authority of the Ministry of Human Resources and Social Security is responsible for testing affairs related to translation, and the Training Center of the State Administration of Foreign Experts Affairs takes charge of testing affairs related to interpretation.

CIPG is responsible for organizing, implementing and administering the test under the guidance of the Ministry of Human Resources and Social Security of the People's Republic of China. It establishes a CATTI leading group, a testing office and the National Translation Test and Appraisal Center responsible for organizing CATTI.

4. CATTI's Languages to Be Tested

CATTI has seven languages to be tested, that is, English, Japanese, Russian, German, French, Spanish, Arabic and other languages.

5. CATTI's Levels and Professional Competence

(1) Senior Translator and Interpreter: Candidates have been engaged in translation and interpretation for a long time, have extensive scientific and cultural knowledge, reach advanced level in bilingual translation and interpretation, can solve major difficult problems arising in translation and interpretation and make great contributions to developing translating and interpreting undertakings and training translators and interpreters in both theory and practice.

(2) Translator and Interpreter of Level 1: Candidates have rich scientific and cultural knowledge and a high competence for bilingual translation and interpretation, can be qualified for extensive and difficult translation and interpretation, solve difficult problems arising in translation and interpretation and are capable of interpreting at important international conferences or finalizing translations.

(3) Translator and Interpreter of Level 2: Candidates have some scientific and cultural knowledge, have a good competence for bilingual translation and interpretation and are capable of translating and interpreting in some areas and with some difficulties.

(4) Translator and Interpreter of Level 3: Candidates have rudimentary scientific and cultural knowledge and a general competence for bilingual translation and interpretation and can accomplish general translation work.

6. CATTI's Methods of Test and Appraisal

The titles of Senior Translator and Interpreter are acquired through the method of appraisal, and candidates for Senior Translator and Interpreter must obtain the Translation and Interpretation Proficiency Qualification Certificates for Translator and Interpreter of Level 1. The titles of Translator and Interpreter of Level 1 are acquired through the method of test and appraisal. The concrete methods of appraisal of Senior Translator and Interpreter and Translator and Interpreter of Level 1 will be formulated separately.

The methods of tests based on uniform outlines, uniform test papers and uniform standards are adopted for Translators and Interpreters of Level 2 and Level 3.

The test for interpreter consists of two parts: Interpreting Comprehensive Aptitude and Interpreting Practice. The Interpreting Practice in the test for Interpreters of Level 2 consists of two specialities: Consecutive Interpreting and Simultaneous Interpreting.

The test for translator consists of two parts: Translating Comprehensive Aptitude and Translating Practice.

The test for Interpreting Comprehensive Aptitude proceeds by listening to the tape and answering questions in writing as required. Consecutive Interpreting and Simultaneous Interpreting in the Interpreting Practice in the test for Interpreters of Level 2 and the Interpreting Practice in the test for Interpreters of Level 3 proceed by on-site recording. The time for the Interpreting Comprehensive Aptitude and Consecutive Interpreting and Simultaneous Interpreting in the Interpreting Practice in the test for Interpreters of Level 2 is 60 minutes. The time for Interpreting Practice for Interpreters of Level 3 is 30 minutes.

Tests for Translating Comprehensive Aptitude and Translating Practice proceed by writing directly on test papers. The time for Translating Comprehensive Aptitude is 120 minutes, and the time for Translating Practice is 180 minutes.

CATTI is designed to test examinees' linguistic knowledge, background knowledge and translation or interpreting skills.

The passing rate for translators of Level 3 is about 20%, the passing rate for translators of Level 2 is about 16%, the passing rate for interpreters of Level 3 is about 13%, and the passing rate for interpreters of Level 2 is about 11%.

If an examinee passes the two parts of the test for translator or interpreter at the corresponding level, that is, he/she gets 60 marks for Translating or Interpreting Comprehensive Aptitude and Translating or Interpreting Practice once, he/she is awarded the Translation and Interpretation Proficiency Qualification Certificate of the People's Republic of China. The Certificate is valid throughout the People's Republic of China. It is one of the prerequisites for translation and interpretation professional and technical post. According to the relevant regulations of the Ministry of Human Resources and Social Security of the People's Republic of China, translation and interpretation proficiency qualification test has been incorporated into the national system of professional qualification certificates. After the test is introduced to the whole country, appraisal of translation and interpretation professional and technical posts for corresponding foreign languages and levels will cease.

In light of needs, employers can give corresponding posts to those candidates who obtain the Translation and Interpretation Proficiency Qualification Certificate for Translator or Interpreter of Level 2 or Translator or Interpreter of Level 3 and who meet qualifications for posts of translator or interpreter or assistant translator or assistant interpreter as prescribed in the Regulations on Posts of Translator and Interpreter for Trial Implementation.

7. Continuation Education and Certificate Management

The system of regular registration is implemented for the Certificate, and registration is handled every three years. A bearer of the Certificate should handle formalities for re-registration in the designated office according to regulations prior to the expiration of the period of validity of the Certificate. The bearer of the Certificate needs to show the certificate for continuation education or professional training at the time of re-registration.

8. CATTI's Advantages

CATTI has the following advantages:

(1) It has won extensive social recognition in China. Examinees in many specialities come from institutions of higher learning, government departments, enterprises, institutions, foreign-funded companies and other sectors of society.

(2) It has won international recognition. People from Japan, Singapore, the Republic of Korea, and the regions of Taiwan and Hong Kong show a great interest in the test. Some examinees from Japan and the regions of Taiwan and Hong Kong have participated in the test and obtained the translation qualification certificates. People in more than 50 countries and regions have visited our website – catti.net.cn.

(3) It helps the Chinese Association of Translators to gradually assume the responsibility of the management of the translation industry. In 2005, the Chinese Association of Translators introduced the new individual membership system. Those examinees at and above Level 3 who have passed CATTI can directly apply to become its individual members. The Chinese

Association of Translators also takes charge of continuation education and translation and interpretation qualification certificate registration.

(4) It helps deepen the reform of China's translation professional title appraisal. It helps select qualified translators and interpreters in a scientific, objective and fair manner, because it is an open test for anyone wishing to become a translator or interpreter, irrespective of age, sex, profession, seniority and schooling.
(5) It helps standardize the national appraisal standards for translators and interpreters, raise their professional competence and establish the translator and interpreter appraisal standards of the People's Republic of China.
(6) It helps standardize the translation market and industry. It helps appraise and select qualified translators and interpreters and encourage them to provide high-quality translation and interpretation services.
(7) It helps standardize the translation and interpretation teaching. It appraises the competence of translators and interpreters and encourages institutions of higher learning to integrate the theory with practice and train and provide qualified translators and interpreters for society.

To sum up, CATTI is of great importance to developing and standardizing China's translation market and industry and draws close attention at home and abroad.

Developing Translation Competence through Peer-Editing

Natalia SIGAREVA / Tatiana YUDINA

Introduction

Alves & Gonçalves see translation competence as "the sum of several sub-competences" and offer the following definition of this notion: "all the knowledge, abilities and strategies a successful translator masters and which will lead to an adequate performance of translation tasks" (Alves & Gonçalves 2003: 4). It is out of the scope of this article to give an account of all sub-competences or discuss the list of them which aimed at developing translation competence. We will focus on editing which is defined here as one of the concepts specific to translation assessment.

Editing and peer editing in particular is important to ensure the mechanical accuracy and preservation of the message content of translations. Peer editing in class not only enables students to easily navigate the revising and editing process but is a very effective way to help students improve their translation competence. It helps to avoid criticizing "bad translation", but to focus on the quality of a translation.

Terminological issues

According to the EN standard: "on completion of the initial translation, the translator shall check his/her own work". This process shall include checking that the meaning has been conveyed, that there are no omissions or errors and that the defined service specifications have been met. The translator shall make any necessary amendments (European Committee for Standardisation 2006: 11).

The idea of improving translation can be expressed in a number of terms: revision, self-revision, checking, re-reading, proofing, proofreading, editing, cross-reading, checking, reviewing etc. There is no unique opinion among the scholars and practitioners on this terminology and most of the terms are used as synonyms.

Setting the objective of this article we believe that the term *revision* can be identified as the most general and a broad one among the others whereas the other terms, including editing can be used as types of revision. To identify each type we have to answer who revises what, when, how, and why (Nord 2005: 41).

In academic set, in the process of translator training two terms – *editing* and *proofreading* – are often confused and therefore we have to make them clear here for further presentation of our ideas. In order to achieve the main communicative goal successfully the translator has to proofread the produced text in search for translation errors that may occur. It is important to distinguish between the two processes: proofreading and editing. More often than not, outsourcers call editing proofreading and vice versa. While most of them do this only because they don't make a difference between the two, a few of them will actually "lure" you into editing a document – at proofreading rates. This comes down to being paid for only half of the work.

Proofreading is a process whereby the text is being scanned for grammar, syntax and spelling errors. The meaning of words and terminology is irrelevant here, as the job focuses only on the correctness of the text. Proofreading is something that is used less and less, as most software nowadays automatically corrects the errors that would be picked up by the proofreader. Editing process concentrates less on the form and more on the terminology. Editing involves checking to make sure that correct terminology was used. This is achieved by researching each term that raises a doubt, or even terms that are unknown to the editor, just to make sure that the right terms were used. This typically involves research – whether online or in specialized dictionaries – accompanied by recommended corrections.

The professional world requires that communication proceed efficiently and expects from professionally trained translators a combination of effectiveness and efficiency in the form of translator competence which is regarded as textual competence.

The aim of editing a translated text is to produce a communicative target text which transmits the message clearly. The message can be distorted or lost if not founded upon appropriate language. But when message and language are made coherent, then communication is natural and effective. Sometimes it presents a considerable challenge. The final texts should not be read like translations but as originally written texts. Therefore the main guidelines to effectively edit a translation are: consistency, accuracy and clarity (Pattison 2009).

Teaching editing in the process of translation training

The translator training process falls into several stages among which the main ones are analytical reading and comprehension of a source text on the basis of source text analysis, target text production, and editing.

At Herzen University the course in editing is a part of a curriculum of the Master programme *Theory of Translation and Interlingual/Intercultural Communication* and 5-year training programme *Translation and Translation Studies*. The aim of the course is to help students acquire professional editing skills and develop awareness that editing does not amount to rewriting everything written by the translator.

The course is resulted from the translation project "Human Technology for Education" undertaken by the trainers of the Translation & Interpreting Department of Herzen State Pedagogical University of Russia (St. Petersburg) in collaboration with the Professor of the University of Westminster (the UK) and a professional editor Ann Pattison.

This was a rewarding experience of translation project management and it was also helpful in terms of Training of Trainers programme which, finally, resulted in designing and implementing a new course for the students of the Translation & Interpreting Department aiming at developing editing skills as a part of translator training.

The main concern was to develop a consistent, coherent and coordinated methodology of training that would determine the translation market value. The idea is to help students turn a draft translation into a smooth, readable, accurate and correct work that is publishable. It requires utmost attention on the part of the editor. This involves applying a series of editing rules to ensure that the translation is accurate and correct.

The basic strategies for editing as the final stage of the translation process to be taught at the university were discussed and developed. They are as follows: verification of terminology and cultural issues; checking of formal aspect and presentation; logic development analysis; checking 'acceptability' and 'informativity' of the target texts; message delivery strategies. In editing classes interdisciplinary approach should be implemented in order to optimize different types of learning. Training editing skills is expected to equip the students with conceptual tools, and to give them an ample opportunity to place more importance to the practical training.

Among the factors that are crucial for producing an appropriate target text is the importance of being a first-rate writer in one's mother tongue which includes clarity and formal correctness in the target language.

In this course students are recommended to use a three-step peer-editing technique that consists of: 1) paying compliments – finding smart solutions; 2) offering suggestions – mapping the discrepancies and revealing mistakes; and 3) making corrections. The main guidelines (consistency, accuracy and clarity) provided are proving helpful and also enable the students to also edit their own translations effectively. In addition the students are given a series of stylistic editing guidelines to ensure that the translation is clear and concise.

The students are given tasks to consider a target text as the whole, and at the same time to take into account all the issues that could be improved: logic, spelling, argumentation, terminology, sense, structure, presentation, style , grammar, and to find the ways of eliminating the problems in order to produce a communicative target text which transmits the message clearly.

Some rather effective computer tools for editing are recommended to the students. For instance, when working in *Word*, the track changes feature is used, and comments are added through the commenting tool of *Word*. The student, whose task is to edit the text, recommends the changes but does not implement them. It is usually up to the original translator to correct their own mistakes.

Another technique is to use track changes, then save that document or send it to the trainer together with the document in which all the changes were accepted. This way, the students have one document with the unimplemented changes, and one with the changes implemented, ready to go to the 'client'. Moreover, both the texts become the subject for critical analysis. So, navigating the editing process which lays the basis for strategic competence, students improve their critical thinking, translation competence, language proficiency and a first-rate writer skills in their own mother tongue.

The opportunity given to edit a translation of a peer student has the advantage to stimulate the intrinsic motivation of the students and hence help them to not only acquire the know-how and the knowledge, but also to store it in their long-term memory and to reuse it. This kind of training increases the competence of the learner, which means that solutions and reflections should be articulated in order to stimulate discussions. The last phase is reflection where the learners compare their respective solutions. This stage aims at stirring up the students' knowledge in all areas related to Translation and Translation Studies and at the same time it presents the advantage to the trainer to stimulate the motivation of the students to enlarge their theoretical background.

Conclusion

Students find editing classes stimulating and rewarding, they help raise their awareness and integrate motivation, develop professional approach to the functional usage of written language, develop professional skills and translator competence, and help achieve the best possible quality of translation.

Bibliography

Alves F., Gonçalves J.L. (2003), "A Relevance Theory Approach to Inferential Processes in Translation". In Alves, F. (ed.) *Triangulating Translation*, Amsterdam/Philadelphia, John Benjamins, 3–24.

European Committee for Standardisation (2006), *Nederlandse norm NEN-EN 15038 (en): translation services: service requirements*. Brussels: Nederlands Normalisatie-instituut.

Nord C. (2005), *Text Analysis in Translation. Theory, Methodology, and Didactic Application of a Model for Translation-oriented Text Analysis*. Amsterdam – New York: Rodopi.

Pattison A. (2009), "The Herzen 'Human Technology' Editing Project". In *Modern Concepts of University Education*, St. Petersburg, 115–121.

3. New Visions

European Master in Translation – Stand des Vorhabens

Reinhard HOHEISEL

Auf dem CIUTI-Forum 2005 in Paris hatte ich Gelegenheit, über die Anforderungen zu sprechen, die die Generaldirektion Übersetzen der Europäischen Kommission an Übersetzerinnen und Übersetzer stellt. Dabei konnte ich auch die Vorstellungen erläutern, die sie zu deren Ausbildung entwickelt hatte. Ich danke der CIUTI dafür, dass ich nun über den Fortgang dieses Vorhabens berichten darf.

Im Vorfeld der EU-Erweiterung von 2004 war klar geworden, dass es in etlichen Ländern keine oder keine universitäre Ausbildung von Übersetzerinnen und Übersetzern gab, oder dass die Absolventen einer bestehenden Übersetzerausbildung nicht die Anforderungen der EU erfüllten. Außerdem traten Universitäten aus künftigen bzw. neuen Mitgliedstaaten an die DGT mit der Bitte heran, sie bei der Ausarbeitung von Studiengängen für Übersetzer zu unterstützen, die den Anforderungen der EU genügen. So entstand der Vorschlag für einen European Master in Translation. Das Projekt wurde auf dem CIUTI-Forum vor zwei Jahren und auch anderswo freundlich aufgenommen.

Knapp gesagt schlägt die DGT den Plan für einen Master-Studiengang als postgraduales Ausbildungsangebot an Absolventen aller Studienrichtungen vor, in dem professionelle Übersetzer ausgebildet werden sollen. Zugangsvoraussetzungen sollen mindestens ein erfolgreiches Bachelor-Studium und die Beherrschung der benötigten Fremdsprachen sein.

Folgende Studieninhalte wurden vorgeschlagen:

Übersetzen als Beruf, Translationstheorie, Text-/Diskursanalyse und Analyse eines Übersetzungsauftrags, Interkulturelle Kommunikation, Terminologiearbeit, Informationstechnologien für das Übersetzen, Sprachbewusstsein und Sprachpflege, Fachgebiete und ihre Fachsprachen, Übersetzungsübungen (in mehr als einem Sprachenpaar).

Mit dem EMT-Projekt verfolgt die DGT folgende Ziele:

1. Ausbildung von genügend qualifizierten Übersetzern, vor allem in den Ländern, in denen sie noch fehlen. Dabei geht es nicht nur um den Bedarf der EU-Organe. Mit dem Beitritt zur EU entsteht erfahrungsgemäß ein Bedarf an Fachübersetzungen, zu dessen Befriedigung qualifizierte, professionelle Übersetzer nötig sind. Mit deren Ausbildung wird auch ein Beitrag zur Wahrung und Stärkung der Vielsprachigkeit in Europa geleistet. Er sollte nicht gering geschätzt werden. Dies bedeutet aber, dass der EMT nicht zu einem Spezialausbildungsprogramm ausschließlich für künftige EU-Übersetzer werden darf. Es muss vielmehr eine gute, ja sehr gute Ausbildung konzipiert werden, deren Absolventen für den professionellen Einsatz bereit sind, wo immer das auch sein mag. Gute Ausbildung aber ist nur mit guten Ausbildern möglich. Auch an die Ausbilder müssen Mindestanforderungen gestellt werden und, wenn nötig, ist für eine entsprechende Ausbildung oder Weiterbildung der Lehrenden zu sorgen.
2. Anregung, inhaltliche Beeinflussung und nach Möglichkeit Unterstützung dieser Ausbildung. Dabei will die DGT keine beherrschende Federführung übernehmen, kein Konsortium bilden und keinen „*closed shop*“ unterstützen, sondern wir wollen möglichst viele Übersetzerausbildungsinstitute vom Inhalt unseres Vorschlags überzeugen und diesen Inhalt mit ihnen diskutieren und verbessern. So kann die Möglichkeit entwickelt werden, dass sich möglichst viel davon de facto verbreitet, und übernommen wird. Es wäre wohl zu optimistisch, anzunehmen, dass quer durch Europa nun Studiengänge für einen EMT aus dem Boden schießen. Wegen der Kompliziertheit (und der Kosten) von Organisation, Zertifizierung, Akkreditierung und Genehmigung

eines neuen Studiengangs dürfte dies wohl nur dann realistisch sein, wenn eine Umstrukturierung oder der Neuaufbau eines Übersetzerstudienganges geplant oder im Gange ist. Aber inhaltlich Gutes bewahren und Anregungen aufnehmen – das dürfte sich auch bei bereits bestehenden Studienprogrammen realisieren lassen. Wenn ein solides Ausbildungsprogramm wie der EMT-Vorschlag oder doch möglichst viele seiner Komponenten mehr und mehr akzeptiert und gemeinsam weiter entwickelt würden, trüge dies auch dazu bei, die Abstimmung, vielleicht sogar auch eine gewisse Aufgabenverteilung zwischen Hochschulen zu erleichtern. Es könnte so ein Beitrag zur Mobilität der Studierenden geleistet werden.

3. Grundlegung der Entwicklung eines allgemeinen Qualitätsstandards für Übersetzerausbildung durch das EMT-Programm. Bei genügender Verbreitung kann das EMT-Programm die Grundlage für die Entwicklung eines inhaltlichen Qualitätsstandards der Übersetzerausbildung bieten, denn es enthält genügend Hinweise darauf, was eigentlich verglichen und bewertet werden sollte. Wenn ich richtig sehe, werden Studienleistungen vor allem dann verglichen, wenn Studierende die Anerkennung anderswo erbrachter Studienleistungen durch die eigene Hochschule beantragen. Die Maßstäbe für die Anerkennung dürften im Dunkeln liegen, vermutlich sind sie formaler Art. Einfacher ist es, wenn die Universität das ECTS *(European Credit Transfer System)* anwendet und anerkennt. Allerdings ist auch dies ein eher formales System, das den erwarteten Arbeitsaufwand der Studierenden widerspiegelt. Die Kriterien, nach denen Lehrveranstaltungen mit Credit-Punkten ausgestattet werden, sind auch nicht immer transparent. Bisweilen drängt sich der Verdacht auf, es werde weniger der erwartete Arbeitsaufwand der Studierenden als vielmehr Rang und Name der Lehrenden honoriert. Das Ziel ist, Einigkeit über einen inhaltlichen Grundkanon einer guten Übersetzerausbildung zu erzielen. Mehr als ein Grundkanon sollte es nicht sein, damit die Hochschulen die Freiheit behalten, besondere Fachrichtungen und Sprachen zu

pflegen, Schwerpunkte zu setzen, örtlichen Verhältnissen gerecht zu werden, sie zu nutzen, sich zu positionieren. In einem solchen Grundkanon kann beschrieben werden, welche Kenntnisse und Fertigkeiten mindestens zu erreichen und dann vielleicht auch, wie sie nachzuweisen sind. Und mit aller gebotenen Bescheidenheit möchte ich sagen, dass wir das EMT-Papier für einen brauchbaren Vorschlag für einen solchen Grundkanon halten. Wenn über Qualitätsstandards gesprochen wird, muss man auch darüber nachdenken, wie das Erreichen und Einhalten dieser Standards sichtbar gemacht werden kann. Die DGT ist keine Zertifizierungsstelle. Sie hat auch nicht die Kompetenz, Studiengänge zu akkreditieren. Und dennoch wird man eine Möglichkeit finden müssen, wie – ich möchte sagen: zitierfähig und zum Vorzeigen – den Instituten und den Studierenden bestätigt werden kann, dass ihr Studium ein Master-Studium ist, das die Anforderungen der DGT, besser noch der EU, erfüllt.

4. Festigung und Anerkennung einer Übersetzerausbildung von hohem Niveau. Dass wir ein Master-Studium vorschlagen, steht im Widerspruch dazu, dass zu unseren Auswahlverfahren – bedauernd und hoffnungsvoll sage ich „noch" – Absolventen eines Bachelorstudiums zugelassen werden. Dass wir dennoch ein Master-Studium vorschlagen, ist unser Bekenntnis zur nötigen Qualität und zum nötigen hohen Niveau der Ausbildung unserer künftigen Mitarbeiterinnen und Mitarbeiter. Und wir meinen und streben an, dass ein europaweiter Qualitätsstandard der Übersetzerausbildung dazu führen wird, dass ein solches Studium auch bei der Einstellung gebührend berücksichtigt wird. So gesehen hat unser Vorschlag zumindest für unser Haus auch einen standespolitischen Aspekt.

Nach eingehender Vorbereitung u. A. durch zahlreiche Einzelgespräche, in denen meine Kollegin Angelique Petrits das Projekt an vielen Übersetzerausbildungsinstituten vorstellte, veranstaltete die GD Übersetzung am 19. und 20. Oktober 2006 eine Hochschulkonferenz mit dem Titel „Auf dem Weg zum Europäischen Master in Übersetzung“. Frau Professor Lee-Jahnke und Herrn Professor Forstner möchte ich an dieser Stelle für die Hilfe und Unterstützung danken, mit der sie dieser Konferenz auf den Weg geholfen haben. Die Konferenz sollte Gelegenheit geben, den Vorschlag der DGT mit Vertretern der Lehre zu erörtern. Eingeladen waren Vertreter von Übersetzerausbildungsinstituten aus allen Mitgliedstaaten, aus der Schweiz und aus Russland. Die Ziele und Möglichkeiten eines Europäischen Masters in Übersetzen wurden erörtert und die Themen und die Problematik der einzelnen Bausteine wurden dargestellt. Aber nicht nur dies, sondern es waren auch ermutigende Berichte über erste Erfahrungen mit dem EMT-Programm und mit internationaler Zusammenarbeit in der Übersetzerausbildung zu hören.

Die EMT-Konferenz wurde eigentlich von allen Teilnehmern als Erfolg gewertet. Auch der Aspekt, dass offenbar erstmals Vertreter der Übersetzerausbildung aus allen EU-Staaten, der Schweiz und sogar aus Russland zur Erörterung eines gemeinsamen Projekts zusammenkamen, wurde als positiv empfunden. Was mir persönlich am wichtigsten ist: das EMT-Papier wurde offenbar von allen Anwesenden als Grundlage für die weitere Arbeit akzeptiert. Zumindest hat niemand widersprochen, obwohl dafür reichlich Gelegenheit gewesen wäre.

Die gesamte Dokumentation zum EMT-Papier und über die Konferenz ist im Internet zu finden: http://ec.europa.eu/dgs/translation/events/emt2006/index_de.htm.

Am Schluss der Konferenz stand eine Reihe von Forderungen und Hinweisen für die weitere Arbeit, aus denen die DGT die Maßnahmen schöpfte, die sie nun einleiten will. Vorsichtshalber muss ich sagen, dass die endgültigen Beschlüsse noch ausstehen, aber die Tendenz, die sich erkennen lässt, dürfte sich kaum ändern.

Folgende Maßnahmen sind ins Auge gefasst:

1. Bildung einer relativ kleinen Taskforce. Im Interesse der Arbeitsfähigkeit sollte sie nicht mehr als ungefähr 10 Mitglieder haben. Sie werden von der DGT ad personam zur Mitarbeit

eingeladen werden. Wir denken an hervorragende Vertreter der Übersetzungslehre. Alte und neue Mitgliedstaaten sollen vertreten sein. Diese Taskforce soll der Motor für die Verwirklichung des EMT-Projekts sein. Erste Arbeitsfelder werden die Präzisierung und Absicherung des Grundkanons, die Möglichkeiten seiner offiziellen Anerkennung, Vorschläge zur Ausbildung der Ausbilder und die finanziellen Aspekte des Vorhabens sein.

Da in einer kleinen Taskforce nicht alle teilnehmenden Länder vertreten sein können, muss auf andere Weise gesichert werden, dass das Projekt in allen beteiligten Ländern verankert wird, dass alle Gesichtspunkte zum Tragen kommen können. Dies soll erreicht werden durch:

2. Bildung eines Netzwerks aus je einem Vertreter jeden Landes und aus Vertretern von Verbänden und Organisationen. Diese prüfen die Vorschläge der Taskforce und äußern sich dazu, vor allem hinsichtlich der Umsetzbarkeit in den jeweils gegebenen Verhältnissen. Außerdem hätten Sie die Verbindung zu den anderen Übersetzerausbildungsinstituten und zu den relevanten Behörden und Regierungsstellen ihrer Länder zu halten oder aufzubauen.
3. bildet die DGT eine interne Unterstützungsgruppe, die einerseits die Beiträge der DGT zur Arbeit der Taskforce und des Netzwerks formuliert und andererseits das EMT-Vorhaben in der DGT selbst verankert.
4. soll zur Erleichterung und Zusammenfassung der Diskussionen für diese drei genannten Gruppen ein Forum im Internet eingerichtet werden, um die Arbeit auch zwischen den Sitzungen der betreffenden Gruppen vorantreiben zu können.

Damit meinen wir, das EMT-Projekt weiterführen zu können. Ihre Meinung dazu ist uns wichtig.

Nun kurz zu einigen Möglichkeiten, wie die CIUTI dieses EMT-Projekt fördern kann. Eines haben sie ja schon getan, und Herrn

Didaoui die Möglichkeit gegeben, eine ähnliche Frage für den Bereich der Vereinten Nationen zu erörtern. Ich meine auch, dass die CIUTI ganz hervorragende Möglichkeiten der Zusammenarbeit bietet, denn sie kennen einander schon und müssen einander nicht erst suchen. Dies kann für die inhaltliche Arbeit am Grundkanon, aber auch für gemeinsame Versuche genutzt werden, in denen Möglichkeiten erprobt werden, beispielsweise, wie eine Anerkennung des EMT erreicht werden kann, die mehr ist als eine Selbsterklärung, aber doch weniger aufwendig als ein regelrechtes Zertifizierungsverfahren. Ich meine, zu recht kann man von der CIUTI eine Vorreiterrolle erwarten.

Erlauben Sie mir nun noch eine Überlegung zur organisatorischen Entwicklung, die wahrscheinlich mit dem EMT-Projekt und der EMT-Konferenz eingeleitet wurde. Gerade eben habe ich über die Mitglieder der künftigen Taskforce gesagt, sie würden von der DGT ad personam eingeladen. Dies hat etwas Willkürliches, undemokratisches, das gefallen mag oder nicht, aber die DGT hat keine andere Wahl. Es wäre ja einfach, wenn es eine europäische oder internationale Organisation gäbe, die die Übersetzerausbildungsinstitute repräsentativ vertreten könnte, denn dann könnte man es ihr anvertrauen, kompetente Vertreter zu benennen. Aber eine solche Organisation gibt es eben nicht und wir vermissen sie schmerzlich. Die CIUTI ist eine einmalige Organisation, die ein hohes Maß von Wissen und Erfahrung in Forschung und Lehre der Translation, von Kenntnissen und etablierten Verbindungen in sich vereinigt. Ihre Mitglieder bieten hervorragende Qualität – zumindest zur Zeit ihrer Aufnahme – Sie nimmt allerdings nur Institute auf, die Übersetzen und Dolmetschen in Forschung und Lehre vertreten. Es gibt aber viele Institute, die nur Übersetzen anbieten, und darin exzellent sind, aber nicht Mitglied bzw. Vollmitglied der CIUTI werden konnen. Diese Feststellung führt zur Schlussfolgerung, dass die CIUTI nicht als repräsentative Vertretung der Über setzerausbildungsinstitute gelten kann. Wenn jedoch diese Institute im Rahmen des EMT-Programms europaweit zusammenarbeiten, dann kann es meiner Meinung nach nicht lange dauern, bis sie erkennen, wie vorteilhaft eine europäische oder internationale Organisation wäre, die sie und ihre Interessen vertritt. Wenn die CIUTI keine Möglichkeit findet, Übersetzungsinstitute aufzunehmen und damit auch für die Welt der Übersetzung repräsentativ zu werden, dann wird es wohl zu einer eigenen Organisation der Übersetzerausbildungsinstitute kommen. Ich überlasse es Ihnen, sich die Folgen für den Einfluss der CIUTI in Angelegenheiten der Übersetzung auszumalen.

Sicherlich kann die CIUTI nun sagen, dass dies ihre eigene, interne Angelegenheit ist, die mich nichts angeht, und sie hätte damit recht. Dennoch bitte ich die CIUTI dringend diesen Aspekt zu bedenken. Es wäre schade, wenn die CIUTI dem Hochadel oder einem feinen Golfclub vergleichbar würde: schwere Aufnahme, exklusiv, vielleicht von hohem Ansehen. Aber Einfluss???

Core Curriculum for a Master's Degree in International Translation

Mohammed DIDAOUI

Objectives

This course aims at providing students with practical competence, developing their research skills and training them in order to be immediately operational at the entry-level in the United Nations System, according to the UN vision based on new telework-inspired non-traditional modes of translation (off-site translation, retainer-contract option, etc.). The new situation would require adequate and tailor-made pre-recruitment outside training. Some of the elements exist already at certain universities and need minor adjustments. The most important part is UN documentation related. For the success of this scheme, staffing by professional and qualified teachers, with UN experience in relation to UN texts and usage, is indispensable. Non-UN-staff teachers, who are assigned to this programme, should be recruited on short term contracts to get acquainted with UN jargon and usage. All future UN translators should transit through the Master's channel and graduates would participate in a new version of competitive examinations with limited scope and lesser costs. A UN contribution to training costs would more be advantageous.

Programme components

Translation history: Aims at reviewing the main trends of thought world-wide on translation and describes profiles of illustrious translators throughout history. It would develop a strong professional identity and pride, emphasize the ethics of the profession and give more insight into the profession mechanisms for a sound professional development.

Translation studies: The objective of this course is to provide students with an overarching view of major theories and lay solid foundations for professional expertise. It gives an overview of the principal concepts and theories and outlines major developments. Students will be acquainted with the most important and authoritative literature in this field. A link between theory and practice will be advisable.

Language aspects of translation: The aim is to equip students with the necessary conceptual tools for text analysis and suitable text-producing. It would rely on the following subsidiary courses:

- Linguistics
- Text linguistics and discourse analysis
- Comparative stylistics
- Advanced grammar
- Rhetoric
- Language studies
- Languages A, B and C literature, etc.

Composition and advanced writing skills: It aims at enabling students to acquire advanced writing skills through learning and practical exercises. Special emphasis will be put on technical writing. This course, which interacts with the one on language aspects as a basis, teaches how to communicate information in texts understandable to others, with fullest possible adaptation to language requirements, high standards of accuracy, consistency and good style. It shows obstacles and interferences in the communication process.

Revision and editing: The course focuses on the quality of translation parameters through practical quality assessment based on structure, style, consistency, etc. It is closely linked to the courses on language aspects and on composition and writing skills.

Critical study of translations: This would develop the student's critical sense by studying and analyzing previous translations in relevant language combinations, including those produced by the United Nations. The translation of philosophical texts is of special interest. This course may be taught in conjunction with the course on translation history to show concretely how eminent translators, who were very often scholars with erudite knowledge, treated their work.

Terminology: It teaches the basic principles of terminology, terminography and lexicology and provides practical skills for terminology management as an essential translation-oriented activity. Students would be involved in preparing specialized terminology, in cooperation with the United Nations, and updating and supplementing DtSearch and UNTERM terminological data bases.

Information technology and CAT tools: The purpose is to make the student aware of all aspects of the state-of-art in the sphere of CAT tools, and in particular as regards available translation memory software and systems, and to prepare him/her for the utilization of those instruments.

Specialized knowledge: The objective is to build up a thematic competence and basic knowledge and learn key concepts in specific fields of knowledge, with special emphasis on LSP. It would adopt an interdisciplinary approach, in collaboration with relevant university departments to deliver necessary credits and would concentrate on sciences, and particularly on mathematics, philosophy and logic.

Thematic courses: The following list of courses, which is not exhaustive, has proved to be very useful and would give an international dimension to training:

- International public law
- Comparative law studies (common law, *shari'a* or Islamic jurisdiction, etc.)
- Constitutional law
- International relations and international organizations
- Regional and inter-regional organizations
- Economics
- Current global issues
- Introduction to media studies

Sight translation and interpretation: To train the student on oral translation and interpretation techniques in order to concentrate on the meaning and gain speed in translation. The interpretative theory will be a basis of this course.

Practicum: This is a fundamental course. It is actually the crux of the whole training programme. It would prepare the student to be functional by translating a wide spectrum of UN documents. Documentation issued in the six official languages of the Organization, and accessible in the Optical Disk System (ODS) via Internet, would be used for comparison and as a reference material.

Graduation memoire: Will consist of the translation of a UN publication or background document. This would be revised within the United Nations, officially evaluated and processed and published as usual as part of normal work flow.

Traineeship: Students would de offered a two-month contract at the TI entry-level, after successfully submitting their memoire, and their performance would be assessed as part of the overall evaluation process for awarding the Master's degree in international translation. A representative of the United Nations would be a member of the board of examiners and the MA in International Translation would be recognized by the United Nations and would qualify for contracts as a UN translator.

What Aphasics Can Tell Us about Translation

The role of interdisciplinary research in translation studies

Annegret STURM

The definition of translation competence

Defining translation competence is one of the most challenging and yet one of the most basic tasks in modern translation studies. It ought to describe the capacity which enables the translator to translate a text correctly from one language into another, i.e. rendering the message conveyed in the source text as equivalent in content, form and style in order to ensure the very same communicative effects in the target situation as the source text would have in this situation.

Seen these manifold equivalence relations which have to be established, translation competence can only be described as a complex concept, which is the reason why it is often defined in the form of sub-competences (e.g. see PACTE 2005, Göpferich 2008, Hurtado Albir & Alves 2009)[1]. This view, however, is not exhaustive: translation competence can be as well considered as a special form of expert knowledge (e.g. see Shreve 2006). Although many publications deal with the issue of translation competence[2], no general and widely accepted definition of it exists up to now. Neither have different theoretical views been compared with respect to their common points.

1 This very fact has even led the European Union to set up a group of experts and develop a set of competencies required for the translator expert. The European Master in Translation is also based on a framework of competences and sub-competences.

2 See Neubert & Shreve (1992), Wilss (1992), Hurtado Albir & Alves (2009).

Any definition existing today is mostly a purely theoretical one and has barely been tested. Most empirical studies on translation competence either dealt with translators or students in translation studies[3]. Therefore, it has to be considered that this does not necessarily prove any component of translation competence. It does rather correspond to checking the results of a university curriculum or the daily experience in dealing with translations respectively.

Furthermore, since there are different, but very few interdisciplinary approaches in translation studies[4], definitions of translation competence continue to grow into complex philosophical constructions without having a clearly proven basis.

A new approach to the definition of translation competence

In order to test a new approach for the definition of translation competence, we decided to create a special study design which would allow for empirical conclusions on the existing theoretical assumptions.

After studying the dense and very complex writings of different translation scholars, we realized that it was impossible to find a concise definition of translation competence that could be tested in an empirical study. To overcome this problem, we created the concept of translation ability, which shall describe the cognitive basis allowing for the acquisition of translation competence. In order to find possible elements, we did search through different publications of translation scholars in order to find out whether

3 See PACTE (2005), Göpferich (2008) and Hurtado Albir & Alves (2009).

4 E.g. see Heiden (2005), Lehr (2006), Lee-Jahnke (1998, 2005).

they mentioned any prerequisite for the acquisition of the competence as they described it. We found elements like memory (especially working memory), empathy (as the hyponym for the ability to interpret the author's intentions and the public's expectations in spite of not being in direct contact with them), the view of oneself (meaning being aware of one's responsibility and the expectations of others concerning our work as a translator), abstraction, creativity, different control- and monitoring- abilities, evaluation (of the work we are doing) and the ability to think logically in order to correctly understand the argumentation structure of the text and in order to correctly re-build it.

As mentioned above, all those possible components of translation ability were found in theoretical works about translation competence and to our knowledge have never been tested, or, if they were submitted to an empirical study, it involved people with a special training in translation. Therefore, these points (memory, empathy, view of oneself, abstraction, creativity, control- and monitoring-abilities, evaluation, capacity of logical thinking) were all to be criticised or, at least, to be proven experimentally before they could be used as elements for our hypothetical definition.

In our research group which unites not only translation scholars from the ETI specialized in translation didactics (such as Prof. Dr. Hannelore Lee-Jahnke), but also neurologists reknown for their work on bilingualism and translation (Prof. Dr. Jean-Marie Annoni) we could built upon the long experience in interdisciplinary research in the history of the Ecole de Traduction et d'Interprétation (ETI in Geneva)[5]. In this project we decided to work together with some neuroscientists. Neurosciences showed a great progress during the last years and offer a unique possibility to investigate the translator's "black box".

In order to find out what the neurosciences' view on translation was, neuroscientific articles on translation performance of bilingual aphasics were compared in order to find common points

5 See: Heiden (2005) & Lehr (2006).

between the different studies described. Although articles were taken from different scientific reviews, we made sure that we would only deal with actual data by choosing only articles of the last 9 years. The decision to carry our research on bilingual aphasics has been taken for the following reasons. First of all, aphasics allow for a negative approach to translation ability and translation competence, since they have reduced language capacities and therefore have to find compensative strategies. Second, they generally have no special translation training so that we could observe how subjects without any previous knowledge of translation would do in a translation task which furthermore would demand them to switch and use both their (impaired) languages at once.

Searching through the articles we found different descriptions of brain areas associated with the different subprocesses of translation[6] such as lexical retrieval, semantic memory, recognition of words, interpretation of double meanings and humour, etc. Mapping each of these functions proven to occur in non-translator-subjects during a translation task allowed for having a detailed picture of the different neurological processes going on during translation. After allocating each of these functions to one of the constituents of the translation process (understanding, processing, production), we tried to map the processing-part as detailed as we could, since only this part was unique to translation because of the different operation chains which ultimately lead to the successful equivalent production in the target language. Then we checked the different elements in the processing-part for possible matches with the elements we had found in the theoretical publications about translation competence. The neurological studies allowed us for confirming the eight elements we had found before.

6 See Stowe, Laurie A. & Haverkort, Marco & Zwarts, Frans (2005), Chee, Michael W.L. (2006), Jefferies, Elizabeth & Baker, Stephen S. & Doran, Mark & Lambon Ralph, Matthew A. (2007) & Wang et al. (2009), Abutalebi & Green (2007), D'Esposito (2008), Perani, Daniela (2005), Green & Abutalebi (2008).

The pilot study

A study with four French-German bilingual patients with chronic aphasia and four bachelor students in translation studies was set up in order to check our hypothesis. If it was true that memory, abstraction, empathy, creativity, control, logical thinking, evaluation and the view of oneself were elements of translation ability, we should find more errors in the translations of the patients consisting in problems with the above mentioned cognitive processes, whereas the students were supposed to show no difficulty in these fields.

As source text for the study, a text from the famous little Nick was chosen, because the story consisted of easy vocabulary so that no special preparation was necessary. Furthermore, the action is told in a very funny way which was supposed to help the subjects with the stress of the test situation. The story plays in school, so that patients as well as students were confronted with a setting which was familiar to them.

The patients had to do the translation in Geneva's University Hospital in the presence of the experimenter. Before they could start with their work on the text, they were asked to fill out two questionnaires concerning their bilingualism in order to make sure that all subjects would have about the same proficiency level in each language. In order to assess their level of aphasia, they had to do a French and a German version of the *Mississippi-Aphasia-Screening Test* (MAST) which allowed for assessing the degree of their impairment in each of their languages. The students were asked to do the two questionnaires and the translation at home, but they were not allowed to spend more than one hour (60 minutes) on the translation.

Three of the patients' mother-tongue was German, whereas French was their second language; one of the patients was a French native speaker with German as a second language. The students were all German native speakers and French was their second language. The study consisted in the very same documents for them as for the patients, except the aphasia tests. All German native speakers were given the French text in order to translate it into German; the French native speaker was asked to translate the German version of the little Nick story into French.

None of the subjects was allowed to use any dictionary or other documentation resource.

Results

All patients experienced the translation as a very frustrating and demanding task, and only one of them did manage to translate the whole text. They had problems understanding the humour and failed to concentrate during the whole task, so that e.g. at the end of a sentence they could not remember its beginning. The same occurred when they had a special problem which they already had found a good solution for in the previous part of the text, but which they could not recall anymore. Neither could they remember that they already had had the very same problem, nor were they aware about the fact that they already solved it.

Furthermore, they were all very oriented towards the source text. They had difficulties in imagining a public for the target text, or were not conscious about the fact that they were acting as mediators between people, that they were supposed to translate the sense and the information of the text. Instead, they apparently perceived the translation as a task consisting of purely linguistic shifts whereas the text contained a distinct quantity of linguistic elements which had to be transferred in their quantitative number.

It is not clear whether patients were able to visualize the story, although it seems in most cases that they did not picture the scene. They mostly used strategies of copying, like calques, and scarcely modulated on the word classes, which may be due, such as the lack of creative solutions, on their apparent inability of abstracting the sense from the words and putting it again into words of another language. Their work on the text did not show any strategy, nor did they try to find any alternative solutions when they had a specific problem (e.g. to solve a double negation with a positive statement).

Discussion

Our study could confirm memory, empathy, the view of oneself, abstraction, creativity, control- and monitoring abilities as possible elements of translation ability, which would mean that all those seven elements have to be present in a subject in order to effectively acquire translation competence. However, the study could not show whether the ability to think logically was an element of translation ability or not, since errors concerning the logical structures of the text only were observed when patients had a general problem either with understanding the passage or with assessing the equivalent terms in the target language.

In general, our study was based on far too small groups so that all findings are not statistically significant. For a profound verification of our results, a third test-group would have been necessary in order to allow for a better comparison between the patients' and the students' group.

One could also imagine that an intralingual translation task would have had an important effect on the comparability of the different samples, so that the ability of translating within one's mother tongue, meaning the ability to paraphrase and to express oneself correctly in different registers could perhaps provide some hints on the capacity to translate between different languages.

The different test conditions for students and patients are another critical point. Since the students worked at home, the experimenter could not verify whether they worked according to the given rules or whether they actually took more time on the translation or whether they used any documentation resources.

Test conditions were not even consistent in the patient's group, since one of the subjects could not write anymore because of his stroke, so that he had to dictate his translation for the experimenter. In consequence, this subject communicated far more with the experimenter and was able to check immediately the reactions of the experimenter on his work. In this way, this test session had a completely different methodological background being rather a kind of a Think-Aloud-Protocol, since the experimenter often had to correct the last written version of the sentence and also could take notes on the verbalized reflections of the patient.

Furthermore, groups were very heterogeneous in different points. First of all, the difference of age was very high in each group since one subject was always significantly older than the rest of the group. Second, the students' group consisted but of women while the patients' group was purely male. We could not create any mixed groups since the majority of aphasia patients is male while the majority of translation students is female.

If there is one remarkable finding in this study, it is the importance of macrostrategies compared to concrete linguistic knowledge in the context of translation ability. None of the MASTs testing the linguistic capacities of the patients in both languages allowed for conclusions on the translation performance. Astonishingly, all macrostrategies are non-linguistic strategies such as empathy and memory and are not only solicited in translation. Most errors, however, can be reduced to an erroneous view of oneself and the responsibility of the translator and misinterpretations or ignorance of the author and the target reader. In sum, one could say that apparently, translators show a broader Theory of Mind, meaning that they are at ease with adapting to the fact of responsibility towards the source text (and the author respectively) and the target reader. The students' works showed that they were able to take different perspectives during their work and that it was mostly this very basic strategy which helped them to find equivalent and good solutions.

Bibliography

Abutalebi, Jubin & Green, David (2007). Bilingual language production: The neurocognition of language representation and control. In: *Journal of Neurolinguistics*. Vol. 20, S. 242–275.

Chee, Michael W.L. (2006). Dissociating language and word meaning in the bilingual brain. In: *Trends in Cognitive Sciences*. Vol. 10, S. 527–529.

D'Esposito, Mark (2008). Working Memory. In: *Handbook of Clinical Neurology* (Series editors: Michael J. Aminoff, François Bohler, Dick F. Swaab). Elsevier, Amsterdam.

Green, David W. & Abutalebi, Jubin (2008). Understanding the link between bilingual aphasia and language control. In: *Journal of Neurolinguistics*. Vol. 21, S. 558–576.

Göpferich, Susanne (2008). *Translationsprozessforschung. Stand – Methoden – Perspektiven*. Tübingen: Gunter Narr: 150.

Heiden, T. (2005). Blick in die Black Box: Kreative Momente im Übersetzungsprozess: eine experimentelle Studie mit Translog. In: *Meta: journal des traducteurs / Metra: translator's journal*, vol. 50, n° 2, (pp. 448–472), sous la direction de Hannelore Lee-Jahnke, André Clas, Presses de l'université de Montréal (ed.).

Hurtado Albir, Amparo & Alves, Fabio: Translation as a cognitive ability. In: Jeremy Munday (ed.): *The Routledge Companion to Translation Studies*. Routledge. Oxon. 2009: 54–74.

Jefferies, Elizabeth & Baker, Stephen S. & Doran, Mark & Lambon Ralph, Matthew A. (2007). Refractory effects in stroke aphasia: A consequence of poor semantic control. In: *Neuropsychologia*. Vol. 45, S. 1065–1079.

Lee-Jahnke, H. (1998). Moderne Hilfsmittel in der Übersetzungslehre am Fallbeispiel medizinische Übersetzung. In: *Equivalences* 97, Tagungsakten, ASTTI, Bern.

Lee-Jahnke, H. (2005). New cognitive approaches in process-oriented translation research. In *Meta: journal des traducteurs / Metra: translator's journal*, vol. 50, n° 2, (pp. 359–377), sous la direction de Hannelore Lee-Jahnke, André Clas, Presses de l'université de Montréal (ed.).

Lehr, C. (2006). *Semantische Priming-Effekte bei Übersetzung unter Einbezug der Expertiseforschung*. Genève: Université de Genève Ecole de traduction et d'interprétation.

Neubert, Albrecht & Shreve, Gregory M. (1992). *Translation as text*. Kent State University Press.

PACTE (2005). Investigating Translation Competence: Conceptual and Methodological Issues. In Meta: *journal des traducteurs / Meta: translator's jour-*

nal, vol. 50, n° 2, (pp. 609–619), sous la direction de Hannelore Lee-Jahnke, André Clas, Presses de l'université de Montréal (ed.).

Perani, Daniela (2005). The neural basis of language talent in bilinguals. In: *Trends in Cognitive Sciences*. Vol. 9, S. 211–213.

Shreve, Gregory M. (2006). Integration of translation and summarization processes in summary translation. In: *Translation and Interpreting Studies*, 87–109.

Stowe, Laurie A. & Haverkort, Marco & Zwarts, Frans (2005). Rethinking the neurological basis of language. In: *Lingua*. Vol. 115, S. 997–1042.

Wang, Y. et al. (2009). Sustained and transient language control in the bilingual brain. In: *NeuroImage*. Vol. 47, S. 414–422.

Wilss, Wolfram (1992). *Übersetzungsfertigkeit. Annäherungen an einen komplexen übersetzungspraktischen Begriff*. Gunter Narr Verlag. Tübingen.

4. *Answers and Solutions*

Information Technology for Translation: Gadget or Must?

The interplay between translator training, professional world and industry[1]

Marcel THELEN

Introduction

The topic of this paper is information technology for translation, in particular in relation to the curriculum of translator training programmes. This can be tackled from a number of angles, one of the most obvious ones being content and place in the curriculum, and weighting in terms of staff and student time to be spent on it and the number of ECTS credits to be earned. I will not walk this road. Instead, this paper will briefly discuss the background of the emergence of information technology for translation and argue that, on the one hand, translation without information technology for translation is unthinkable, and, on the other, that circumstances are becoming more and more favourable for intensive use of this technology by the various parties involved in translation.

1 This paper is based on the presentation (with the same title as this paper) that I gave at the DGT-Universities conference "Towards a European Master's in Translation" (Brussels, 19–20 October 2006). It is supplemented by insights and ideas based on later developments, in particular as regards place and role of IT, CAT tools, and localisation tools in the curriculum of the Department of Translation and Interpreting of the Maastricht School of International Communication of Zuyd University, and the involvement of the professional world and the tools manufacturing industry in the curriculum.

Actually, not only was the introduction of this technology an answer to growing demands on the translator, it also brought about (and is still doing so) a considerable change in his activities. All this makes it all the more compelling to make information technology an important and integral part of the curriculum of translator training programmes. The focus of this paper will be on the interplay between the parties involved in translation vis-à-vis information technology.

Information technology for translation will be addressed from a purely practical, i.e. non-technical, point of view. First, a short survey will be given of the various types of tools available. These will not be viewed from the point of their technology, e.g. I will not try to answer such questions as: how are the various tools built, how do they work, what do they do, which tool is the best? Instead, I will view the various tools from the point of their importance and usefulness in the practice of a professional translator. This will be followed by a discussion of the role of translator training in relation to information technology for translation. Here such questions play a role as: can a training institute afford not to include tools in its curriculum, what tools should be included in the curriculum and with what objectives, how should they be taught, when and where in the curriculum should technical resources be taught, and should they be part of BA or MA programmes? An important part in this discussion is reserved for the input from the professional world in the training, and the position of the tools manufacturing industry in this.

In this paper, I will deal with specialised translation[2] only, i.e. exclude literary translation. Although a number of the tools that I

2 The label "specialised translation" is a cover term for the translation of all those texts that are not literary by nature. Specialised translation thus covers a number of domains, of which the following are perhaps the most well-known and best examples: administration/business/economics, biology/medicine, science/technology/IT, and law/politics. For the term "specialised translation" see Thelen (2002: 21).

will discuss may be suited for application to literary translation, quite a few of them are not. As far as I know, these tools have been (and still are being) developed in the first place with an eye to their application to specialised translation[3].

1. Information Technology. What's in a name?

For my presentation at the conference I was asked to speak about "Information technology for translators". I adopted this title also for this paper. The term "information technology" is, however, not really appropriate since it is not precise enough. According to the New Oxford Dictionary of English, information technology is:

> The study or use of systems (especially computers and telecommunications) for storing, retrieving, and sending information.

Clearly, "study" or "systems" do not apply to tools, and these tools are not computers, but programmes that are run on computers. Moreover, telecommunications is not appropriate here either. The same dictionary defines telecommunications as:

> [treated as sing.] the branch of technology concerned with such communication;
> [count noun] formal a message sent by such means,

where "telecommunication" is defined as:

> communication over a distance by cable, telegraph, telephone or broadcasting.

3 It would, however, be a challenge to investigate if the tools that are purely meant for specialised translation could also be suitable for literary translation, and if so, what the impact would be on the nature of the translations thus produced, and if not, why not. However, this is beyond the scope of this paper.

Clearly, none of these definitions applies here. Therefore, I suggest to use "technical resources for translators" instead of the term "information technology", because this is exactly what is meant here. For the term "technical resources for translators" I refer to the new European standard on translation services, EN 15038: 2006. "Translation Services – Service Requirements". This standard "encompasses the core translation process and all other related aspects involved in providing service, including assurance and traceability" (p. 4).

In this standard, "technical resources for translators" is defined as:

> requisite equipment for the proper execution of the translation projects as well as for safe and confidential handling, storage, retrieval and disposal of documents and data;
> Requisite communications equipment as well as hardware and software;
> Access to relevant information sources and media (p. 7).

From this definition it appears that the term "technical resources for translators"[4] is an all-encompassing term covering all the different tools and resources that the translator will use in the various activities that he carries out between the first contact with his client to the delivery of the translation and its aftercare, ranging from what I would call "basic IT activities" to "translation activities" to "administrative activities". In what follows, I will first give a survey of relevant resources for the various activities and stages.

4 Austermühl (2001) employs the term "electronic tools for translators".

2. Technical resources for translation

2.1 Relevant technical resources for basic IT activities

In this survey, I will not go into technical details. Nor do I claim it to be exhaustive. Among the most common technical resources that the translator will use for basic IT activities are:

1. operating systems (e.g. MS Windows)
2. word processing tools (e.g. MSWord)
3. presentation tools (e.g. MS PowerPoint)
4. tools for calculating (e.g. MS Excel)
5. internet tools (e.g. MS Internet Explorer)
6. file formats (e.g. RTF, pdf) and file converting tools (e.g. ScanSoft pdf Converter)
7. communication tools (e.g. MS Outlook, MSN Messenger)
8. scanning tools (e.g. OCR)

In order for the translator to be able to work in a professional way, he must have these tools at his disposal and be skilled in using them. These tools form the precondition for translating and are the very basic tools for:

1. file and document handling,
2. processing the target text,
3. information retrieval necessary for the processing of the target text, and
4. communicating (about) the ultimate translation results.

2.2 Relevant technical resources for translation activities

Translation activities form the core of the whole process from the first translator-client contact to aftercare. The tools relevant to these activities are the tools that the translator actually uses to produce and formulate his translation. Unlike the tools used for processing the target text mentioned in the previous section (the modern and contemporary counterparts of the traditional feather & ink, and the typewriter), these tools actually help the translator in formulating the translation. These tools can be subdivided into smaller classes in line with the type or mode of translating: translating, subtitling, localisation. Again, this list is not meant to be exhaustive (for additional tools, see e.g. Austermühl 2001).

A) *Tools for translating*
   1. translation memory tools (e.g. Trados-SDL, aligning, tagging, concordancing)
   2. machine translation tools (e.g. Systran)
   3. speech recognition tools (e.g. Dragon)

B) *Tools for subtitling:*
   1. subtitling tools (e.g. FAB, Spot)

C) *Tools for localisation:*
   1. localisation tools (e.g. Passolo).

The tools for translating and for subtitling are sometimes placed into one category under the name of "CAT tools" (for computer aided, or assisted, tools). Subtitling is sometimes subsumed under localisation.

In addition to the tools mentioned, there are terminology management tools (e.g. Trados-SDL MultiTerm) and term extraction tools (e.g. WordSmith, SystemQ). These tools can be used in combination with any of the above three categories.

In particular in the case of web translating, i.e. the translation of web pages, the translator should be familiar with and skilled in a mark-up language (e.g. html, sgml, xml).

Some of the tools mentioned can be combined into "integrated packages". These are combinations of a series of tools that – applied together – offer the translator a means to translate more efficiently and faster, and deliver high quality translations. An example of such an "integrated package" is SDL Knowledge-based

Translation System. As the producer of this system puts it: "The power of the solution lies in the combination of sophisticated machine translation technology with other translation automation technologies and human linguistic skills" (http://www.sdl.com/en/products/products-index/kbts.asp). Such "integrated packages are particularly useful for large companies in need of fast and high-quality translations of 'high volumes of content'" *(ibid.)*. Another example of such an integrated package is Euramis, in use with the DGT of the European Commission (http://ec.europa.eu/dgs/translation/bookshelf/tools_and_workflow_en.pdf).

The tools for the translation activities are essential for translators. Without them, translators would not be able to cope with the translation demands of the modern communication society.

2.3 Relevant technical resources for administrative activities

The third class of technical resources for translators is made up of tools for administrative purposes such as book keeping (e.g. MS Excel) and workflow management (e.g. LTC, SDL TeamWorks). Since the new European standard for translation services also requires documented procedures for the administrative processing of translation projects, such tools are indispensable for translators. This is not to say that all translators, great and small, must have and use existing tools. In particular freelance translators very often develop their own tools for book keeping and workflow management.

Since the tools mentioned in (2), (3) and (4) are essential to the three most important activities in the translation service chain, they form the minimum set of technical tools that must be included in the curriculum of a translator training programme that envisages to train and deliver professional translators.

3. The importance of technical resources in the practice of the professional translator

3.1 Technical resources and the professional world

The translation market has seen a number of developments and drastic changes over the years that had and are still having a great impact on translation in general and the activities of the individual translator[5] in particular. In this section, I will discuss the developments and changes that took (and are taking) place in the professional world.

These are the times of quality, quality assurance and quality management. One of the drives behind the call for quality is – for Europe at least – the changed position of the EU vis-à-vis the rest of the world, laid down in a number of EU declarations, such as:

A) *For education:*
1. the Bologna Declaration (19 June 1999) (see http://www.bologna-berlin2003.de/pdf/bologna_declaration.pdf).

B) *For economic and social renewal of Europe:*
1. the Lisbon Strategy (March 2000). Available at: http://ec.europa.eu/growthandjobs/pdf/lisbon_en.pdf.

This is not to say that these declarations were the sole or most important causes for these changes, yet they reinforced and perhaps accelerated them. Although both declarations pertain to different areas, a common basic element in them is the urge for competiveness of the EU, which can best be achieved by offering quality and setting up quality management systems. All this had its effect on translation and the translation market, too. Con-

5 With "translator" I not only mean to refer to the individual translator, freelance or employed, but also to the individual translation department, translation company or translation bureau.

comitant developments, especially in the translation market, were/are:

1. *intensified cost negotiation:* commissioners of translations try to negotiate the lowest prices possible;
2. *growing necessity to shorten time to market of translations:* commissioners increasingly want translations to be ready as fast as possible and submit texts for translation later; as a result, translators have to work faster;
3. *increasing output:* the volume of translations is increasing enormously; as a result translators have to translate more;
4. *more emphasis on product liability:* like in other sectors, translators are held liable for their translations;
5. *quality assurance:* to avoid being held liable, translators have to deliver and guarantee quality; this development is "supported" by international standards, e.g. the new European standard on translation services;
6. *"Taylorisation":* in order to comply with the demands and developments described in (1)–(5), translators are forced to work as efficiently as possible, where every detail of the translation and service process has to be processed very carefully.

Austermühl (2001: 4–6) mentions another three factors that have an influence on translation and the translation market, viz.:

1. globalisation;
2. automation, and
3. digitisation.

It will be clear that in this situation, technical resources are a good solution and more than welcome. In fact, it is becoming increasingly difficult for a translator to meet these changing requirements when not making use of technical resources. Putting it differently, not only are conditions in the translation market favourable for further introduction of technical resources, this situation also affects the translator in general: using technical resources has become a must and a translator cannot afford not to use them.

The technical resources that the modern translator has to master and use are in particular the resources for translation activities, but also those for administrative activities (see sections [3] and [4] above). However, in order to be able to work with these profitably, the translator must be IT-literate and master at least most of the resources for basic IT activities (section [2] above).

3.2 Technical resources and the translator

More in detail, the developments and requirements outlined in [5] also affect the activities of the translator. Because of the growing impact and importance of technical resources and the changing market conditions, the nature of the focus of activities is changing. Indications for this come from various sources.

Among the new activities of translators are:

1. systematic automated term extraction;
2. terminology management;
3. controlled language;
4. interaction with machine translation;
5. intensified interaction with content management systems.

These activities were mentioned at the international conference "Qualifying translators: the role and responsibilities of Higher Education" (Rennes, France, 22–23 September 2006), and later in a meeting of the professional advisory board of the department of Translation and Interpreting, Maastricht School of International Communication, Zuyd University.

In order not to lag behind, the translator is forced to familiarise himself continuously with new technical resources and keep track of developments.

One of the most obvious advantages of these resources, on the other hand, is that they enable the translator to improve his speed of working. Generally, technical resources will

1. make translating more attractive;
2. make work better organised/organisable;
3. enable multi-tasking;
4. boost consistency & accuracy;
5. boost speed of work, which is important for meeting deadlines;
6. make work traceable, retrievable & repeatable;
7. make work comparable & "assessable";
8. raise the quality of work delivered;
9. enable further specialisation & excellence;
10. make the translator receptive to new IT developments;
11. enhance documentation strategies;
12. enable research;
13. enhance client satisfaction.

The relation between translator and technical resources is diverse: on the one hand, these technical resources are indispensable tools for the translator to meet the new demands from commissioners and to cope with tight deadlines, on the other they are important means to deliver and guarantee quality. In addition, they make the translator more "tool literate" and "computer minded" for him to become more open to new technical developments and specialise/excel in particular areas or skills, thus improving his market position.

At present, it is still too early to speak of an IT generation of professional translators since by far not all translators actually use technical resources, but gradually this is changing. As it is now, various types of translator (partly due to technical developments and partly due to ignorance of technical resources), and various types of translation(-related) activities can be distinguished:

1. *traditional "resourceless" translators*;
2. *resource-using translators*; these are the translators using the "basic" technical tool viz. a translation memory;
3. *resource-driven translators*: the way of working and translating of these translators is to a large extent determined by the

resources that they use, such as speech recognition systems, localisation tools, subtitling tools, and machine translation tools (see "raw machine output editors" below), etc.;
4. *"raw machine output" editors*; these are the persons that interpret and edit the output of machine translation;
5. *"end of line" translators*; these are highly specialised translators of "last-resort" that do their job at the very end of a knowledge-based system-like production line.

4. Translator training and technical resources

4.1 The student translator

Student translators are, like any other students, more and more computer-minded. Very often they have become familiarised with computers and become computer-literate at an earlier stage in their educational careers. In any case, most of them are familiar with computer games and therefore are not "afraid of computers". In other words, they are ripe for technical resources. This means that they more or less expect to work with computers and computer programmes and that computers will be involved in their training. In fact, they tend to be bored with the traditional non-computer ways of training. This is an important and favourable precondition to introduce technical resources in the curriculum. Let me call this precondition "predisposition". There are a number of other equally important reasons why it is necessary to introduce technical resources in the curriculum:

1. *predisposition:* see above;
2. *potential*: students have an increased ability for multi-tasking and have no problems with technical resources. Instead, they very often have problems with handling long stretches of text

(they very often do not have an overview of a text, lack consistency when having to formulate longer texts, etc.). Whatever their potential, student translation need technical resources in the curriculum to help them become professional translators;

3. *variation*: operating tools introduces variation in working (using a mouse, typing on a keyboard, looking at a screen, etc.); technical resources fit very well with their growing need for variation;
4. *competence-based learning:* this has become one of the most common and widely spread learning strategies. Technical resources fit very well in competence-based learning;
5. *student expectations:* student translators expect to be prepared for a professional career. Since technical resources are essential for professional translation, they cannot be left out from the curriculum; they are a help and a must.

4.2 *The translator trainer*

As a logical consequence of the foregoing, translator trainers should be at least as resource-literate as student translators. This is to say, not only those trainers who are actually involved in the teaching of the use of technical resources, but – more importantly – also all the trainers that are involved in the teaching of translation and terminology. Only then will the student translators receive the training that is necessary for them to become professional translators. The necessary goals to achieve by latter group of trainers are:

1. *to increase their resource literacy*;
2. *to become certified in the use of technical resources* (see [4.3.2] below); only then will they know enough to train their students well enough in the proper and profitable use of technical resources;
3. *to apply the tools that they train their students in themselves*; only then they will know all the tricks and bugs of these tools;

4. *to introduce tools in assignments*; this is important because the more student translators work with tools, the better they will master them.

Introducing technical resources in the curriculum where these translator and terminology trainers are not capable to use these resources themselves and where they do not introduce these resources in as many assignments as possible and relevant, would not make any sense, at least not achieve the effect envisaged by this introduction.

4.3 The professional world and the tools manufacturing industry

The third party, to be more precise, the training-external party that is important for technical resources to be introduced in the curriculum is formed both by the professional world and the tools manufacturing industry.

4.3.1 The professional world

The professional world has an interest in the introduction of technical tools in translator training curricula because it requires for a translator to work professionally and in accordance with common practice that he is capable of working with these resources. And since the professional world will be the future "employer" of student translators, these should be resource-literate to be "hired on".

4.3.2 The tools manufacturing industry

The interest of the tools manufacturing industry is of a different nature. Not only does the industry want their products to be bought by as many professional translators as possible, it also seeks to have their products introduced in the curriculum of as many translator training institutes as possible, since these are the cradles of future buyers of their products. An additional interest of the industry is to encourage the users of their products to acquire the appropriate knowledge and skills needed for the optimal use and application of these products and thus lay the basis for the assimilation of new updates and upgrades of these products. This can best be done by training institutes.

To this end, the tools manufacturing industry offers a number of certification options, viz.

1. the tools manufacturing company SDL offers a three-level certification programme for individual certification for competence in working with SDL products (see http://www.sdl.com/en/services/certification/default.asp); such programmes would, of course, be ideal for both student translators and translator trainers;
2. the Institute of Localisation Professionals (TILP)[6] offers two types of CLP[7] certification programmes:
   - for individuals (= certification proper);
   - for course providers, modules, and whole programmes (= accreditation).

   For more information see http://www.tilponline.org/CLP/about clp.shtml).

Such certification programmes are interesting both for student translators and translator trainers.

The SDL programme specifically aims at translators, whereas the TILP programmes aim at engineers, project managers and linguists, the latter not necessarily being translators. Whatever the target group, these programmes show that the tool producing industry certainly has an interest in translator training.

6 TILP "represents localisation industry professionals and professionals active in localisation related areas. These include: (1) software publishers and publishers of other material using electronic media, (2) eContent providers, (3) localisation service providers, (4) tools developers, (5) trainers and educators (including third level colleges), and (6) researchers". For more information on TILP, see (http://www.tilponline.org/TILP%20Brochuref1.pdf).

7 CLP stand for "Certified Localisation Professional".

5. Technical resources and the curriculum

5.1 General

From the foregoing it will be clear that technical resources are indispensable for the curriculum of translator training, i.e. for all three types of activities that are important for translation: (1) basic IT activities, (2) translation activities, and (3) administrative activities (see [2.1–2.3] above). These resources should be prominently omnipresent in the whole curriculum. Translator training simply cannot lag behind and has a duty to fulfil towards the student translators on the one hand and the professional world and the tools manufacturing industry on the other.

Along with these resources, translation quality assurance should be introduced, i.e. with a focus not only – as is usual for translator training institutes – on "resources for translation", "translation as a product" and the "translation process", but also on the "translator" and in particular the "translation service" (or translation as service). This comes down to including the new European standard in the curriculum. This is rather a must since in this standard all the other focal points are included and related to one another. This would give the student translator a good insight into professional translation.

5.2 Implementation in the curriculum

Since technical resources are vital to translation, it is necessary that all resources are taught as early in a training programme as possible so as to enable student translators to apply them as often and as extensively as possible right after they have first encountered them, in order for them to become highly skilled in their use and make the most of them. From the first instruction onwards, technical resources should, as much as possible and relevant, be part and parcel of every translation assignment to be done, so that they become the student translator's "second nature". In most cases it would suffice to train students in the use of one specific tool for translation activities (more would be welcome, but two would be enough), with the idea that it would be better to master one or two tools perfectly well and on the basis of this mastery be able to familiarise oneself with other tools fairly quickly, than to know about more tools and master them only superficially. However, this is not enough. The proper use of technical resources should also be part of assessments (perhaps even as much as 50 %).

These ideas derive from the type of translator training that the Department of Translation and Interpreting of the Maastricht School of International Communication (Zuyd University, the Netherlands) is: a four-year professionally-oriented training programme at bachelor level that – by law – is forced to deliver graduates that are skilled enough to enter the professional translation market as young and starting translators. Given a programme such as this, it would be only natural to have all practical training at BA level and further specialisation and theorising at MA level.

Across Europe, training programmes, i. e. their nature (academic *vs.* professional) and the division in years between BA and MA, differ, however, and therefore other options may well be appropriate and necessary.

5.3 Input from the professional world

Given the fact that the professional world can only benefit from that type of translator training that trains students to become translators that would be able to function in this professional world, it would be no more than obvious for the professional world to participate in such a training programme and for the training institute to make this possible. This certainly goes for technical resources for translation.

The traditional options for the professional world are:

1. giving guest lectures;
2. giving workshops;
3. offering student placements.

In [6] below I will mention a number of new opportunities that are actually being implemented in the curriculum of the Department of Translation and Interpreting of the Maastricht School of International Communication.

5.4 Input from the tools manufacturing industry

What goes for the professional world, also goes for the tools manufacturing industry, be it that here technical resources play an even more important and central role. The tools manufacturing industry, too, can actively participate in translator training programmes. In addition to the three traditional ways mentioned in [5.3] above, the supply of licenses for technical resources at as low a price as possible is, of course the number one of these traditional ways. The extent to which the industry is willing to do this depends on the nature of the cooperation with the training institute (see [6] below). Whatever is the case, in general, the tools manufacturing industry attaches great importance to collaboration with training institutes. A case in point here is that Lionbridge has made its translation tool Logoport freely available for academic use in translation education[8]. Another example is that more and more companies establish contact points for cooperation with training institutes (e.g. SDL University Alliance Program).

8 Source: Rudy Tirry, Country Manager Lionbridge Belgium in his presentation "Translation resource management in a global company" at the LISA-Lessius conference "Teaching Localization for Global Business Readiness", Antwerp, 10–12 December 2007.

6. Technical resources: new opportunities for the curriculum

As mentioned in [5.3] and [5.4] above, technical resources open up a number of interesting new opportunities for the curriculum in terms of cooperation with the professional world and the tools manufacturing industry. One of the most basic conditions here is that there is a sound balance between supply and demand on the side of professional world and tools manufacturing industry on the one hand and the training institute on the other, in other words, there should be no one-way traffic from professional world and tools manufacturing industry to training institute.

Let me give a few examples from the Department of Translation and Interpreting of the Maastricht School of International Communication.

The Department has very good contacts with both the professional world and the tools manufacturing industry. These contacts have opened up new ways of cooperation:

1. work placements for translator trainers, where the trainers actually work along with staff of the host translation bureau;
2. active involvement of both professional world and industry in curriculum development;
3. involvement of both professional world and industry in the development of training materials.

In addition to this, both professional world and industry cooperate with the Department in the in-house simulated translation bureau. This is a simulated translation bureau that is run and staffed by fourth-year students under the supervision of a lecturer-director and coached by an external professional translator. For more information about this translation bureau, see e.g. Thelen (2006). This bureau takes on simulated, but also realistic jobs ranging from translation and localisation, to subtitling, interpreting, DTP, terminology work, etc. The cooperation options here are:

1. Both professional world and industry submit jobs to the bureau that they themselves have already dealt with as if they are new jobs. Students process these as professionally as possible and send them back. The student results are then compared with the results of professional world and industry and feedback is given to the students. This gives both professional world and industry the opportunity to look among fourth-year students for potential for future vacancies to be filled.
2. In this way, both professional world and industry can also be involved in student assessment.

These are only a few examples. They make clear that close cooperation is possible between professional world and industry and training institutes on the point of technical resources. Technical resources are "binding elements".

7. Who benefits from technical resources?

From the foregoing it will be clear that there are no losers, only winners, when it comes down to technical resources. These will be beneficial to:

1. the professional world,
2. the individual professional translator,
3. the student translator,
4. the translator trainer,
5. the tools manufacturing industry,
6. the translator training curriculum,
7. the cooperation between the various parties,

and, last but certainly not least:

8. the profession.

8. Epilogue

In this paper, I discussed technical resources for translation. They are both necessity and a blessing, and will certainly help to raise the status of the profession of translation. Therefore, and for all the reasons mentioned in this paper, technical resources cannot and must not be omitted from translator training programmes. On the contrary, they must form an essential core element and be present from beginning to end.

References

Austermühl, F. (2001). *Electronic Tools for Translators.* Manchester/U.K.: St. Jerome Publishing.

CLP certification programmes of TILP. Information available at: http://www.tilponline.org/CLP/aboutclp.shtml (visited last: 3 January 2008).

EN 15038: 2006. "Translation Services – Service Requirements". CEN, 13 April 2006. Available at: http://www.cen.eu/esearch/extendedsearch.aspx (visited last: 28 December 2007).

Euramis. See: http://ec.europa.eu/dgs/translation/bookshelf/tools_and_workflow_en.pdf (visited last: 28 December 2007).

Knowledge-based Translation System. See http://www.sdl.com/en/products/products-index/kbts.asp (visited last: 28 December 2007).

SDL certification programme. Information available at: http://www.sdl.com/en/services/certification/default.asp (visited last: 3 January 2008).

The Bologna Declaration (19 June 1999). Available at: http://www.bologna-berlin2003.de/pdf/bologna_declaration.pdf) (visited last: 28 December 2007).

The Institute of Localisation Professionals (TILP). Information avalailable at: http://www.tilponline.org/TILP%20Brochuref1.pdf (visited last: 3 January 2008).

The Lisbon Strategy (March 2000). Available at: http://ec.europa.eu/growthandjobs/pdf/lisbon_en.pdf (visited last: 28 December 2007).

The New Oxford Dictionary of English (1998). Oxford: Clarendon Press. Ed. J. Pearsall & P. Hanks.

Thelen, M. (2002). "Translation Studies in the year 2000: the state of the art. Terminology theory and practice". In: Lewandowska-Tomaszczyk, B. & M. Thelen (eds.), *Translation and Meaning*, Part 6. Proceedings of the Łódź Session of the 3rd International Maastricht-Łódź Duo Colloquium on 'Translation and Meaning', Held in Łódź, Poland, 22–24 September 2000. Maastricht: Hogeschool Zuyd, Maastricht School of Translation and Interpreting, 21–39. For more information about the *Translation and Meaning* book series, see http://www.hszuyd.msti.translation-and-meaning.nedweb.com.

Thelen, M. (2006). "Going European: a plea for building a network of simulated translation bureaus". In: Forstner, M. and H. Lee-Jahnke (eds.), *CIUTI-Forum Paris 2005. Regards sur les aspects culturels de la communication*. Bern: Peter Lang, pp. 219–236.

Machine Translation as an Aid in Identifying Translation Difficulties for Texts Used in Introductory Translation Courses

Diane HOWARD

Introduction

The texts selected for translation in introductory courses provide students with their first experience of the expectations placed on professional translators. Therefore, instructors need to ensure that texts not only reflect market demand and different stylistic conventions, but also provide students with a means of both progressively building skills and of realistic self-assessment. This is particularly important because, according to the U.S. *2003 National Assessment of Adult Literacy*, only 31% of U.S. college graduates read at the proficient level, defined as "reading lengthy, complex, abstract prose texts as well as synthesizing information and making complex inferences" (National Center for Education Statistics [NCES] 2003: 15). A sample task typical of this level is "comparing two editorials." While one might argue that this situation is peculiar to the United States, results from the 2003 Programme for International Student Assessment (PISA) suggest that the situation may be even more dire in some European countries (OECD 2004: 281), including Germany, Italy, and Spain.[1] As a result, instructors need to consider not only the reading level of the mate-

1 The PISA studies are directed at young adults (aged 15 years), while the NCES targeted multiple age ranges, so the studies are not comparable. However, the results of both surveys suggest a lack of high-level reading skills among both students and the general population.

rials they use in class, but also the reading abilities of incoming students.

While defining the exact set of competencies required for translation remains a work in progress (the competencies set out by the European Master's in Translation expert group is a recent contribution [EMT Expert Group 2009]), we can probably agree that translators need to be able to synthesize information, make inferences, and read reasonably complex prose; in short, to read and perform the types of tasks set out at the NCES "proficient level." This ability is likely to be more in demand as machine translation improves and now that computer programs can write well enough to turn raw data into publishable articles.[2] The lower end of the translation market – the level at which the majority of students is comfortable reading – is being lost to automation and so for students to flourish in the future translation environment, they will need to be able to do two things: function at a higher level than computers and post-edit machine translation output.

We should be able to safely assume that people – by definition – read their *A* language better than their *B* language. So, if two-thirds of the students in a given class are probably not reading at a proficient level in their first language, we can expect the percentage to be even lower for their second language. The numbers probably drop even more when there is a great deal of linguistic and cultural distance between the source and target languages, as for example, between Chinese and Japanese and English.

As a result, we should abandon phrases such as "perfect command" of language (does anyone actually achieve that?) and replace them with "ability to read and analyze complex texts in both languages." Then, rather than thinking of comprehension

2 Stats Monkey, developed at Northwestern University, generates quite readable articles about baseball games. See http://infolab.northwestern.edu/projects/stats-monkey/ for information about the project and http://singularityhub.com/2009/11/09/is-software-set-to-replace-sports-journalists/ for a sample article (both sites visited June 2010).

difficulties primarily as a matter of inadequate second language training, trainers should consider improving reading comprehension – with the accompanying textual awareness – a global issue to be built into course objectives. In order to realize that objective, the texts used in introductory translation courses should be of carefully considered increasing levels of difficulty.

Text difficulty

Several authors of books on translator training and education have noted that materials used in class should be of increasing difficulty (Kussmaul 1995; Nord 2005; Kiraly 2000; Kelly 2005), but how to measure difficulty remains an open question, as does what features constitute a translation difficulty. Nord, for example, distinguishes between *translation difficulties* and *translation problems*, arguing that a *problem* is objective and must be solved by all translators undertaking a given translation task (examples include puns, structural differences between languages, etc.). A *difficulty*, on the other hand, is subjective and related to individual translators and specific working conditions (2005: 166–167). From this description, it appears that Nord's *problems* are inherent in the text, while *difficulties* occur as the result of the dynamics of individual translators in specific setting, for example, having to work under unrealistic time constraints, without appropriate information about the source text, or without proper references and resources. Although *problem* is the pedagogically preferable word it's much nicer to spend one's day solving problems than in the exhausting task of overcoming difficulties – here I will call problems existing in the text *difficulties* with the caveat that this descriptor can continue to be applied to textual elements even when the specific difficulty does not, or not longer, interferes with rapid processing and translation by a given translator.

Sandra Hale and Stuart Campbell have published several articles on text difficulty in translation at the lexis and grammar level focusing on processing effort and decision-making, with number of available translation options and lack of a target language lemma, and grammatical metaphor (Campbell 1999; Campbell and Hall 1999; Hale and Campbell 2002). They also make the sensible distinction between comprehension and production difficulties:

> there are two loci of difficulty. The first locus is comprehension, and difficulty is likely to be fairly universal [i. e., it will be the same across target languages for a single source language]. The second locus is production, and here there are likely to be different levels of difficulty depending on the lexis and grammar of the target language. (Campbell and Hale 1999)

While I suspect that the modification pattern in Chinese – in which all modifiers precede a head noun – is an example of a production difficulty for translation into English, which has limited toleration for noun stacking, the discussion here will not specifically separate comprehension and transfer difficulties.

In their 2002 paper, Hale and Campbell cite a model set out by Katharina Reiss (1982: 12) that ranks difficulty by text type and subject matter. Reiss has proposed a grid with five aspects – subject matter, register, type of language function, pragmatics, and historical cultural context – ranged at four levels. For example, the levels attached to subject matter are first, *general transcultural*; second, *general culture specific*; third, *specialized transcultural*, and fourth, *specialized culture specific*. As Hale and Campbell note, the model is not empirically based and one might well argue that the above third level – specialized transcultural – can be actually easier to translate than the second level, general culture specific. (Precisely because the texts belong to a transcultural professional group, the difficulties in translating medical journal articles are almost entirely terminological and can be solved with the appropriate references. Resolving the difficulties inherent in making patient education materials culturally sensitive can be much greater, particularly when coupled with writing at a specific grade level.)

Reiss's third aspect – type of language function – is similar to a model proposed by James Child that also views language function as an indicator of text difficulty. According to Child, the orientation mode, with a one-to-one correspondence of language and content is easy to read. The instructive mode, which offers straightforward information about the real world, is relatively easy. The evaluative mode, which requires analysis and evaluation against a "backdrop of shared information" (in short, the sort of materials involved in the NCES "proficient" reader tasks). The final mode – projective – is the most difficult because texts are the result of extensive author shaping.

Child's modes are an elaboration of the Interagency Language Roundtable (ILR) rating system, which was originally meant to rank achievement in the four skills for second language learning, with translation proficiency and interpretation proficiency recently added (ILR 2010). Although descriptors of second-language reading difficulty do not necessarily equate to translation difficulty, in a preliminary study, I found that the features of the reading levels in the ILR scale appear to identify problem areas in the source text (Howard 2009). Therefore, I propose using the ILR reading level scale as the initial basis for selecting texts of increasing difficulty in introductory courses. In the following, I will discuss a possible way of ranking text difficulty that combines the ILR scale with machine translation output. The goal is not simply to describe difficulty, but to do it in a way that allows students to develop textual awareness, self-awareness, and revision skills.

Setting course objectives

As was suggested above, primary objectives of an introductory translation course include:

- improving students' reading skills in both languages;
- introducing the idea of different types of textual difficulties;
- providing students with tools for resolving such difficulties;
- sensitizing students to future market conditions, including the need for post-editing skills; and
- developing the ability to self-assess.

Students entering translation programs are often quite naïve about what translation entails, the nature of texts, and their own abilities. Translation is often seen as a word-swapping operation that should follow the source text as closely as possible, sometimes even down to the punctuation. Many students have never been exposed to notions of text types, register, and function, and have not considered that various linguistic elements work differently in different languages. In addition, students can be quite defensive about their language skills, both in terms of ability to read the source language and to write in the target language. And, based on the NCES statistics – as well as personal experience – we can assume that the majority of entering students do not read either the source or target language well enough to function at minimal level of professional performance, as defined by the ILR "Skill Level Descriptions for Translation Performance":

> Can translate texts that contain not only facts but also abstract language, showing an emerging ability to capture their intended implications and many nuances. Such texts usually contain situations and events which are subject to value judgments of a personal or institutional kind, as in some newspaper editorials, propaganda tracts, and evaluations of projects. (ILR 2010)

So, perhaps the greatest challenge for the instructor is to tactfully promote improved reading skills and the ability to self evaluate and self correct without making the students defensive or causing them to lose confidence. Two axioms to keep in mind are that people don't want to be told that they can't read as well as they thought they could and it's easier to see and correct other people's mistakes than one's own. So, in the following the use of a straw-man proposal approach is set out, with Google Translate as the foil.

Using machine translation output to screen and generate texts for use in an introductory course has two benefits: in conjunction with a difficulty rating system like the ILR levels it allows instructors to identify difficulties in texts and then permits students to critique and work through the difficulties without any focus on personal abilities. At the same time, this approach sensitizes students to the revision process early in their training and to doing something they are likely to be doing in their later careers: post-editing machine translated texts. And perhaps most importantly, students usually think that correcting Google is fun.

The following examples are taken from texts I have used in introductory online courses for the University of Denver University College (Japanese to English) and the University of Chicago Graham School (Chinese to English).

Simple general texts: ILR Reading Level 1

Texts at this level have short, simple sentences usually written in the orientation mode, that is texts that "make information immediately available" (Child 1999: 91). Since these texts are categorized as elementary level, they are – by definition – easy to read. Possible translation difficulties should only exist at the lexical level; textual structure should be clear.

A weakness of the ILR system is that it does not address vocabulary difficulties in any meaningful way. Therefore, one needs to turn to other sources in thinking about translation difficulties at the word level. Hale and Campbell (2002) have alerted us to possible lexical problems with official terms that have no equivalent in the target language culture. Another potential problem is depth of vocabulary knowledge (also called "quality of vocabulary knowledge"); i.e., do readers know multiple meanings of a word or only the most common meaning? According to John Read, quality of vocabulary is an understudied area, particularly since exploratory studies have shown that less than 60 % of university students and school teachers tested had *deep* knowledge of words in English (Read 2000: 90–91). Lack of deep vocabulary knowledge may account for both comprehension and production problems in translation.

The Japanese text below was taken from the Web site of the Kyoto City Zoo and contains straightforward information about admission times and prices. The original is followed by the Google Translate translation. The last sentence includes a list of people qualifying for free admission and the documents they need to present. If we use Nord's terminology, this section is a difficulty only when the translator does not have access to the appropriate resources. Translations of the terms are readily available on the Web (but not so available in bilingual dictionaries – a good lesson in resource management). A lexical item with multiple meanings – and so requiring deep vocabulary knowledge – is 以下 *ika*, which can mean *less than*, *below*, *under*, and *the following*, among other things.

Original
開園時間 ・ 3 月～11 月の期間 AM9:00～PM5:00 ・ 12 月～2 月の期間 AM9:00～PM4:30 □入園できるのは閉園する 30 分前まで 休園日 ・ 月曜日 (月曜日が祝日の場合はその翌日) ・ 年末年始 (12 月 28 日～1 月 3 日)

入園料金

・ 一般 500 円 (団体 30 名以上 400 円)

・ 中学生 300 円

□小学生以下，土・ 日曜日の市内中学生，市内 70 歳以上の京都市敬老乗車証等をお持ちの方は本人無料，

市内７０歳以上の介護保険被保険者証をお持ちの方は本人及び介護者１名無料，

身体障害者手帳，療育手帳，戦傷病者手帳，被爆者健康手帳，精神障害者保護福祉手帳等を

お持ちの方は本人，及び介護者 1 名無料 (動物園入口にて上記証明書をお見せください。)

Machine Translation

Opening hours
– During the months of March to 11 AM9: 00 ~ PM5: 00
– During the months of December – 2 AM9: 00 ~ PM4: 30
□ Can admission 30 minutes before closing
Sun Closed
* Monday (the following day if Monday is a holiday)
– New Year (December 28 – January 3)

Admission Prices
– 500 yen (400 yen more than 30 groups)
Teens – 300 yen
The following elementary □, Saturday and Sunday the city junior high school, etc. If you have a boarding card for senior citizens over the age of 70 in Kyoto City are free person, If you have insurance card over 70 years of nursing-care insurance free local person and one caregiver,
Physical disability, care book, notebook sick casualties, hibakusha, to protect the mentally disabled and welfare handbook
If you have a person of one's free and caregivers (Please show the above certificates at the zoo entrance.)

Google Translate had the expected lexical difficulties, translating *ika* as *the following* ("elementary school students and younger" is a possible rendering) and making a hash of the official terms in the last sentence, as well as providing a nice collection of errors for students to critique without having made the mistakes themselves and without needing to feel defensive. The list includes the failure to change *11* and *2* to *November* and *February*, the placement of *AM* and *PM*, and the use of Japanese punctuation (~; students often do this). "Can admission 30 minutes before closing" is a rich point for discussion, as possible solutions include the more grammatically acceptable "Entry permitted until 30 minutes before zoo closing" or a phrase taken from parallel documents, such as "Ticket sales stop 30 minutes prior to closing time." *Hibakusha* are atomic bomb victims as defined by Japanese law.

After critiquing Google's output and discussing text type, level, and purpose, students can be asked to revise the translation for publication in a brochure to be given to English-speaking visitors to the zoo. A possible topic of discussion is whether to omit the section on people eligible for free admission in light of providing complete information and the possible linguistic abilities of caregivers.

Informational texts: ILR Reading Level 2

Material written at ILR Reading Level 2 is factual, often meant to instruct, and can contain main ideas supported by details. Texts are written for the general reader and presented in a straightforward, predictable manner. Such texts may include the sorts of lexical problems cited above and, with the increased amount of information, have a greater chance of containing culturally specific items. Because longer compound and/or complex sentences begin to appear at this level, modification within sentences may start to be a difficulty, particularly in languages with radically different structures, such as Chinese and Japanese (head noun languages) and English (which avoids extensive noun stacking, but does distinguish between restrictive and nonrestrictive clauses). The ILR Translation Performance descriptors for Level 2 state that, "Expression in the target language may be faulty, frequently reflecting the structure and word order of the source language" (ILR 2010), which suggests that even if students read at this level, beginning translators will still have production difficulties. Maintaining source language structure is certainly true of machine translation output at this level. Students, on the other hand, should begin to be aware of register and the range of word choice and how those elements affect the final target text.

Because translation errors at this level are likely to be at the sentence level, they will probably be language specific, i.e., related to the sentence structure and modification patterns of the source and target languages involved. Students in introductory courses may have never thought about structural differences between languages, and analyzing why a machine translation "sounds funny" can be an initial step in making them aware of this translation challenge. A predictable error in Chinese-to-English translation is noun stacking, as can be seen in the following:

Original
中国著名整形专家"广州第一人造美女"和"江城第一人造美女"主刀医生汪良明介绍，目前男士整形美容开始在中国日渐盛行，如隆鼻、增高、抽脂等，但大规模、多部位且公开身份整形美容的至今还没有先例。
Machine Translation
Famous plastic expert "in Guangzhou the first man-made beauty" and "River City the first man-made beauty," chief surgeon Dr Wang Liangming, at present the men's plastic surgery began in China with the growing popularity, such as nose jobs, higher, liposuction, etc., but large-scale, multi- site and the public so far as plastic surgery of no precedent.

The original sentence is typical of Chinese sentence structure. The underlined section modifies the head noun, Wang Liangming, and Google Translate has faithfully reproduced this structure. It has also flagged a Level 1 difficulty by translating 江城 as “River City”; a Web search should tell students that this is another name for Wuhan. Students next need to realize that the second half of the sentence should be restructured so that the examples of types of plastic surgery are close to the noun they modify. The computer has also highlighted two vocabulary items that have – somewhat to my surprise – been a difficulty in student translations: 增高 and 多部位. The first, translated above as *higher* refers to surgery to increase height; the second indicates that plastic surgery is done on multiple body parts. However, the pairing with 大规模, “large scale,” (better translated *extensive* in the example above) seems to pull Google Translate and some students into thinking about “large-scale, multi-site clinical trials,” which is not appropriate in this passage.

Another difficulty beginning students have is identifying the core sentence. This is generally true in both the source and target language. In addition to exercises like sentence diagramming and drawing sentence trees, critiquing machine translations can help alert students to the necessity of being aware of precise sentence structure. The following example is taken from a newsletter on environmental regulations in China and is an example of a sentence embedded in another sentence as a definition:

Original
条例规定，放射性物品是指含有放射性核素，并且其活度和比活度均高于国家规定的豁免值的物品。
Machine Translation
Regulations, radioactive substances is radioactive nuclide, and its activity and specific activity were higher than the value set by the state exempted items.

Google Translate has missed both sentences in this example. The initial four characters are the main subject and verb (and not synonyms for *regulations*): *The Regulations define. Radioactive substances* are what is being defined, with the definition the string of underlined modifiers before the head noun: *radioactive substances are substances that A and B*. Students, like machine translation programs, have a tendency to break the sentence at *and* (¦}¥B) instead of seeing that there are two parts to the definition. However, analyzing what went wrong with the machine translation should help them realize why identifying the core sentence is important in achieving acceptable translations.

Another sensitizing exercise that can be done with the examples above is assessing the time that revision requires. The example at ILR Reading Level 1 can be revised fairly quickly when students have been pointed at the appropriate resources for translating the official terms at the end of the passage. However, a question to ask students concerning the sentences given here is whether it would take more time to revise or retranslate the examples. This sort of exercise should help them become aware of the consequences of bad translation, the challenges involved in revision, and the likely tolerance level of future clients. At the same time, examples of good machine translation at this level should be provided to illustrate that materials which are easier to translate and for which there are parallel documents are likely to be done by machine. A study of the ability of machine translation to convey meaning noted that:

> Overall, we have found that Level 2 texts are a natural fit for successful machine translation. The MT systems seem to show an ability to convey concrete factual information that can be retrieved and used by the reader who does not need to understand the style, tone, or organizational pattern used by the writer. (Jones et al. 2009: 45)

This suggests that the easier end of the translation market is likely to be lost to machine translation and that students need to be able to function at higher levels of reading and translation in which they can convey style and tone, and recognize organizational patterns.

Difficulties above the sentence level: ILR Reading Level 3

Discussions of translation difficulty above the sentence level have focused on text type and subject matter. Nord classifies texts by function, but does not rank these by difficulty. Child, on the other hand, writes that:

> The term *mode*... is intended to express the ways in which language is realized according to the purposes of users. As such it is not necessarily intended as a hierarchical system. As a matter of convenience, however, it has been useful to present the modes as a scheme of increasing complexity and, in this context, to refer to them as textual levels corresponding roughly to the ILR skill levels. (1999: 91)

Hatim and Mason quote Gülich and Raible as saying "different text types seem to place different demands on the translator," and further note that news reports are less demanding than editorials because they are expository texts, while editorials are argumentative. As a result, news reports are structured in a more straightforward manner, have unmarked patterns of connectivity and theme-rheme development. The texture in editorials and other argumentative texts "tends to be opaque and to be manipulated for rhetorical effect," making literal approaches – the cognitively easier approach one might add – inappropriate (1997: 181).

Editorials are typical of such "demanding" material and also correspond to ILR Reading Level 3, the point at which the language learner is able to "relate ideas and 'read between the lines'." We have also seen that the ability to compare two editorials is the mark of a proficient reader in the native language. Therefore, despite the argument that editorials are rarely translated – which may not be true if one includes opinion pieces under the same heading and considers the various purposes (including governmental, think tank use, lawsuits, reference material) for which such materials are commercially translated – editorials are appropriate materials for introductory courses. This is particularly true when course objectives include improving reading ability in both languages and self-evaluation skills. In addition, as noted above the description of ILR Translation Professional Performance at Level 3 essentially sets editorials as the touchstone for emerging translation proficiency. Put differently, translators at Performance Level 3 should be able to translate Reading Level 3 texts. However, the descriptors for both reading ability and translation performance suggest that textual understanding and translation performance are still works in progress.

At the same time, instructors should be aware that not all members of a class may be able to read at the editorial level in their A language. Therefore, reading and analyzing source language editorials should be a part of an introductory curriculum and should be introduced before setting translation assignments with material at this degree of difficulty. If a student is clearly having trouble reading at this level, the student, instructor, and institution need to consider what remedial steps can be taken or if translation is a wise career choice for that individual. As a result, it is important that materials clearly at ILR Reading Level 3 be included in first year courses to allow everyone involved an opportunity to realistically assess the challenges involved in professional translation as well as individual aptitude and degree of preparation.

The difficulties likely to be encountered at Reading Level 3 include cultural references that may require explication and – most strikingly – cohesion patterns as expressed through tense, choice of grammatical subject in the case of Chinese and Japanese, as well as antecedents to pronouns. We can also expect that machine translation will start to break down at this level of textual difficulty.

The following passage – taken from a Japanese editorial concerning Japanese reluctance to screen a Chinese-made film about the Yasukuni shrine – illustrates difficulties with subjects, pronouns, and tense.

Original
これは言論や表現の自由にとって極めて深刻な事態である。中国人監督によるドキュメンタリー映画「靖国　ＹＡＳＵＫＵＮＩ」の今月公開を予定していた東京と大阪の五つの映画館が、すべて上映中止を決めた。来月以降の上映を準備しているところも数カ所あるが、今回の動きが足を引っ張ることにもなりかねない。
Machine Translation
This is a very serious situation for freedom of speech and expression. Chinese documentary film directed by "Yasukuni YASUKUNI" five cinemas in Tokyo and Osaka had planned to release this month decided to cancel all screenings. There are also several places where screening is preparing next month, it could lead to dampen this movement.

The first word of the passage and of the editorial is *kore* (これ), which Google Translate has correctly translated as "this." In Japanese, the pronoun refers to the general situation set out in the title ("靖国"上映中止—表現の自由が危うい [Refusal to Screen *Yasukuni* Threatens Freedom of Expression]), which is then described in detail in the second sentence. This pattern of presenting information is not particularly marked or uncommon in Japanese. However, because English requires closer noun-pronoun connections, starting an editorial with "this" is both confusing and an example of weak writing. Nevertheless, the impulse toward literalness – perhaps coupled with inadequate knowledge of target language conventions – often leads students to start their translations with "this." Tracing the relational patterns in the Japanese and why the literal machine translation reproduction of these does not work helps students improve reading skills in both languages and so also comprehension and production skills.

Determining the correct English tense for translation is often a problem for students. In the present case, Google Translate performed better than some beginning translators and did not use a form of the present tense for 予定していた ("had planned"). In the last sentence, Google Translate opted for two dummy subjects, highlighting a frequent problem in student translations. Because

Japanese is a null subject and pro-drop language, students tend to over use dummy subjects in their initial translations. Google's choice to do the same thing provides a good opportunity for discussing the different grammatical and stylistic requirements of Japanese and English.

Because machine translation – like many freelance translators – does not receive a translation brief, the translation is entirely out of context. Because of the importance of context and inference at higher reading levels, the lack of context can be thought to be partly responsible for the poor quality of most machine translation at ILR Reading Level 3 and above. In the setting of the discussion here, critiquing machine translation in light of context provides another teachable moment, in which the instructor can ask questions such as: What difference does having a brief make? How does the translator make choices when no context is given? The discussion can be expanded to include cohesion and coherence markers in both languages and the ways in which these are contextually determined.

Conclusion

I have suggested ways of introducing students to the idea of different types of textual difficulties through the use of machine translation as an initial straw man for critique. I have also pointed out that – given recent statistics concerning general reading ability – both students and instructors need to be realistic about reading skills. Students need to be aware that machine translation is not just a "straw man," but is also a growing presence in the translation world and that they need to be able to translate better than the machines. They also need to have enough awareness of target text conventions to be able to post-edit machine translations. Finally, I hope that, by moving the focus of criticism from student work to machine output, students will have a safe place in which to work out their initial approach to translation without feeling that their early output is under excess scrutiny.

References

Campbell, Stuart (1999). "A Cognitive Approach to Source Text Difficulty in Translation." *Target* 11: 1 33–63.

Campbell, Stuart & Sandra Hale (1999). "What Makes a Text Difficult to Translate?" *Refereed Proceedings of the 23rd Annual ALAA Congress.* (19 April 1999).

Child, James R. (1981). "Language Proficiency Levels and the Typology of Texts." Unpublished paper, given at a pre-conference workshop on language testing sponsored by the Georgetown University Language Roundtable on Languages and Linguistics.

Child, James R. (1999). "Analysis of Texts and Critique of Judgment." *Georgetown University Round Table on Languages and Linguistics* 1999: 88–97. Available at http://tiny.cc/asccb/. Visited June 2010.

EMT Expert Group (2009). *Competences for Professional Translators, Experts in Multilingual and Multimedia Communication.* Available at http://ec.europa.eu/dgs/translation/programmes/emt/index_en.htm. Visited June 2010.

Hale, Sandra and Stuart Campbell (2002). "The Interaction Between Text Difficulty and Translation Accuracy." *Babel* 48: 1 14–33.

Hatim, Basil and Ian Mason (1997). *The Translator as Communicator.* London: Routledge.

Howard, Diane (2009). "What Was So Hard About That?" In *Translation Research Projects* 2, edited by Anthony Pym and Alexander Perekrestenko. Tarragona: Intercultural Studies Group, Universitat Rovira I Virgili, pp. 83–91.

Interagency Language Roundtable (2010). *Homepage.* http://www.govtilr.org/. Entry point for information about the ILR skill levels. Visited June 2010.

Jones, Doug, Wade Shen, Martha Herzog, Sabine Atwell, Hussny Ibrahim, Dan Ding (2009). "Using United States Government Language Proficiency Standards for MT Evaluation." Available at http://tiny.cc/4z7lq/. Visited June 2010.

Kelly, Dorothy (2005). *A Handbook for Translator Trainers.* Manchester: St. Jerome Publishing.

Kiraly, Don (2000). *A Social Constructivist Approach to Translator Education: Empowerment from Theory to Practice.* Manchester: St. Jerome Publishing.

Kussmaul, Paul (1995). *Training the Translator*. Amsterdam: John Benjamins Publishing Co.
Nord, Christiane (2005). *Text Analysis in Translation: Theory, Methodology, and Didactic Application of a Model for Translation-Oriented Text Analysis*, 2nd *Ed*. Amsterdam: Rodopi.
National Center for Education Statistics (2003). *2003 National Assessment of Adult Literacy* (NCES 2006-470). Available at http://www.oecd.org/dataoecd/1/60/34002216.pdf. Visited June 2010.
Organization for Economic Co-operation and Development (OECD) (2004). *Learning for Tomorrow's World: First Results from PISA 2003*. Available at http://www.oecd.org/dataoecd/1/60/34002216.pdf. Visited June 2010.
Read, John (2000). *Assessing Vocabulary*. Cambridge: Cambridge University Press.

Vergleich der Schweizer Gesetzesbestimmungen über die internationale Schiedsgerichtsbarkeit mit den entsprechenden Vorschriften in Frankreich und Deutschland – eine interdisziplinäre Analyse

Suzanne Ballansat / Gunhilt Perrin

Einleitung

Der folgende Beitrag hat den Vergleich von Schiedsgesetzen in deutscher und französischer Sprache zum Gegenstand, die einerseits im mehrsprachigen Rechtssystem der Schweiz und andererseits in den einsprachigen Rechtssystemen Frankreichs und Deutschlands entstanden sind. Ziel dieses Vergleichs ist es, die Zusammenhänge zwischen Inhalt und Sprache dieser Schiedsgesetze aufzuzeigen[*].

In Kapitel 1 werden wir kurz Entstehung, Zielsetzung und Anwendungsbereich dieser Gesetze darstellen und die Vergleichskriterien besprechen. In Kapitel 2 werden wir als Grundlage für unseren Vergleich einige allgemeine Merkmale der Gesetzgebung in der Schweiz, in Frankreich und in Deutschland in Erinnerung rufen. Die Kapitel 3, 4 und 5 sind dem Vergleich der Schiedsgesetze auf makro- und mikrostruktureller Ebene gewidmet.

* Dieses Thema war Gegenstand eines Vortrags der Autorinnen am Kongress *Researching Language and the Law: Intercultural Perspectives*, der vom *Centro di Ricerca sui Linguaggi Specialistici (CERLIS)* an der Universität Bergamo vom 18.–20. Juni 2009 organisiert worden war.

1. Untersuchungsgegenstand und Methode

1.1 Untersuchungsgegenstand

1.1.1 Schiedsgesetze in der Schweiz (IPRG/LDIP), in Frankreich (CPC) und in Deutschland (ZPO)

In unserem Beitrag werden wir einerseits die deutschsprachige und die französischsprachige Fassung der Schweizer Gesetzesbestimmungen über die internationale Schiedsgerichtsbarkeit (Kapitel 12 des Bundesgesetzes über das Internationale Privatrecht, Artikel 176–194, in Kraft seit 1.1.1989[1], im Folgenden: IPRG) einander gegenüberstellen und dabei das Phänomen der Mehrsprachigkeit kurz beleuchten. Andererseits werden wir die Schweizer Gesetzesbestimmungen mit den entsprechenden Normen in Frankreich (Code de procédure civile, livre IV, articles 1492–1507, in Kraft seit 12.5.1981[2], im Folgenden CPC) und in Deutschland (Zivilprozessordnung, Buch 10, §1025–1066, in Kraft seit 1.1.1998[3], im Folgenden ZPO) vergleichen.

1 Bundesgesetz vom 18. Dezember 1987 über das Internationale Privatrecht IPRG, Systematische Sammlung SR 291, http://www.admin.ch/ch/d/sr/c291.html.
Loi fédérale du 18 décembre 1987 sur le droit international privé LDIP, Recueil systématique RS 291, http://www.admin.ch/ch/f/rs/c291.html.

2 Code de procédure civile (CPC), Livre IV, arbitrage international, articles 1492–1507, eingefügt durch: Décret n° 81-500 1981-05-12 art. 5 JORF 14 mai 1981rectificatif JORF 21 mai 1981, JORF 14 mai 1981 p. 1380. http://legifrance.gouv.fr/affichCode.do?cidTexte=LEGITEXT000006070716&dateTexte=20090120.

3 Zivilprozessordnung (ZPO) http://www.bundesrecht.juris.de/zpo/BJNR005330950.html.
Neufassung durch das Schiedsverfahrensgesetz (SchiedsVfG) vom 22.12.1997 (BGBl 1997, I S. 3224).

1.1.2 Entstehung, Zielsetzung und Anwendungsbereich dieser Schiedsgesetze

Zahlreiche Staaten wollten anlässlich der Revision ihrer Schiedsgesetze in den zwei letzten Jahrzehnten des 20. Jahrhunderts ein attraktives Forum für Schiedsverfahren zur Verfügung stellen und dadurch den Wirtschaftsstandort fördern (Burger-Scheidlin 2007: 5). In den drei erwähnten Ländern wurde dieses Ziel auf verschiedene Weise angestrebt. Deutschland setzte wie viele andere Staaten das im Rahmen der UNO am 11.12.1985 von der Vollversammlung verabschiedete UNCITRAL-Modellgesetz (Model Law, im Folgenden ML[4]) um, doch Frankreich und die Schweiz bevorzugten ein eigenständiges, besonders schiedsfreundliches und flexibles Gesetz. In Deutschland hielt man zur Förderung der internationalen Schiedsgerichtsbarkeit eine möglichst umfassende Regelung für angebracht (Berger 1998: 45; Kulpa 2005: 336–337), in Frankreich (Boisséson 1983: 402) und der Schweiz (Lalive 1989: 273, 280) hingegen eine möglichst knappe Regelung.

Bezüglich Anwendungsbereich und systematischer Einordnung der drei Schiedsgesetze sind folgende Unterschiede hervorzuheben. In der Schweiz kam auf Bundesebene nur eine knappe Regelung der internationalen Schiedsgerichtsbarkeit im Rahmen des internationalen Privatrechts in Frage, weil der Bund damals nicht für das Zivilprozessrecht zuständig war (Hochstrasser/Blessing 2007: 1466). Die interne Schiedsgerichtsbarkeit wird durch das Konkordat[5] geregelt. In Frankreich und Deutschland ist die Schiedsgerichtsbarkeit hingegen in der Zivilprozessordnung normiert. Bezüglich des

4 General Assembly Resolution 40/72 vom 11.12.1985; englische Fassung des ML: http://www.uncitral.org/pdf/englisch/texts/arbitration/ml-arb/07-86998_Ebook-pdf.
Es handelt sich um ein Rahmengesetz zur Harmonisierung der Bestimmungen über die internationale Schiedsgerichtsbarkeit auf internationaler Ebene.

5 Konkordat über die Schiedsgerichtsbarkeit vom 29. März 1969, Amtliche Sammlung AS 1995 31. Das Konkordat wird ab 1.1.2011 durch die Art. 353–399 der neuen Schweizerischen Zivilprozessordnung vom 19.12.2008 ersetzt.

Anwendungsbereichs ist zu beachten, dass man in Deutschland von einer monistischen Konzeption ausging (die oben erwähnten Bestimmungen der ZPO gelten sowohl für die interne wie auch für die internationale Schiedsgerichtsbarkeit), während man in Frankreich wie in der Schweiz einer dualistischen Konzeption folgte (die oben aufgeführten Bestimmungen des CPC sind nur auf die internationale Schiedsgerichtsbarkeit anwendbar, für die interne Schiedsgerichtsbarkeit gelten hingegen die Artikel 1442–1491 CPC).

1.2 Methode

Für unsere interdisziplinäre Untersuchung werden wir das linguistische Kriterium der Explizitheit von Texten[6] mit dem juristischen Gesichtspunkt der Normierungsdichte von Gesetzestexten (zu diesem Begriff siehe 2.1.1) verbinden.

1.2.1 Das Merkmal der Explizitheit

Je expliziter ein Text ist, desto mehr Informationen sind ausdrücklich im Text untergebracht. Explizitheit ist eine graduelle Eigenschaft, die von anderen Grössen der Kommunikationssituation (v. Hahn 1998: 383) und insbesondere vom Kontextwissen des Rezipienten abhängt. Je expliziter ein Text, je weniger Kontextwissen muss der Rezipient zusätzlich einbringen, um den Text zu verstehen. Ein in einer bestimmten Kommunikationssituation angemessen expliziter Text besitzt genau den Grad an Informativität, der zum Erfolg der Kommunikation nötig ist.

Das pragmatische Merkmal der Explizitheit schlägt sich in erster Linie in den syntaktischen Strukturen eines Textes nieder. Wenn Explizitheit mit grosser Informationsdichte einhergeht, bedeutet dies, dass Sätze oft länger und komplexer sind, denn zusätzliche

6 Siehe den Vergleich von ZPO und IPRG unter den Gesichtspunkten der Explizitheit und Vagheit bei Heller (2003b: 599f und 2003a: 288).

Informationen können in Form von Attributen, Adverbialen oder Nebensätzen in einen Satz eingefügt werden (Heller 2003b: 602). Andererseits kann Explizitheit auch die Anzahl der Sätze eines Textes erhöhen.

Explizitheit betrifft zudem andere Sprachebenen (v. Hahn 1998: 384). Auf semantisch-lexikalischer Ebene kann z.B. das Ersetzen von Pronomen durch ihre Referenten einen Text expliziter machen (v. Hahn 1998: 385, 388). Auf Textebene wird die äußere Darstellung und Gliederung als wichtiges Explizitheitsmerkmal der logischen Anordnung des Textinhalts betrachtet (v. Hahn 1998: 386). Schliesslich kann Explizitheit auf intertextueller Ebene in Form von expliziten Verweisen auf andere Texte vorkommen.

An dieser Stelle sei auch kurz auf die von v. Hahn beschriebene Unterscheidung zwischen Explizitheit und Präzision hingewiesen. Präzision wird erreicht durch Entfernung von semantisch vagen Ausdrücken wie z.B. unbestimmten Rechtsbegriffen, nicht durch Explizierung (v. Hahn 1998: 384). Explizitheit dagegen bedeutet Hinzufügen, bzw. Spezifizieren von Information. Präzisierung von Vagheit ist in diesem Sinne etwas anderes als Erhöhung des Informativitätsgrades einer Aussage[7] und soll daher in diesem Beitrag nicht weiter behandelt werden.

1.2.2 Explizitheit bei Gesetzestexten[8]

Explizitheit bei Gesetzestexten bedeutet insbesondere Verringerung von Allgemeingültigkeit und Abstraktheit durch grössere Spezifizierung oder – auf intertextueller Ebene – ausdrückliches Verweisen auf andere Textstellen (siehe 3.2). Dies führt in syntaktischer Hinsicht zu zahlreichen Konditionalnebensätzen (Heller 2003a: 295; Heller 2003b: 602), Adverbialen, Attributen, oder – im Fall expiziter Verweise – auch zu Parenthesen.

7 Zur Unterscheidung von Präzisierung und Spezifizierung siehe Pinkal (1985: 14, 18–19).

8 Zum Problem der Vagheit in normativen Texten, siehe u.a. Heller (2003b), Heller (2005), Engberg/Heller (2008), Gotti (2005), Gotti (2008a).

2. Allgemeine Merkmale der Gesetzgebung in der Schweiz, in Frankreich und in Deutschland

2.1 *Gesetzgebungstradition*

Unsere Untersuchung zeigt, dass die Gesetzgebungstradition der drei Länder in den analysierten Schiedsgesetzen weiterlebt. Sie geht auf die Kodifikationen des Privatrechts zurück, nämlich in Frankreich auf den *Code Civil (Code Napoléon)* von 1804, in Deutschland auf das Bürgerliche Gesetzbuch (BGB) von 1900 und in der Schweiz auf das Zivilgesetzbuch bzw. den *Code civil suisse* (ZGB/CCS) von 1912.

2.1.1 Gesetzgebungstechnik

Der Gesetzgeber stellt generell-abstrakte Normen auf, d.h. Bestimmungen, die auf eine unbegrenzte Zahl von Fällen und Personen anwendbar sind. Angesichts der Vielfalt des Lebens sind Gesetze gezwungenermassen lückenhaft, und es ist Aufgabe der Gerichte, sie weiter zu entwickeln, um im konkreten Fall eine Lösung zu finden. Der Gesetzgeber hat also zu entscheiden, wie weitmaschig ein Gesetz sein soll und wie viel Spielraum dem Richter bei der Anwendung eingeräumt wird, d.h. welche Normierungsdichte angestrebt werden soll (Emmenegger 2006: 213–218; Forstmoser/Vogt 2008: 118; Dullion 2007: 58–59)[9].

9 In der Schweiz wird im Gesetzgebungsleitfaden des Bundesamtes für Justiz in der deutschsprachigen Fassung (Rz 723) der Ausdruck *Regelungsdichte* verwendet, in der französischsprachigen Fassung, dem *Guide de législation*, der Ausdruck *densité normative* (Rz 723). http://www.bj.admin.ch/bj/de/home/themen/staat_und_buerger/legistik.gesetzgebungsleitfaden.html.
http://www.bj.admin.ch/bj/fr/home/themen/staat_und_buerger/legistik/gesetzgebungsleitfaden.html.
Dullion (2007: 58) spricht in diesem Zusammenhang von *précision normative*.

Die Kodifikationen des Privatrechts haben bezüglich der Normierungsdichte in den drei Ländern verschiedene Traditionen begründet[10]. Der *Code civil* ist prägnant formuliert und enthält zahlreiche Generalklauseln, die der Rechtsprechung grossen Spielraum lassen. Das ZGB folgte mit seiner geringen Normierungsdichte dem Vorbild des *Code Napoléon*, doch wurde dem Richter sogar ausdrücklich die Befugnis zuerkannt, bei Gesetzeslücken selbst eine allgemeine Regel aufzustellen (Art.1 Abs. 2 ZGB). Die Verfasser des BGB strebten hingegen nach Vollständigkeit, Genauigkeit und innerer Folgerichtigkeit und wollten mit dieser grösseren Normierungsdichte die Rolle der Rechtsprechung gerade einschränken, indem sie Generalklauseln und unbestimmte Rechtsbegriffe vermieden (Gmür 1965: 28–30).

2.1.2 Gesetzessprache

Die drei Länder haben nicht nur bezüglich der Normierungsdichte, sondern auch bezüglich der Gesetzessprache eine andere Tradition. Während das BGB mit seiner wissenschaftlichen Ausdrucksweise sich an den Rechtsspezialisten richtet (Gmür 1965: 28), sind der *Code Napoléon* und das ZGB in einem anschaulicheren, bürgernäheren Stil geschrieben (Lasserre 2006: 219; Gmür 1965: 40).

2.2 Mehrsprachigkeit der Schweizer Gesetzgebung

Die Mehrsprachigkeit als besonderes Merkmal der Schweizer Gesetzgebung beruht auf Artikel 70 der Bundesverfassung[11], wonach Deutsch, Französisch, Italienisch und, im Verkehr mit Personen rätoromanischer Sprache, auch Rätoromanisch Amtssprachen des

10 Siehe den Vergleich dieser drei Gesetzbücher bei Dullion (2007: 47–69) und Lasserre-Kiesow (2004: 213–223) sowie den Vergleich BGB/ZGB bei Gmür (1965), zum Unterschied *common law/civil law* siehe Gotti (2008a: 100–101).

11 Bundesverfassung der Schweizerischen Eidgenossenschaft vom 18. April 1999 (SR 101).

Bundes sind. Nach Art. 14 Abs. 1 des Publikationsgesetzes[12] werden Erlasse des Bundes gleichzeitig in den drei Amtsprachen Deutsch, Französisch und Italienisch veröffentlicht, wobei alle drei Fassungen in gleicher Weise verbindlich sind. Im Zweifelsfall muss ermittelt werden, welche der drei gleichberechtigten Fassungen den Normsinn am zutreffendsten wiedergibt. In dieser Hinsicht stellt die Mehrsprachigkeit eine Auslegungshilfe dar (Forstmoser/Vogt 2008: 123).

3. Vergleich der Textstruktur und Verweistechnik in den drei Schiedsgesetzen

3.1 Makrostruktur

Gliederungssignale in Gesetzestexten erleichtern die Übersicht und erhöhen die Explizitheit und Verständlichkeit (Nussbaumer 2007: 55). Sie sind ausserdem ein Hilfsmittel für die Auslegung nach der Gesetzessystematik. In den drei verglichenen Schiedsgesetzen stellt man wesentliche Unterschiede bezüglich der Gliederungssignale fest. So werden in der ZPO Untertitel zu jedem Paragraphen, im IPRG Randziffern zu jedem Artikel verwendet, im CPC tragen hingegen nur die Kapitel Überschriften. Zudem sind im CPC die Absätze im Gegensatz zur ZPO und zum IPRG nicht nummeriert. Der französische Gesetzestext ist in dieser Hinsicht also weniger leserfreundlich.

Bezüglich des Textumfangs und der Informationsdichte wird auf den schon bei Heller (2003b: 606) und Engberg/Heller (2008: 154–155) vorgenommenen Vergleich verwiesen. In der folgenden Tabelle wird dieser Vergleich auf die Gesetzestexte in französischer Sprache erweitert.

12 Bundesgesetz über die Sammlungen des Bundesrechts und das Bundesblatt PublG (SR 170.512).

Hinsichtlich des Textumfangs der verglichenen Schiedsgesetze ergibt sich, dass die ZPO ungefähr 4.6 Mal mehr Wörter umfasst als der CPC und 4.3 Mal mehr Wörter als die deutsche Fassung des IPRG:

Gesetz	IPRG	LDIP	CPC	ZPO
Wörter	1191.00	1358	1118	5148
Artikel/§	19	19	16	42
Absätze	42	42	22	120
Art./§: 1 Abs.	5 (26,31%)	5 (26,31%)	10 (62,5%)	7 (16,66%)
Art./§: 2 Abs.	5 (26,31%)	5 (26,31%)	6 (37,5%)	11 (26,19%)
Art./§: 3 Abs.	8 (42,10%)	8 (42,10%)	0 (0%)	11 (26,19%)
Art.§ :+ 3 Abs.	1 (5,26%)	1 (5,26%)	0 (0%)	13 (30,95%)
Sätze	47	47	26	186
Abs. mit 1 Satz	40 (95,23%)	40 (95,23%)	18 (81,81%)	73 (60,83%)
Abs. mit 2 Sätzen	2 (4,76%)	1 (2,38%)	4 (18,18%)	37 (30,83%)
Abs. mit + 2 Sätzen	0 (0%)	1 (2,38%)	0 (0%)	10 (8,33%)
Wörter/Satz (Durchschnitt)	25,34	28,89	43	27,6
Absatzlänge (Min./Max)	7/77	9/81	9/79	7/246
Satzlänge (Min/Max.)	6/77	5/81	9/79	6/246

Tabelle 1. Vergleich von Textumfang und Informationsdichte.

Betrachtet man zum Vergleich der Informationsdichte die Aufteilung der Gesetzesartikel bzw. -paragraphen in Absätze und Sätze, so stellt man fest, dass die in der Schweiz geltende Grundregel, wonach der besseren Verständlichkeit wegen ein Artikel höchstens drei Absätze, ein Absatz höchstens einen Satz und jeder Satz höchstens einen Gedanken enthalten soll[13], im IPRG/LDIP bis auf wenige Ausnahmen eingehalten wurde.

13 Diese Grundregel geht auf Eugen Huber, den Verfasser des ZGB, zurück und ist im Gesetzgebungsleitfaden *(Guide de législation)* des Bundesamtes für Justiz enthalten (siehe Rz 8235 und 8241 der deutschsprachigen Fassung und Rz 8235 der französischsprachigen Fassung); Quellenangaben siehe Fn 9.

Im CPC ist die Informationsdichte pro Artikel wesentlich geringer als im IPRG/LDIP; zehn Artikel des CPC enthalten nur einen einzigen Absatz, sechs Artikel zwei Absätze, doch kein einziger Artikel drei oder mehr Absätze. Diesbezüglich ist zu erwähnen, dass in Frankreich im *Guide de Légistique* empfohlen wird, nur eine Regel pro Artikel aufzustellen und zu lange Artikel mit zu vielen Absätzen zu vermeiden[14]. Die Informationsdichte pro Absatz des CPC ist hingegen im Vergleich zum IPRG/LDIP insofern etwas grösser, als die meisten Absätze des CPC zwar wie jene des IPRG/LDIP nur einen Satz, einige Absätze jedoch zwei Sätze enthalten. Auffällig ist, dass der CPC für eine dem IPRG/LDIP analoge Anzahl Wörter nur 26 Sätze gegenüber den 47 Sätzen im IPRG/LDIP aufweist. Damit stimmt überein, dass die Sätze im CPC im Durchschnitt wesentlich länger sind als im LDIP (durchschnittlich 43 Wörter pro Satz anstatt 28,89). Es ist anzunehmen, dass die durchschnittliche Informationsdichte der Sätze des CPC grösser ist als im LDIP, was z.T. mit komplexeren syntaktischen Strukturen verbunden ist (siehe 5.3).

In der ZPO ist die Informationsdichte pro Paragraph sehr gross. Zahlreiche Paragraphen umfassen mehr als drei Absätze (bis zu 6 Absätzen!). Absätze mit zwei oder mehr Sätzen sind häufig. Diese Informationsdichte hält sich im Rahmen der Empfehlungen, die das deutsche Bundesministerium der Justiz im Handbuch der Rechtsförmlichkeit (1.7. Rz 105)[15] formuliert, wonach ein Paragraph nicht mehr als fünf Absätze und ein Absatz nicht mehr als drei Sätze enthalten soll.

14 *Guide de légistique*, 2. Auflage 2007, Ziffer 3.2.2. http://www.legifrance.gouv.fr/html/Guide_legistique_2/accueil_guide_leg.htm.

15 Handbuch der Rechtsförmlichkeit. Empfehlungen des Bundesministeriums der Justiz zur einheitlichen rechtsförmlichen Gestaltung von Gesetzen und Rechtsverordnungen nach § 38 Abs. 3 GGO II / hrsg. vom Bundesministerium der Justiz, 3. neu bearbeitete Auflage 2008 http://www.bmj.de/rechtsfoermlichkeit/.

Welche Faktoren beeinflussen die Länge der verglichenen Gesetzestexte? Erstens entspricht die grössere Normierungsdichte der ZPO der nach der Gesetzgebungstradition in Deutschland verwendeten Gesetzgebungstechnik (siehe 2.1.1), wobei ausserdem zu bedenken ist, dass die ZPO sich am ML orientiert, das entsprechend der angelsächsischen Tradition detaillierter ist (Heller 2003a: 290–291; Heller 2003b: 597; Gotti 2008b). Zweitens ist für einen sinnvollen Vergleich der unterschiedliche Anwendungsbereich zu berücksichtigen. Da die ZPO auch für die interne Schiedsgerichtsbarkeit gilt, muss sie für letztere detailliertere Regeln enthalten (siehe insbesondere §1041–1050 über das Schiedsverfahren). Bezüglich Frankreich und der Schweiz ist schliesslich zu beachten, dass manche Bestimmungen über die interne Schiedsgerichtsbarkeit durch explizite Verweise für anwendbar erklärt werden. Damit wird der Gesamtumfang der anwendbaren Bestimmungen vergrössert (siehe Art. 1493, 1495, 1500 CPC; Art. 176 Abs. 2, 179 Abs. 2 IPRG).

3.2 *Intertextualität*

Intertextualität ist eine wichtige Eigenschaft von Rechtstexten, durch die Information aus einem Text in einen anderen integriert wird (Hebenstreit 1997: 113). In Gesetzesbestimmungen finden sich insbesondere explizite Verweise auf andere Vorschriften im gleichen oder einem anderen Gesetz. Sie haben den Vorteil, dass unnötige Abweichungen vermieden und die Zusammenhänge zwischen unterschiedlichen Regelungsmaterien aufgezeigt werden, doch sie beeinträchtigen den Lesefluss (Handbuch der Rechtsförmlichkeit, siehe Fn 15, 4.2. Rz 225, *Guide de Légistique*, siehe Fn 14, Ziffer 3.4.2.).

Nach der Gesetzgebungstradition sind explizite Verweise in deutschen und französischen Gesetzen häufig (Emmenegger 2006: 203–204; Dullion 2007: 57; Cornu 2005: 305), in der Schweiz wird hingegen wenn möglich darauf verzichtet (Gesetzgebungsleitfaden, siehe Fn 9, Rz 8351; Nussbaumer 2007: 55; Forstmoser/Vogt 2008: 120).

Berücksichtigt man den unterschiedlichen Umfang der analysierten Schiedsgesetze, so fallen die 14 expliziten Verweise im CPC rein zahlenmässig stärker ins Gewicht als die 46 expliziten Verweise in der 4.6 Mal längeren ZPO. Kennzeichnend für die deutsche Gesetzessprache ist die Häufung von expliziten Verweisen (z.B. zehn in § 1025 ZPO, siehe 5.1). Das IPRG/LDIP enthält dagegen nur sieben explizite Verweise.

Neben den expliziten Verweisen finden sich in Gesetzestexten häufig implizite Verweise durch Gebrauch von Begriffen, die in einem andern Gesetz definiert sind (Hebenstreit 1997: 113). Diese verringern die Explizitheit eines Gesetzes (z.B. Art. 176 Abs.1 IPRG *Wohnsitz:* impliziter Verweis auf Art. 23 ZGB; §1031 Abs. 5 ZPO *Verbraucher*: impliziter Verweis auf §13 BGB).

4. Mikrostruktureller Vergleich der deutschsprachigen und französischsprachigen Fassung des Schweizer Schiedsgesetzes

4.1 *Terminologische Abweichungen*

4.1.1 Art. 187 Abs. 1 IPRG/LDIP

Diese Norm bestimmt, dass die Parteien das auf den Streitfall anwendbare Recht wählen können, doch werden in den beiden Sprachfassungen diesbezüglich nicht deckungsgleiche Begriffe verwendet. In der deutschsprachigen Fassung wird der Ausdruck *Recht* verwendet, was bedeutet, dass die gesamte Rechtsordnung eines Staates zu wählen ist. In der französischsprachigen Fassung ist hingegen der Ausdruck *règles de droit* zu finden, der auf die Möglichkeit hindeutet, auch andere Rechtsregeln wie Handelsbräuche *(lex mercatoria)* und allgemeine Rechtsgrundsätze zu wählen.[16]

(1) Art. 187 Abs. 1 IPRG Anwendbares Recht
1 Das Schiedsgericht entscheidet die Streitsache nach dem von den Parteien gewählten *Recht* oder, bei Fehlen einer Rechtswahl, nach dem *Recht*, mit dem die Streitsache am engsten zusammenhängt.

(2) Art. 187 al. 1 LDIP Droit applicable
1 Le tribunal arbitral statue *selon les règles de droit* choisies par les parties ou, à défaut de choix, selon *les règles de droit* avec lesquelles la cause présente les liens les plus étroits.

Der engere deutsche Begriff würde zu einer ungewollten Einschränkung des Spielraums der Parteien führen. In der Rechtslehre wird darauf hingewiesen, dass die französischsprachige Fassung den Normsinn zutreffend ausdrückt (Kulpa 2005: 363–364; Poudret/Besson 2002: 616). Diese Auffassung lässt sich durch die Entstehung des Gesetzes begründen. Art. 187 IPRG wurde von den Experten im Vorentwurf ursprünglich in französischer Sprache abgefasst (Poudret/Besson 2002: 616; Kulpa 2005: 362), doch anschliessend wurden Teile des Gesetzentwurfs auf Deutsch und andere auf Französisch erarbeitet (Šarčević 1997: 99; von Overbeck 1984: 977). In der Parlamentsdebatte wurde vor allem der französische Text verwendet, der den korrekten Ausdruck *règles de droit* enthielt. Zur vorliegenden Abweichung im endgültigen Text kam es wohl dadurch, dass die deutschsprachige Fassung von der parlamentarischen Redaktionskommission unter Zeitdruck bereinigt werden musste (Hochstrasser/Blessing 2007: 1465). Die Mehrsprachigkeit erweist sich in diesem Fall als wertvolle Auslegungshilfe, um den richtigen Normsinn zu ermitteln (siehe 2.3).

16 Im Folgenden werden in den zitierten Gesetzesbestimmungen die besprochenen Passagen durch kursive Schrift markiert.

4.1.2 Art. 178 Abs. 1 und 2 IPRG/LDIP

Absatz 1 dieser Norm regelt die formelle Gültigkeit *(Form, forme)*, Absatz 2 die materielle Gültigkeit der Schiedsvereinbarung, wobei die Bezeichnung für die materielle Gültigkeit im Französischen klarer ist *(im Übrigen, quant au fond)*.

(3) Art. 178 Abs. 1 und 2 IPRG Schiedsvereinbarung
1 Die Schiedsvereinbarung hat schriftlich, durch Telegramm, Telex, Telefax oder in einer anderen *Form* der Übermittlung zu erfolgen, die den Nachweis der Vereinbarung durch Text ermöglicht.
2 Die Schiedsvereinbarung ist *im Übrigen* gültig, wenn sie dem von den Parteien gewählten, dem auf die Streitsache, insbesondere dem auf den Hauptvertrag anwendbaren oder dem schweizerischen Recht entspricht.

(4) Art. 178 Abs. 1 und 2 LDIP Convention d'arbitrage
1 *Quant à la forme*, la convention d'arbitrage est valable si elle est passée par écrit, télégramme, télex, télécopieur ou tout autre moyen de communication qui permet d'en établir la preuve par un texte.
2 *Quant au fond*, elle est valable si elle répond aux conditions que pose soit le droit choisi par les parties, soit le droit régissant l'objet du litige et notamment le droit applicable au contrat principal, soit encore le droit suisse.

Die Auslegung dieser Norm aufgrund der Gesetzessystematik ergibt, dass in der deutschsprachigen Fassung in Absatz 2 im Gegensatz zu der in Absatz 1 behandelten formellen Gültigkeit die materielle Gültigkeit gemeint sein muss. Der präzisere französische Text ist auch in diesem Fall Auslegungshilfe zur Ermittlung des Normsinns.

4.2 Unterschiedlicher Grad der Explizitheit

An manchen Stellen ist eine der Fassungen expliziter, doch ist dies sprachlich bedingt und inhaltlich nicht relevant.

4.2.1 Explizitere Formulierung im Französischen

An vier Textstellen wird eine französische Infinitivkonstruktion zur Satzverkürzung im Deutschen durch ein abgeleitetes Verbalsubstantiv nominalisiert (siehe auch Art. 176 Abs. 2, 177 und 182 Abs. 3 IPRG/LDIP):

(5) Art. 183 Abs. 3 IPRG Vorsorgliche und sichernde Massnahmen
3 Das Schiedsgericht oder der staatliche Richter können die *Anordnung* vorsorglicher oder sichernder Massnahmen von der Leistung angemessener Sicherheiten abhängig machen.

(6) Art 183 al. 3 LDIP Mesures provisionnelles et mesures conservatoires
3 Le tribunal arbitral ou le juge peuvent subordonner les mesures provisionnelles ou les mesures conservatoires *qu'ils ont été requis d'ordonner* à la fourniture de sûretés appropriées.

4.2.2 Explizitere Formulierung im Deutschen

Die deutschsprachige Fassung weist einige Hinzufügungen auf (Art. 182 Abs. 3, 177 Abs. 2 und 181).

In drei Fällen entspricht eine französische Präpositionalphrase im Deutschen einer längeren Formulierung, nämlich einem Nebensatz (siehe auch Art. 179 und 183 Abs. 1 IPRG/LDIP):

(7) Art. 181 IPRG Rechtshängigkeit
Das Schiedsverfahren ist hängig, sobald eine Partei mit einem Rechtsbegehren den oder die in der Schiedsvereinbarung bezeichneten Schiedsrichter anruft oder, *wenn die Vereinbarung keinen Schiedsrichter bezeichnet*, sobald eine Partei das Verfahren zur Bildung des Schiedsgerichts einleitet.

(8) Art. 181 LDIP Litispendance
L'instance arbitrale est pendante dès le moment où l'une des parties saisit le ou les arbitres désignés dans la convention d'arbitrage ou, *à défaut d'une telle désignation*, dès que l'une des parties engage la procédure de constitution du tribunal arbitral.

Auffällig ist in zwei Artikeln die Wiederaufnahmen durch Pronomen in der französischsprachigen Fassung, wogegen in der deutschsprachigen Fassung an den gleichen Stellen die Kohärenz explizit durch Wiederholung der Substantive markiert ist (siehe auch Art. 183 Abs. 2 IPRG/LDIP):

(9) Art. 190 Endgültigkeit, Anfechtung
1 Mit der Eröffnung ist der Entscheid endgültig.
2 Der *Entscheid* kann nur angefochten werden [...]

(10) Art. 190 Caractère définitif. Recours
1 La sentence est définitive dès sa communication.
2 *Elle* ne peut être attaquée que [...]

Die deutschsprachige Fassung entspricht der Empfehlung im deutschsprachigen Gesetzgebungsleitfaden (siehe Fn 9, Rz 8351), die Wiederholung von Substantiven der Verwendung von Pronomen vorzuziehen, was zu einer gewissen Eintönigkeit führt. Der französischsprachige *Guide de législation* enthält hingegen keine derartige Empfehlung.

Zusammenfassend stellt man auf lexikalischer und syntaktischer Ebene eine grosse Übereinstimmung der beiden Sprachfassungen fest. Die etwas grössere Wortanzahl in der französischsprachigen Fassung (siehe Tabelle 1) hat unseres Erachtens sprachstrukturelle Gründe. So vermindern z.B. die zahlreichen Wortzusammensetzungen im Deutschen die Wortanzahl, während der obligatorische Gebrauch der Determinanten im Französischen sie erhöht.

5. Mikrostruktureller Vergleich des schweizerischen, französischen und deutschen Schiedsgesetzes

Im Folgenden werden ausgewählte Normen der drei Schiedsgesetze verglichen (wobei die Berücksichtigung des LDIP nur in 5.3. relevant ist). Bei dieser interdisziplinären Analyse bildet der Vergleich des Normgehalts und des Anwendungsbereichs die Grundlage, um den Explizitheitsgrad der verglichenen Bestimmungen zu beurteilen und ihre syntaktische Komplexität zu untersuchen.

5.1 Anwendungsbereich

(11) Schweiz Art. 176 Abs. 1 und 2 IPRG
1 Die Bestimmungen dieses Kapitels gelten für Schiedsgerichte *mit Sitz in der Schweiz*, *sofern* beim Abschluss der Schiedsvereinbarung wenigstens eine Partei ihren Wohnsitz *oder* ihren gewöhnlichen Aufenthalt nicht in der Schweiz hatte.
2 Die Bestimmungen dieses Kapitels gelten nicht, *wenn* die Parteien schriftlich die Anwendung dieses Kapitels ausgeschlossen *und* die ausschliessliche Anwendung der kantonalen Bestimmungen über die Schiedsgerichtsbarkeit vereinbart haben. [60 Wörter]

(12) Deutschland § 1025 ZPO
(1) Die Vorschriften dieses Buches sind anzuwenden, *wenn* der Ort des schiedsrichterlichen Verfahrens *im Sinne des §1043 Abs.1* in Deutschland liegt.
(2) Die Bestimmungen der §§ 1032, 1033 und 1050 sind auch dann anzuwenden, *wenn* der Ort des schiedsrichterlichen Verfahrens im Ausland liegt *oder* noch nicht bestimmt ist.
(3) *Solange* der Ort des schiedsrichterlichen Verfahrens noch nicht bestimmt ist, sind die deutschen Gerichte für die Ausübung der *in den §§ 1034, 1035, 1037 und 1038 bezeichneten* gerichtlichen Aufgaben zuständig, *wenn* der Beklagte *oder* der Kläger seinen Sitz *oder* seinen gewöhnlichen Aufenthalt in Deutschland hat. [94 Wörter]

(13) Frankreich Art. 1492 CPC
Est international l'arbitrage qui met en cause des intérêts du commerce international. [12 Wörter]

Die Bestimmungen über die Abgrenzung des Anwendungsbereichs entsprechen sich in den drei Schiedsgesetzen inhaltlich nicht. Im Rahmen unserer interdisziplinären Betrachtungsweise kann vom unterschiedlichen Umfang der Gesetzesbestimmungen nicht auf eine unterschiedliche Explizitheit geschlossen werden.

Art. 176 Abs. 1 IPRG und §1025 Abs. 1 ZPO definieren den örtlichen Anwendungsbereich aufgrund des gleichen territorialen Kriteriums, nämlich des Sitzes des Schiedsgerichts bzw. des Orts des schiedsrichterlichen Verfahrens (Poudret/Besson 2002: 86; Berger 1998: 47). In Art. 176 Abs. 1 IPRG wird das territoriale Kriterium im Hauptsatz durch ein spezifizierendes Präpositionalattribut („[...] mit Sitz in der Schweiz [...]") ausgedrückt, in §1025 Abs. 1 ZPO durch einen Konditionalnebensatz mit einer Spezifizierung in Form einer Adverbiale, die einen expliziten Verweis enthält („wenn der Ort des schiedsrichterlichen Verfahrens im Sinne des § 1043 Abs. 1 in Deutschland liegt").

Allerdings ist für die Anwendung des IPRG Voraussetzung, dass eine Partei ihren Wohnsitz oder gewöhnlichen Aufenthalt nicht in der Schweiz hat. Diese Einschränkung wird in Art. 176 Abs. 1 durch einen einschränkenden Konditionalnebensatz mit einer durch *oder* angezeigten Alternative formuliert. Die ZPO enthält diese Einschränkung gerade nicht, da sie auch für interne Fälle gilt (siehe 1.1.2).

Auch die in Art. 176 Abs. 2 und § 1025 Abs. 2 und 3 enthaltenen Einschränkungen entsprechen sich inhaltlich nicht. In der Schweiz geht es um ein *opting out* der Parteien zugunsten des Konkordats, in Deutschland um die Mitwirkung des staatlichen Richters im Schiedsverfahren.

Während in beiden Gesetzen jeweils die zweiten Absätze in Bezug auf ihre syntaktische Komplexität vergleichbar sind – beide enthalten einen nachgestellten, zweiteiligen Konditionalnebensatz –, erscheint §1025 Abs. 3 besonders komplex; das Satzgefüge beginnt mit einer temporalen Angabe in Form eines Nebensatzes; der Hauptsatz enthält ein erweitertes Partizipialattribut, durch das wiederum explizit auf andere Paragraphen verwiesen wird („[...] der in den §§ 1034, 1035, 1037 und 1038 bezeichneten gerichtlichen Aufgaben [...]"); der nachgestellte Konditionalnebensatz schliesst zwei Alternativen ein.

Mit 44 Wörtern ist dieser letzte Absatz der ZPO doppelt so lang wie die mittlere Satzlänge, die im Handbuch der Rechtsförmlichkeit auf Grund des menschlichen Kurzzeitgedächtnisses empfohlen wird (siehe Fn 15, 1.6 Rz 95). Auch die expliziten Verweise auf andere Paragraphen machen die Sätze syntaktisch komplizierter.

Art. 1492 CPC enthält gerade keine Definition des territorialen Anwendungsbereichs. Für die Unterscheidung zwischen internationaler und interner Schiedsgerichtsbarkeit wird das materielle Kriterium des internationalen Handels *(commerce international)* verwendet (Schröder 2007: 19; das IPRG und die ZPO gelten hingegen für alle vermögensrechtlichen Streitigkeiten). Sobald ein französisches Gericht angerufen wird, gelten die Artikel 1492–1507 CPC ohne Rücksicht auf den Sitz des Schiedsgerichts für alle internationalen Fälle (Poudret/Besson 2002: 88). Die Legaldefinition in Art. 1492 dient dazu, die Anwendung der restriktiveren Artikel 1442–1491 CPC über die interne Schiedsgerichtsbarkeit auszuschliessen.

Syntaktisch frappiert Art. 1492 CPC, da er nur aus einem einzigen Satz besteht, nämlich einem Hauptsatz, der mit dem Prädikat in Erststellung beginnt und von einem Relativsatz gefolgt ist. Diese sprachlich ungewöhnliche, sehr einfache Struktur ist für französische Legaldefinitionen charakteristisch. Die Norm ist keineswegs explizit, da ihre Tragweite erst unter Berücksichtigung der Gesetzessystematik erkannt werden kann.

5.2 Form der Schiedsvereinbarung

(14) Schweiz Art. 178 Abs.1 IPRG
1 Die Schiedsvereinbarung hat *schriftlich, durch Telegramm, Telex, Telefax oder in einer anderen Form der Übermittlung* zu erfolgen, *die* den Nachweis der Vereinbarung durch Text ermöglicht. [26 Wörter]

(15) Deutschland § 1031 Abs. 1 ZPO
(1) Die Schiedsvereinbarung muß *entweder* in einem *von den Parteien unterzeichneten Dokument oder* in zwischen *ihnen gewechselten Schreiben, Fernkopien, Telegrammen oder anderen Formen der Nachrichtenübermittlung, die* einen Nachweis der Vereinbarung sicherstellen, enthalten sein.

(2) Die Form des Absatzes 1 gilt auch dann als erfüllt, *wenn* die Schiedsvereinbarung in einem *von der einen Partei der anderen Partei oder von einem Dritten beiden Parteien übermittelten Dokument* enthalten ist *und* der Inhalt des Dokuments *im Fall* eines nicht rechtzeitig erfolgten Widerspruchs *nach der Verkehrssitte* als Vertragsinhalt angesehen wird.
(3) *Nimmt* ein *den Formerfordernissen des Absatzes 1 oder 2 entsprechender* Vertrag auf ein Dokument Bezug, *das* eine Schiedsklausel enthält, so begründet dies eine Schiedsvereinbarung, *wenn* die Bezugnahme *dergestalt* ist, *daß* sie diese Klausel zu einem Bestandteil des Vertrages macht.
(4) Eine Schiedsvereinbarung wird auch *durch die Begebung eines Konnossements* begründet, *in dem* ausdrücklich auf die in einem Chartervertrag enthaltene Schiedsklausel Bezug genommen wird.
(5) Schiedsvereinbarungen, *an denen* ein Verbraucher beteiligt ist, müssen in einer von den Parteien *eigenhändig unterzeichneten* Urkunde enthalten sein. Die schriftliche Form *nach Satz 1* kann durch die elektronische Form *nach § 126a des Bürgerlichen Gesetzbuchs* ersetzt werden. Andere Vereinbarungen als *solche*, *die* sich auf das schiedsrichterliche Verfahren beziehen, darf die Urkunde *oder* das elektronische Dokument nicht enthalten; dies gilt nicht bei notarieller Beurkundung.
(6) Der Mangel der Form wird durch die Einlassung auf die schiedsgerichtliche Verhandlung zur Hauptsache geheilt. [230 Wörter]

(16) Frankreich CPC
[keine Bestimmung]

Im CPC wird die Form der Schiedsvereinbarung, die an anderer Stelle erwähnt wird (Art. 1493), nicht geregelt. Es gilt also der Grundsatz der Formfreiheit und es steht den Parteien völlig frei, mündliche oder stillschweigende Schiedsvereinbarungen abzuschliessen (Poudret/Besson 2002: 174). Nicht dem Gesetzestext, sondern der Rechtsprechung und Lehre ist zu entnehmen, dass die für die interne Schiedsgerichtsbarkeit vorgesehene Schriftform (Art. 1443 und 1449 CPC) nicht anwendbar ist, da der Verweis in Art. 1495 auf das interne Recht in diesem Fall nicht gilt (Poudret/Besson 2002: 168–169).

Dagegen ist in §1031 Abs. 1 ZPO und in Art. 178 Abs.1 IPRG die gleiche Formvorschrift verankert, nämlich die vereinfachte Schriftform. Es ist also nicht unbedingt ein unterzeichnetes Dokument erforderlich, sondern es genügt eine sonstige Textform (Poudret/Besson 2002: 164, 161, 162). §1031 Abs. 1 ZPO ist diesbezüglich expliziter als 178 Abs. 1 IPRG, da er in Form erweiterter Partizipialattribute erwähnt, dass sowohl die unterzeichnete („[...] in einem von den Parteien unterzeichneten Dokument [...]") wie die nicht unterzeichnete Form („[...] in zwischen ihnen gewechselten Schreiben, Fernkopien, Telegrammen oder anderen Formen der Nachrichtenübermittlung [...]") gültig ist. Die Alternative wird betont durch den Gebrauch der zweigliedrigen Konjunktion *entweder – oder*. Art. 178 Abs. 1 IPRG begnügt sich mit dem Adverb *schriftlich*, erläutert durch drei Beispiele und die Verallgemeinerung „[...] *oder in einer anderen Form der Übermittlung* [...]".

Die ZPO regelt im Sinne einer grösseren Normierungsdichte zahlreiche Sonderfälle ausdrücklich (§1031 Abs. 2–6), was sich sprachlich in fünf weiteren Absätzen mit verschiedenen erweiterten Attributen, Adverbialen, Konditional- und anderen Nebensätzen ausdrückt. In der Schweiz findet man dagegen nicht im Gesetzestext, sondern in der Rechtsprechung eine Antwort auf diese Fragen (diese bejaht wie §1031 Abs. 2 die Gültigkeit einer Schiedsvereinbarung durch Verweis, doch verneint anders als §1031 Abs. 3 die Zulässigkeit einer stillschweigenden Schiedsvereinbarung.) Der Verbraucherschutz (§1031 Abs. 5) ist nur in Deutschland relevant, weil die Norm auch für interne Fälle gilt (siehe 1.1.2).

5.3 Bildung des Schiedsgerichts

(17) Schweiz Art 179 IPRG Schiedsgericht 1. Bestellung

1 Die Schiedsrichter werden *gemäss der Vereinbarung der Parteien* ernannt, abberufen oder ersetzt.

2 *Fehlt eine solche Vereinbarung*, so kann der Richter am Sitz des Schiedsgerichts angerufen werden; er wendet *sinngemäss* die Bestimmungen des kantonalen Rechts über die Ernennung, Abberufung oder Ersetzung von Schiedsrichtern an.

3 *Ist* ein staatlicher Richter mit der Ernennung eines Schiedsrichters betraut, so muss er diesem Begehren stattgeben, ***es sei denn***, eine summarische Prüfung ergebe, dass zwischen den Parteien keine Schiedsvereinbarung besteht. [76 Wörter]

(18) Schweiz Art 179 LDIP Tribunal arbitral: 1.Constitution
1 Les arbitres sont nommés, révoqués ou remplacés conformément à la *convention des parties.*
2 *A défaut d'une telle convention*, le juge du siège du tribunal arbitral peut être saisi; il applique *par analogie* les dispositions du droit cantonal sur la nomination, la révocation ou le remplacement des arbitres.
3 *Lorsqu*'un juge est appelé à nommer un arbitre, il donne suite à la demande de nomination qui lui est adressée, *à moins qu*'un examen sommaire ne démontre qu'il n'existe entre les parties aucune convention d'arbitrage. [85 Wörter]

(19) Deutschland §1034 ZPO Bildung des Schiedsgerichts
(1) Die Parteien können die Anzahl der Schiedsrichter vereinbaren. *Fehlt eine solche Vereinbarung*, so ist die Zahl der Schiedsrichter drei.
(2) *Gibt* die Schiedsvereinbarung einer Partei bei der Zusammensetzung des Schiedsgerichts ein Übergewicht, *das* die andere Partei benachteiligt, so kann diese Partei bei Gericht beantragen, den *oder* die Schiedsrichter abweichend von der erfolgten Ernennung *oder* der vereinbarten Ernennungsregelung zu bestellen. Der Antrag ist spätestens bis zum Ablauf von zwei Wochen, *nachdem* der Partei die Zusammensetzung des Schiedsgerichts bekannt geworden ist, zu stellen. §1032 Abs. 3 gilt entsprechend.

§ 1035 Bestellung der Schiedsrichter
(1) Die Parteien können das Verfahren zur Bestellung des Schiedsrichters oder der Schiedsrichter vereinbaren.
(2) *Sofern die Parteien nichts anderes vereinbart haben*, ist eine Partei an die durch sie erfolgte Bestellung eines Schiedsrichters gebunden, *sobald* die andere Partei die Mitteilung über die Bestellung empfangen hat.
(3) *Fehlt* eine Vereinbarung der Parteien über die Bestellung der Schiedsrichter, wird ein Einzelschiedsrichter, *wenn* die Parteien sich über seine Bestellung nicht einigen können, *auf Antrag* einer Partei durch das Gericht bestellt. In schiedsrichterlichen Verfahren *mit drei Schiedsrichtern* bestellt jede Partei einen Schiedsrichter; diese beiden Schiedsrichter bestellen den dritten Schiedsrichter, *der* als Vorsitzender des Schiedsgerichts tätig wird. *Hat* eine Partei den Schiedsrichter nicht *innerhalb eines Monats nach Empfang einer entsprechenden Aufforderung durch die andere Partei* bestellt *oder* können sich die beiden Schiedsrichter *nicht binnen eines Monats nach ihrer Bestellung* über den dritten Schiedsrichter einigen, so ist der Schiedsrichter *auf Antrag einer Partei* durch das Gericht zu bestellen.

(4) *Haben* die Parteien ein Verfahren für die Bestellung vereinbart *und* handelt eine Partei nicht entsprechend diesem Verfahren *oder* können die Parteien *oder* die beiden Schiedsrichter eine Einigung *entsprechend diesem Verfahren* nicht erzielen *oder* erfüllt ein Dritter eine *ihm nach diesem Verfahren übertragene* Aufgabe nicht, so kann jede Partei bei Gericht die Anordnung der erforderlichen Maßnahmen beantragen, *sofern* das vereinbarte Bestellungsverfahren zur Sicherung der Bestellung nichts anderes vorsieht.

(5) Das Gericht hat bei der Bestellung eines Schiedsrichters *alle nach der Parteivereinbarung für den Schiedsrichter vorgeschriebenen* Voraussetzungen zu berücksichtigen *und* allen Gesichtspunkten Rechnung zu tragen, *die* die Bestellung eines *unabhängigen und unparteiischen* Schiedsrichters sicherstellen. Bei der Bestellung eines Einzelschiedsrichters *oder* eines dritten Schiedsrichters hat das Gericht auch die Zweckmäßigkeit der Bestellung eines Schiedsrichters *mit einer anderen Staatsangehörigkeit als derjenigen der Parteien* in Erwägung zu ziehen. [372 Wörter]

(20) Frankreich Art 1493 CPC

Directement *ou* par référence à un règlement d'arbitrage, la convention d'arbitrage peut désigner *le ou les* arbitres *ou* prévoir les modalités de leur désignation.

Si pour les arbitrages *se déroulant en France ou* pour ceux *à l'égard desquels* les parties ont prévu l'application de la loi de procédure française, la constitution du tribunal arbitral se heurte à une difficulté, la partie la plus diligente peut, *sauf clause contraire*, saisir le président du tribunal de grande instance de Paris *selon les modalités de l'article 1457*. [84 Wörter]

Die Gesetzesbestimmungen zur Bildung des Schiedsgerichts weisen einen sehr unterschiedlichen Explizitheitsgrad auf. Während die ZPO die Zusammensetzung des Schiedsgerichts in einem Paragraphen mit zwei Absätzen und 86 Wörtern und die Bestellung des Schiedsrichter in einem weiteren Paragraphen mit fünf Absätzen und 286 Wörtern (insgesamt 372 Wörter) regelt, behandeln das IPRG und der CPC beide Themen in einem Artikel mit 3 bzw. 2 Absätzen (85 Wörter für LDIP, 76 Wörter für IPRG, 84 Wörter für CPC). Allerdings muss bei diesem Vergleich des Textumfangs berücksichtigt werden, dass mittels expliziter Verweise in Art. 179 Abs. 2 IPRG/LDIP und Art. 1493 Abs. 2 CPC zusätzlich Information in den Text integriert wird (siehe 1.2.1 und 3.2).

Den drei Gesetzestexten ist gemeinsam, dass sie die Parteiautonomie bezüglich der Anzahl der Schiedsrichter und ihrer Bestellung gewährleisten. In der ZPO werden im vorliegenden Beispiel vorangestellte Konditionalnebensätze zum Ausdruck der Parteiautonomie gebraucht (§1034 Abs. 1, §1035 Abs. 2, 3, 4). Im IPRG wird diese sowohl anhand eines vorangestellten Konditionalnebensatzes formuliert (Art. 179 Abs. 2 „Fehlt eine solche Vereinbarung [...]") als auch – wie an anderen Stellen im IPRG – in Form einer Präpositionalphrase (Art. 179 Abs. 1 „[...] gemäss der Vereinbarung der Parteien [...]"). Im LDIP werden an dieser Stelle die im Französischen häufigeren Präpositionalphrasen (Abs. 1 „[...] conformément à la convention des parties[...]"; Abs. 2 „[...] à défaut d'une telle convention[...]")[17] gebraucht, genau wie im CPC (Art. 1493 „[...] sauf clause contraire [...]")[18].

Die Parteiautonomie wird durch den Gleichheitsgrundsatz eingeschränkt, der ein Übergewicht einer Partei bezüglich der Bestellung der Schiedsrichter verbietet. Diese Einschränkung ist in §1034 Abs. 2 ZPO ausdrücklich formuliert, wonach die benachteiligte Partei beim Richter eine abweichende Bestellung beantragen kann. In der Schweiz ist diesbezüglich keine Bestimmung vorgesehen (Peter/Legler 2007: 1565; die Ablehnung des Schiedsrichters oder Anfechtung des Schiedsspruchs sind möglich). In Frankreich gilt der Gleichheitssatz aufgrund der Rechtsprechung der *Cour de cassation* (Poudret/Besson 2002: 359–360). In dieser Hinsicht sind Explizitheit und Normierungsdichte im schweizerischen und französischen Gesetz geringer als im deutschen.

Die ZPO ist auch insoweit expliziter, als sie subsidiär eine Anzahl von drei Schiedsrichtern vorsieht (§ 1034 Abs. 1). In Art. 179 Abs 2. IPRG ist diesbezüglich ein expliziter Verweis auf das Konkordat enthalten, welches ebenfalls drei Schiedsrichter vorsieht. Die Anwendung des kantonalen Rechts unterliegt allerdings der

17 Andere Beispiele: Art. 181, 183, 188, 189 LDIP; doch treten im LDIP auch Konditionalnebensätze auf (Art. 180, 182).

18 Andere Beispiele: Art. 1494, 1495, 1496.

Parteiautonomie. Im CPC ist keine subsidiär gültige Anzahl von Schiedsrichtern vorgesehen, doch ist Art. 1493 Abs. 1 insoweit expliziter als das IPRG/LDIP, als er ausdrücklich die Möglichkeit eines Einzelschiedsrichters („[...] le ou les arbitres [...]") und die eventuelle Bezugnahme auf eine Schiedsordnung („[...]par référence à un règlement d'arbitrage [...]") erwähnt und zwischen Ernennung und Ernennungsmodalitäten unterschiedet („[...]la convention d'arbitrage peut désigner *le ou les* arbitres *ou* prévoir les modalités de leur désignation"). Syntaktisch ist der CPC durch diese Reihung von drei Alternativen komplexer als das IPRG/LDIP

In allen drei Ländern kann der Richter aufgefordert werden, die Schiedsrichter zu ernennen. In §1035 Abs. 3 Satz 1 ZPO ist explizit die Wahl eines Einzelschiedsrichters durch das Gericht vorgesehen, was sich syntaktisch in einem komplexen Satzgefüge mit zwei Konditionalnebensätzen und einem Hauptsatz mit zwei Adverbialen niederschlägt (§1035 Abs. 3, Satz 1). In §1035 Abs. 3 Satz 2 und 3 wird ausserdem die Bestellung eines Kollegiums von 3 Schiedsrichtern durch die Parteien oder gegebenenfalls durch das Gericht statuiert. Syntaktisch liegt hier eine Satzperiode vor, bestehend aus einem Einfachsatz, der durch Strichpunkt mit einem Satzgefüge verbunden ist (Abs. 3, Satz 2) sowie ein sehr komplexes Konditionalgefüge, das mehrere durch mehrgliedrige Attributketten spezifizierte Adverbialen enthält (Abs. 3, Satz 3).

In Frankreich ist die Anrufung des Richters kraft Art. 1493 Abs. 2 CPC möglich, der explizit auf die Bestimmungen des internen Rechts verweist (Art. 1457 CPC, der seinerseits auf die Art. 1444, 1453 und 1455 weiter verweist; den beiden letztgenannten Normen ist schliesslich zu entnehmen, dass ein Einzelschiedsrichter oder eine ungerade Anzahl Schiedsrichter vorgesehen sind oder bei gerader Anzahl Sonderregelungen gelten). In der Schweiz verweist Art. 179 Abs. 2 auch auf die internen Bestimmungen, nämlich auf Art. 12 des Konkordats. Die weitaus grössere Explizitheit der ZPO bewirkt, dass man anders als in Frankreich und der Schweiz ohne Berücksichtigung anderer Bestimmungen die Anzahl der Schiedsrichter und deren Bestellungsverfahren zur Kenntnis nehmen kann.

6. Fazit

In unserer Untersuchung haben wir Gesetzestexte verglichen, die einerseits in einem mehrsprachigen und andererseits in einem einsprachigen Umfeld entstanden sind.

Aus der Darstellung der allgemeinen Merkmale der Gesetzgebung in den drei betroffenen Ländern in Kapitel 2 und dem Vergleich der Makrostruktur der untersuchten Schiedsgesetze in Kapitel 3 ergibt sich, dass nicht nur die Gesetzgebungstradition, sondern auch der Anwendungsbereich die Textlänge beeinflussen.

In Kapitel 4 konnten wir beim mikrostrukturellen Vergleich der deutschsprachigen und französischsprachigen Fassung des IPRG/LDIP feststellen, dass diese zwar an einigen Stellen nicht die gleiche Explizitheit in der Formulierung aufweisen und dass einige Terminologieunterschiede bestehen, dass jedoch eine weitgehende Parallelität der Sprachfassungen erreicht wurde.

Im Rahmen unseres mikrostrukturellen Vergleichs der drei Schiedsgesetze hat unsere Analyse der Bestimmungen über den Anwendungsbereich (5.1) ergeben, dass in den drei Ländern erhebliche inhaltliche Unterschiede in dessen Umschreibung bestehen und dass deshalb im Rahmen einer interdisziplinären Betrachtungsweise von der unterschiedlichen Textlänge nicht auf einen unterschiedlichen Explizitheitsgrad geschlossen werden darf.

Die Bestimmungen bezüglich der Form der Schiedsvereinbarung (5.2), die sich in Deutschland und der Schweiz inhaltlich grundsätzlich entsprechen, illustrieren hingegen gerade die grössere Explizitheit deutscher Gesetze. In diesem Punkt wird die Tradition der grösseren Normierungsdichte in Deutschland und die wichtigere Rolle der Rechtsprechung in der Schweiz bestätigt. Der in Frankreich geltende Grundsatz der Formfreiheit unterscheidet sich inhaltlich völlig von den anderen beiden gesetzlichen Regelungen und ergibt sich nur implizit aus dem Gesetzestext.

Was die Bestellung des Schiedsgerichts angeht (5.3), wurden in allen drei Ländern inhaltlich analoge Normen aufgestellt, doch die dualistische Konzeption in Frankreich und der Schweiz führte zu Verweisen auf die internen Bestimmungen, während in Deutschland aufgrund der monistischen Konzeption der ZPO eine sehr explizite Regelung vorliegt. Das Kriterium des Anwendungsbereichs ist bei der Betrachtung der Explizitheit also ausschlaggebend.

In syntaktischer Hinsicht ist die ZPO insgesamt eindeutig am komplexesten, was mit einem hohen Explizitheitsgrad einhergeht. Der Vergleich zwischen CPC und IPRG/LDIP führt zu folgender Feststellung: Der CPC kann bei maximaler Implizitheit extrem einfache syntaktische Strukturen aufweisen (5.1), er kann aber auch inhaltlich expliziter sein als das IPRG/LDIP, was dann komplexeren syntaktischen Strukturen entspricht (5.3).

Abschliessend möchten wir festhalten, dass sich unseres Erachtens ein Vergleich der Explizitheit von Gesetzestexten auf eine genaue Analyse der inhaltlichen Entsprechung der Normen und ihres Anwendungsbereichs stützen muss. Es wäre aufschlussreich, diese Methode auf umfangreichere Vergleiche neuer Spezialgesetze anzuwenden, um zu verifizieren, inwieweit die unterschiedlichen Gesetzgebungstraditionen weiterleben.

7. Bibliographie

Berger, Klaus Peter 1998. Das neue deutsche Schiedsverfahrensrecht. *Deutsche Zeitschrift für Wirtschaftsrecht*, 45–55.

Bhatia, Vijay K. 1993. *Analysing Genre. Language Use in Professional Settings.* London/New York: Longman.

Boisséson, Matthieu de 1983. *Le droit français de l'arbitrage*. Paris: Gide, Loyrette, Nouel.

Burger-Scheidlin, Maximilian 2007. Einleitung. In Torggler, Hellwig (Hg.) *Praxishandbuch Schiedsgerichtsbarkeit*. Wien: Nomos, 3–7.

Cornu, Gérard 2005. *Linguistique juridique*. Paris: Montchrestien.

Dullion, Valérie 2007. *Traduire les lois, un éclairage culturel. La traduction en français des codes civils allemand et suisse autour de 1900*. Cortil-Wodon: E. M. E. et InterCommunications sprl.

Emmenegger, Sigrid 2006. *Gesetzgebungskunst*. Siebeck/Tübingen: Mohr.

Engberg, Jan / Heller, Dorothee 2008. Vagueness and Indeterminacy in Law. In Bhatia, Vijay K. / Candlin, Christopher, N. / Engberg, Jan (Hg.) *Legal Discourse across Cultures and Systems*. Hong Kong: University Press, 145–168.

Forstmoser, Peter / Vogt, Hans-Ueli 42008. *Einführung in das Recht*. Bern: Stämpfli.

Gotti, Maurizio 2005. Vagueness in the Model Law on International Commercial Arbitration. In Bhatia, Vijay K. / Engberg, Jan / Gotti, Maurizio / Heller, Dorothee (Hg.) *Vagueness in Normative Texts*. Bern: Peter Lang, 227–253.

Gotti, Maurizio 2008a. Customising the Model Law on International Commercial Arbitration. In Wagner, Anne / Cacciaguidi-Fahy, Sophie (Hg.) *Obscurity and Clarity in the Law, Prospects and Challenges*. Aldershot: Ashgate, 89–108.

Gotti, Maurizio 2008b. The Formulation of Legal Concepts in Arbitration Normative Texts in a Multilingual, Multicultural Context. In Bhatia, Vijay K. / Candlin, Christopher N. / Evangelista Allori, Paola (Hg.) *Language, Culture and the Law*. Bern: Peter Lang, 23–45.

Gmür, Rudolf 1965. *Das Schweizerische Zivilgesetzbuch, verglichen mit dem deutschen Bürgerlichen Gesetzbuch*. Bern: Stämpfli.

Hahn von, Walther 1998. Das Postulat der Explizitheit für den Fachsprachengebrauch. In Hoffmann, Lothar / Kalverkämper, Hartwig / Wiegand, Herbert Ernst (Hg.) *Fachsprachen: ein internationales Handbuch zur Fachsprachenforschung und Terminologiewissenschaft / Languages for special purposes: an international handbook of special-language and terminology research*. Berlin [etc.]: de Gruyter, 1. Halbband 383–389.

Hebenstreit, Gernot 1997. Terminus – Weltbild – Intertextualität: Translatologische Überlegungen zu juristischen Fachtexten. In Grbic, Nadija / Wolf, Michaela (Hg.) *Text – Kultur. Kommunikation, Translation als Forschungsaufgabe*. Tübingen: Stauffenburg, 97–116.

Heller, Dorothee 2003a. Prinzipien der Textgestaltung und der Gebrauch von Konditionalsätzen im deutschen Schiedsverfahrensrecht. In Bhatia, Vijay K. / Candlin, Christopher N. / Gotti, Maurizio (Hg.) *Legal Discourse in Multilingual and Multicultural Contexts. Arbitration Texts in Europe*. Bern: Peter Lang, 287–312.

Heller, Dorothee 2003b. Zur dualen Ausrichtung gesetzlicher Bestimmungen. *L'Analisi linguistica e letteraria* 11, 595–618.

Heller, Dorothee 2005. Zwischen Bestimmtheit und strategischer Offenheit: Zur sprachlichen Qualifizierung deutscher und schweizerischer Sanktionsnormen. In Bhatia, Vijay K. / Engberg, Jan / Gotti, Maurizio / Heller, Dorothee (Hg.) *Vagueness in Normative Texts*. Bern: Peter Lang, 357–378.

Hochstrasser, Daniel / Blessing, Marc 2007. Einleitung zum zwölften Kapitel: Grundlagen der Internationalen Schiedsgerichtsbarkeit. In Honsell, Heinrich *et al.* (Hg.) *Basler Kommentar, Internationales Privatrecht.* Basel: Helbing & Lichtenhahn, 1409–1501.

Kulpa, Norman Norbert 2005. *Das anwendbare (materielle) Recht in internationalen Handelsschiedsgerichtsverfahren.* Bern: Peter Lang.

Lalive, Pierre / Poudret, Jean-François / Reymond, Claude 1989. *Le droit de l'arbitrage international en Suisse.* Lausanne: Payot.

Lasserre-Kiesow, Valérie 2004. Die Theorie der drei Fiktionen, Die Diskussion um die Verständlichkeit des Code civil und des BGB. In Lerch, Kent D. (Hg.) *Recht verstehen. Verständlichkeit, Missverständlichkeit und Unverständlichkeit von Recht.* Berlin/New York: de Gruyter, 213–223.

Nussbaumer, Markus 2007. Gesetze verständlicher machen – dass ich nicht lache! In Lötscher, Andreas / Nussbaumer, Markus *Denken wie ein Philosoph und schreiben wie ein Bauer. Sprache, mit der ein Staat zu machen ist.* Zürich: Schulthess, 43–65.

Overbeck von, A. E. 1984. L'interprétation des textes plurilingues en Suisse. *Les cahiers de Droit* 25/4, 973–988.

Peter, Wolfgang / Legler, Thomas 2007. Einleitung zum zwölften Kapitel: Grundlagen der Internationalen Schiedsgerichtsbarkeit. In Honsell, Heinrich *et al.* (Hg.) *Basler Kommentar, Internationales Privatrecht.* Basel: Helbing & Lichtenhahn, 1560–1576.

Pinkal, Manfred 1985. *Logik und Lexikon: die Semantik des Unbestimmten.* Berlin / New York: W. de Gruyter.

Poudret, Jean-François / Besson, Sébastien 2002. *Droit comparé de l'arbitrage international.* Bruxelles: Bruylant. Paris: LGDJ. Zürich: Schulthess.

Šarčević, Susan 1997. *New Approach to Legal Translation.* The Hague: Kluwer Law International.

Schröder, Hans-Patrick 2007. *Die lex mercatoria arbitralis, Strukturelle Transnationalität und transnationale Rechtsstrukturen im Recht der internationalen Schiedsgerichtsbarkeit.* München: Sellier.

An Investigation Report of Corpus Construction Chinese-English Translation of Signs

Lu Jiang

With China's integration into the global economy and the increasing international exchanges, English language starts influencing into work, life, culture and almost all aspects in China. As an important social component of language with its self-evident social function, the sign is a more unique style of application. There are huge Chinese-English signs in public places. However, a variety of errors and irregularities abound also. And translation of signs is thus a comparatively new field of study. Throughout the country there launched a massive error correction on bilingual signs as well as corresponding regulatory actions. Many experts and scholars have joined the research project and achieved gratifying results.

In September 2004, "A Chinese-English Dictionary on Signs" (LU Hefa & SHAN Liping of BISU: co-editor in chief) was published by the Commercial Press.

In September 2005, the Translators Association of China (TAC), the China Daily, the China National Institute of Standardization, and Beijing International Studies University (BISU) co-sponsored "The 1st National Symposium in C-E Signs in a Global Context" in BISU. At the meeting, LIU Xiliang, president of TAC delivered a speech entitled "Purification of English Environment and Promotion of Cultural Exchanges," and HUANG Youyi, vice president and secretary general of TAC, vice president of the International Federation of Translators (FIT) made a speech on "From Translators Power to International Communication". Experts and scholars further discussed issues such as the theoretic research and work practice on C-E translation of signs.

In July 2005, "Chinese-English Translation of Signs" (WANG Ying & LU Hefa of BISU: co-editor in chief, another 20 university teachers of BISU working as members of editorial board) was published by China Publishing Group and China Translation & Publishing Corporation. Key members of the group took the advantage of studying or traveling abroad, participating in international academic conferences to collect data in Britain, France, Germany, the

Netherlands, Belgium, Austria, Luxembourg, Italy, Finland, Sweden and Vatican. The book demonstrates new perspectives, new areas, new breakthroughs through the study and application of signs, such as safety warnings, commercial promotions, rules and requirements etc, and more than 400 well selected pieces of full-color photographs precisely provide a visual representation of the authentic application context. It is taken as preliminary results of the C-E signs corpus, has become the domestic standard-setting source of the local standard of Beijing and Guangdong.

In February 2006, C-E Signs Research Center of BISU was set up, and the center has been engaged itself in giving itinerate speeches in universities and colleges ever since.

In July 2007, "The 2nd National Symposium in C-E Signs in a Global Context" was held in Tongji University, more than 200 representatives from universities, research institutions and enterprises attended the opening ceremony. BISU sent out a strong line-up of over 30 professors and experts to attend the meeting. Wang Ying, director of C-E Signs Research Center of BISU, was invited at the meeting to make a keynote speech, entitled "C-E Translation of Signs in China". In her report, Dr. Wang pointed that, since May 2006, C-E Signs Research Center of BISU carried out an empirical research on the translation and use of signs across the country. This research project is meant to find out how foreign residents and visitors feel about C-E translation of signs in China, to compare the Chinese approach to sign translation with those adopted by other countries, to identify functional and pragmatic deficiencies in English versions of signs in China, and to otherwise reflect on general issues in this area of concern. The researchers propose a number of ways to improve and standardize the translation of signs, urging the translators to be more responsive to the target audience's feelings, to take the global language context more seriously, and to be more practical and creative in searching for solutions to existing problems. A collaboration between Chinese translators and native English speakers in China is recommended as the most effective and the most interculturally sensitive model in the translation of signs. The researchers also call on TAC and other institutions concerned to work together and take actions to set up adequate information services in popular tourist destinations and major cities in China. The research consists of three parts. The first part is the survey and analysis of the status quo of signs, the second part is the questionnaire survey and analysis of foreigners who reside and travel in China, and the third is the qualitative and quantitative assessment of foreigners on the mistranslation issues in signs. And JIANG Lu, professor of C-E Signs Research Center of BISU, made a speech on corpus construction in the sub-forum.

In the occasion of the opening of 2008 Beijing Olympic Games, the Corpus of Chinese-English Signs by C-E Signs Research Center of BISU was incorporated into the power networks. It not only better serves the humanity and bilingual language environment construction of the 2008 Olympic Games and the 2010 Shanghai World Expo, but also provides intelligence service for the international Beijing and the construction of a tourist destination.

The Online Corpus of C-E Signs incorporates over 50,000 items of Chinese and/or English signs, relating to food, lodging, transportation, travel, entertaining, and all the other aspects. At the same time, it touches some special collections for the needs of society, including social development, newborn things, crisis management, urban management, business promotion, etc. The use of modern media reflects the latest research in this area.

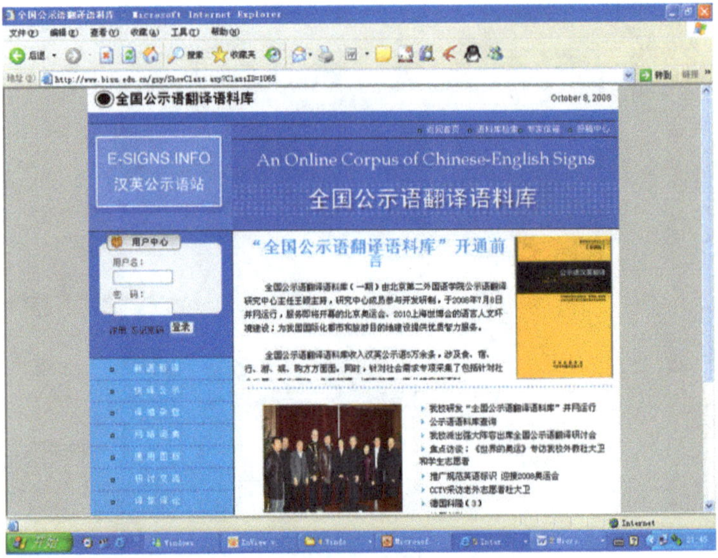

http://www.bisu.edu.cn/gsy/ShowClass.asp?ClassID=1065

http://www.bisu.edu.cn/e-signs/main.asp

The 18th FIT World Congress was held in August 2008 at the Shanghai International Convention Center. 1,500 translators and scholars from 76 countries and regions attended the opening ceremony. Invited by the Organizing Committee, BISU undertook the third sub-forum, the theme of which was "Specialized Translation & Sign Translation". Over 20 scholars of BISU attended the convention and presented academic papers.

In October 2008, the report meeting for concluding the Corpus of C-E Signs (1st phase) was held, which was sponsored by WANG Ying, director of the C-E Signs Research Center, BISU. The assessment team of experts agreed that: the project researchers seek truth from facts, boldly explore cross-cultural new features of theoretical and applied aspects under the conditions of globalization. Sign corpus and site-building is commendable and of strong practical significance, particularly in interoperability. It is easy to be used, sought and interacted for sign translators, researchers and users, also it is conducive for norms of sign translation to be in popularity and the best combination of production, teaching and research.

The corpus collects 20,000 items of signs, over 5,000 pictures, with total words of more than 500,000, which is the largest Corpus of C-E Signs throughout the country. Results of the research are of great enlightenment and inspired demonstration in standardization of sign translation. The established corpus realizes the group's research objectives, the accumulation of talents, information and experience. At the same time, the chairperson and members also completed a number of innovative and much-needed academic achievements of high value. They take the initiative to combine translation research with important issues facing the open and development of the nation, in favor of Chinese culture's going out to enhance the nation's "soft power", and the realization of cross-cultural understanding and integration. The expert team unanimously agreed to end the project.

In January 2009, Professor LU Hefa of C-E Signs Research Center, BISU won the Grand Prize in the activity "International Language Environment Construction" held by the Foreign Affairs

Office of Beijing Municipal People's Government. His award-winning thesis is entitled "High-touch Construction of a Greater Beijing International Language Environment".

So far, the second phase of the Corpus of C-E Signs is being built. Based on a large number of first-hand sources of live pictures obtained in the field research from different cities, the focus is the use of signs in the United States to reveal the history, definitions, anecdotes, and other issues of signs.

References

北京第二外国语学院公示语翻译研究中心，全国公示语翻译现状的调查与分析。中国翻译，2007 (4).

赵 湘，公示语翻译研究综述。外语与外语教学，2006 (12).

Authors

BALLANSAT, Suzanne: Lehrbeauftragte (Universität Genf), Juristin und dipl. Übersetzerin (MA jeweils Universität Genf)

DIDAOUI, Mohammed: Dr. phil. Traducteur freelance, Ancien chef de section ONU Genève

FIORITO, Mariana: Sworn Translators' Association of the City of Buenos Aires, Argentina

FORSTNER, Martin: Univ. Prof. Dr. phil. habil. Johannes Gutenberg-Universität Mainz; Generalsekretär CIUTI

GRATCHEV, Vladimir: Director, UNOG Conference Services Division, Geneva

HOHEISEL, Reinhard: ehemaliger Sprachkoordinator Deutsch, Generaldirektion Übersetzung der Europäischen Kommission

HOWARD, Diane: PhD Student, Specialized translator Chinese/Japanese – English

LEE-JAHNKE, Hannelore: Univ. Prof. Dr. phil., Universität Genf, Präsidentin der CIUTI

LU, Jiang: Chinese-English Signs Research Center, Beijing International Studies University, Beijing, China

LU, Min: National Translation Test and Appraisal Center of China International Publishing Group

PERRIN, Gunhilt: Lic. ès lettres, Lehrbeauftragte (Universität Genf) und dipl. Übersetzerin (Universität Genf)

PRUNČ, Erich: Univ. Prof. Dr. phil. habil., Universität Graz

SAINT-ROBERT, de, Marie-Josée: Chef de Service linguistique auprès de l'office des Nations Unies, Genève

SIGAREVA, Natalia: PhD, Herzen State Pedagogical University of Russia

STURM, Annegret: PhD Student, University of Geneva

TATE, Nicolas: Dr. Director-General, International Schools, Geneva

THELEN, Marcel: Maastricht School of International Communication Zuyd University

WANG, Lidi: PhD, Dean, Beijing Foreign Studies University

YUAN, Jianhua: Director International Relations, Beijing Foreign Studies University

YUDINA, Tatjana: PhD, Dean, Herzen State Pedagogical University of Russia

FSC
www.fsc.org
MIX
Papier | Fördert gute Waldnutzung
FSC® C083411

Kolibri 360 GmbH
Ferdinand-Jühlke-Straße 7
99095 Erfurt, Deutschland
produktsicherheit@kolibri360.de